WITHDRAWN

Wisdom and Wilderness:
The Achievement of Yvor Winters

WISDOM AND WILDERNESS

The Achievement of
Yvor Winters

BY DICK DAVIS

The University of Georgia Press
Athens

Designed by Francisca Vassy
Set in 10 on 12 point Bembo type
Printed in the United States of America.

The paper in this book meets the guidelines for
permanence and durability of the Committee on
Production Guidelines for Book Longevity of the Council
on Library Resources.

Library of Congress Cataloging in Publication Data

Davis, Dick, 1945–
    Wisdom and wilderness.

    1. Winters, Yvor, 1900–1968—Criticism and inter-
pretation. I. Title.
PS3545.I765Z62   811'.52   82-4809
ISBN 0-8203-0631-2   AACR2

For permission to quote from previously published
material the author and the publisher gratefully
acknowledge Janet Lewis, the editors of the *Southern
Review* (in which Chapter 3, "The Change of Direction,"
first appeared in Fall 1981 under the title "Turning
Metaphysician: Winters' Change of Direction"), and the
publishers of the following works: Yvor Winters, *Collected
Poems of Yvor Winters*. Copyright 1943 by New Directions
Publishing Corporation. Reprinted by permission of New
Directions. Elizabeth Isaacs, *An Introduction to the Poetry of
Yvor Winters*. Copyright © 1981 by Ohio University Press.
Reprinted by permission of Ohio University Press.

To Tony Tanner
with gratitude and affection

Wisdom and Wilderness are here at poise.

YVOR WINTERS
"To a Portrait of Melville in My Library"

Contents

Acknowledgments

Many people have helped me in the writing of this book, either by discussing particular problems with me or by helping me find material difficult to obtain. The opinions in the book are of course my own, and I am sure that some of them are not held by some of those who have assisted me. I should like to thank, particularly, Edgar Bowers, Dana Gioia, Thom Gunn, Janet Lewis, Grosvenor Powell, and Donald Stanford. My especial thanks are due to Joshua Odell, who provided me with a copy of *The Case of David Lamson*, by Frances Theresa Russell and Yvor Winters, and to James Davis of the University Research Library, Los Angeles, who very kindly tracked down a great deal of information for me, in particular on the scholar H. B. Parkes. I should also like to thank the Arts Council of Great Britain for financial assistance.

D. D.

Introduction

In retrospect it seems to me that I was fortunate in reading Yvor Winters's poetry before I got to know his criticism. I remember as an undergraduate picking up his *Collected Poems* in a bookshop, and the pages falling open at "The California Oaks." It was only later, when I mentioned my new enthusiasm to one of my teachers, that I learned I had been reading the poetry of a famous critic. This intrigued me, but I still thought of him principally as a poet; I still do.

My experience was not, I think, typical. I would guess that most readers of his work begin with the criticism and only if they find themselves largely in agreement with its methods and premises do they try his poetry. I have met many teachers of English and American literature who were familiar with a great deal of his criticism but who had never heard that he had published a line of his own verse. If readers of his criticism do try his poetry it is often with the expectation that it will be "academic," the passionless verse of a critic rather than the poetry of a "real" poet; and, as men frequently find in literature what they are looking for, the even tone and understated language of most of Winters's poetry apparently confirm their suspicions.

I had none of these expectations and I could value the poetry simply for itself. I think the first thing that impressed me as an undergraduate was the tone of deeply affectionate love—almost reverence—for the poems' subjects, which I thought I detected in poems like "The California Oaks," "The Marriage," "John Sutter," and "On a View of Pasadena from the Hills." Here was an author far more interested in the world about him than in himself, whose language hardly ever drew attention to itself, whose verse seemed visionary but never eccentric, intense but never self-obsessed. Yet, paradoxically, for all their lack of idiosyncratic language and violently dramatic effects, the poems did exude a definite character: they never seemed anonymous or simply ordinary; they implied a specific personality. When, later, I began to read Winters's criticism this personality seemed to clarify for me; the famous pugnacity became apparent, the passion for the precise use of language, the impatience with sloppiness of diction or thought, and the insistence that the one always implied the other. The driving force of the criticism seemed to be a passion to *understand*. Winters remarks of Henry James's novels that they all contain a character whose virtually sole function is to try and unravel what is going on around him—in his criticism Winters often seems to be this character himself. But I found myself thinking back to the poetry: the desire for understanding did not appear to be the ruling passion of most of the poems I especially admired; in these poems the mind often seemed less active than passive, less an organ of reasonable analysis than of rapt contemplation. The dichotomy seemed summed up by the lines of Winters's poem "Summer Commentary":

> Some old penumbra of the ground
> In which to be but not to find.

The poetry was about being, the criticism about finding. But the poem in which these lines occur showed me that this was too simple a description: the poem was to some degree a rejection of being in favor of finding; it recorded a progress from one to the other. So if the poetry was principally about being, not all of it felt equally happy with being. There had been a change at some point.

The edition of Winters's poems I had bought as an undergraduate was the edition prepared by Winters himself, and it contained very few of his early free-verse poems. Still, it did contain enough for the reader to notice a remarkable change from the extremely minimal early work—sometimes consisting of single-line poems—and the later sonnets and heroic couplets. Here was another dichotomy, a sudden and inexplicable break in poetic style. How had Winters passed from writing single-line poems like "Sleep" to poems in heroic couplets like "The Journey"? And *why* had he done it? Surely the more usual progress in twentieth-century American poetry had been from traditional verse forms to free verse, and not vice versa. When, later on, I came to know the extent of Winters's free-verse writings, and their evident authority and commitment to the principles of the form as it was practiced in America during the early decades of this century, the change became even more puzzling. Though I never doubted that I preferred the later poems, I felt curious as to how and why someone who had been writing like William Carlos Williams had come to produce them. I seemed to have found two, if not exactly contradictions, at least interesting cleavages in Winters's work: between the fiercely logical tone of the criticism and the rapt, contemplative tone of much of the poetry, and between the minimal free verse of Winters's earliest poems and the more discursive and traditional forms of his later work.

There is a group of verses in the *Collected Poems* which, I would guess, are rarely those that the new reader of Winters's poetry chooses as the most attractive. It takes perhaps a certain familiarity with the rest of his oeuvre, and a sympathy with his preoccupations, to fully appreciate them. They are often occasional poems—for example, the three written around the Lamson trial and the poems to William Dinsmore Briggs—but what chiefly unites them is their concern with understanding and wisdom. Unlike the poems which had initially attracted me, they seemed at one with the atmosphere of Winters's prose—or the difference in tone was slight, the poems showing perhaps marginally less confidence in the strategies of reason than the prose.

The majority of these poems were written fairly late in Winters's career. They exist at the opposite extreme, chronologically, thematically, and technically, from the free verse of his early period. This early verse is imagist and concerned with the clean evocation of the natural world. It mentions virtually no human artifacts; indeed it often seems to exclude humanity altogether and to record a prehuman landscape, a wilderness where man has hardly trod, except perhaps as a passive observer. By contrast, the later poems concerned with wisdom rarely mention the natural world: their concern is wholly with abstractions like justice and probity and the ways in which these abstractions inform, or fail to inform, human life. The concern has moved from the evocation of the American wilderness to the formulation of the nature of human wisdom.

I came to realize that this was a fundamental dichotomy which underlay Winters's work. He was a poet from his late teens until his mid fifties, though few poems were written after his early forties. He was only spasmodically a critic during his twenties, but he continued to write criticism until shortly before his death. In general, then, his energies can be said to have passed gradually from poetry to criticism (as was the case with Matthew Arnold, a poet-critic with whom he had much in common), and this is paralleled by the development within his poetry from being to finding, from wilderness to wisdom. There was a period, during his thirties, when the two extremes seemed to be held in balance, and to this decade belong his most-applauded works of criticism and, in my opinion, most of his finest poetry. In a poem addressed to Herman Melville he wrote, "Wisdom and wilderness are here at poise," and the phrase sums up with remarkable accuracy both the nature of his own concerns and that integration of their opposing claims which informs his best work.

This book discusses his writings in terms of his development from being to finding, from wilderness to wisdom. Throughout I have treated Winters not as a critic who happened to write poetry but as a poet who also wrote criticism, often in order to clarify for himself and others the situation in which he and his contemporaries functioned as poets. This was, I believe, the way Winters saw his situation. A man is, of course, far more complex than his published writings, and it is to those writings that I address myself. My chief concern has been to explicate what I take to be the most important preoccupations evident in his published work, and incidentally to bring to the reader's attention—if he is not already aware of them—those works which seem to me especially fine: the book is in no sense a biography, or even a "biographical explanation" of Winters's oeuvre.

Biographical Note

Yvor Winters was born in Chicago in 1900, the son of a fairly prosperous stockbroker. When he was still a child his family moved to Pasadena, California, and the landscape of this area was to be an important feature of his later poetry. But by the time Winters was in his mid teens his family had returned to Chicago, and it was here, during his last year of high school, that he became interested in contemporary poetry. He began to subscribe to *Poetry, A Magazine of Verse*, the *Little Review*, and *Others*, all publications promoting the then new imagist poetry. In 1917 he entered the University of Chicago and joined the Poetry Club, through which he met the editor of *Poetry*, Harriet Monroe.

A year later Winters discovered that he had tuberculosis and was forced to move to a drier and warmer climate. He returned briefly to Pasadena and then lived for almost three years at Sunmount Sanatorium, near Santa Fe, New Mexico. A great deal of this period was spent in enforced rest, particularly irksome to Winters as he had been comparatively athletic as an adolescent, with a particular interest in boxing. Toward the end of his life he alluded briefly to his experience during this period, "the only known cure, and this was known to only a few physicians, was absolute rest, often immobilized rest. The disease filled the body with a fatigue so heavy that it was an acute pain, pervasive and poisonous" (*Forms of Discovery*, p. 329). His first book of poetry and most of his second were written at this time.

During his convalescence Winters had a protracted quarrel (over his choice of friends) with his parents, and when he left the sanatorium in 1921 he could no longer count on their financial support. He became a schoolteacher in the mining town of Madrid, New Mexico, and the following year he taught in the neighboring town of Los Cerrillos. This was a period of uncongenial work in relatively squalid surroundings, and Winters seems to have been extremely lonely. A French priest living in Santa Fe, twenty miles away, gave him lessons in French; Winters used his new knowledge to read Rimbaud, of whose poetry the priest strongly disapproved.

Between leaving the sanatorium and taking up his duties as a schoolteacher Winters briefly revisited Chicago and there met his future wife, Janet Lewis. In 1922 she too was forced to interrupt her studies at the University of Chicago because of tuberculosis, and like Winters before her she moved to Sunmount Sanatorium.

By 1923 the breach with his parents had been healed, and with their financial support Winters was able to enter the University of Colorado, where he studied French, Spanish, and Latin. He achieved consistently high grades and in 1925 was awarded his M.A. with the thesis "A Method of Critical Approach to Works of Literature Based Primarily upon a Study of the Lyric in French and English." Part of this thesis was taken up by the essay "Testament of a Stone," a concise statement of his early (imagist) beliefs as to the nature of poetry.

Winters himself admitted (in the introduction to his *Early Poems*) that though he could read French and Spanish well at this period he could not speak them; nevertheless, he taught both languages for two years at the University of Idaho, Moscow. Despite the presence of the university Moscow was still a very small town, and he was almost as isolated there as he had been at Madrid and Los Cerrillos. In 1926 he married Janet Lewis. During the first year of their marriage she was still undergoing treatment at Sunmount, and Winters lived alone in Idaho.

The poet's late teens and early twenties were obviously an upsetting and difficult period: his severe illness, his interrupted education, the quarrel with his parents, which resulted in two years of uncongenial work and loneliness, and his wife's illness, which prevented their living together during the first year of their marriage, give an impression of a dislocated and unsettled life. But by 1926 he had published his first two volumes of poetry, received his M.A., and was in touch, at least by letter, with some of the most important poets of his own generation, including Hart Crane, Allen Tate, and Marianne Moore.

In 1927 Winters entered Stanford University as a graduate student in English; he was to stay associated with Stanford for the rest of his working life. From this time on he rarely left California and almost never traveled east of Chicago. He never visited Europe, or indeed anywhere else outside the United States. Though it is apparent from his poetry that he had a deep affection for the California landscape and its history, nevertheless his initial move there was perhaps partly prompted by his wife's illness. When Hart Crane visited the Winters household during Christmas of 1927, "Janet Lewis was still convalescing from tuberculosis and was confined to bed each day until four o'clock" (Thomas Parkinson, *Hart Crane and Yvor Winters: Their Literary Correspondence*, p. 108). Finding a suitable climate for his wife must have played as large a part in Winters's decision as the desire to return to the scenes of his childhood. There are hints in Crane's letters to Winters (Winters's letters to Crane have been lost) that Winters felt himself to be cut off from the literary movements flourishing in less (at least in the 1920s) conspicuously provincial parts of the country. As he later (1966) wryly commented, "In the 'twenties I was not in Paris, nor even at Harvard. After a year as a student at Stanford I became a full-time instructor of English. . . . I have remained on the same English faculty since" (*Collected Poems*, p. 15).

This sense of separateness from literary fashion, at first partially enforced, later deliberately cultivated, was to remain with Winters throughout his life and is an important factor in his stance on many literary issues. He belonged to no clique (though one was later to gather about him), and he felt that this gave him a clear perspective where others had been carried away by cant or fashion. His deliberately literal reading of texts, his earnest common sense and refusal to be hoodwinked by specious rhetoric have about them much of the sturdy independence of the skeptical outsider, and more than a hint of the down-to-earth provincial unmoved by the meretricious and glib. His nonliterary pursuits—the breeding of Airedales, the keeping of goats and a large vegetable garden, the continued interest in boxing (though he could no longer participate in the sport), his deep sympathy for the culture and life of the American Indian, all support the picture of a self-reliant man wary of cabals and movements. His sympathy for the independent outsider is evident in two of his most moving later poems—significantly, on figures from California history, John Sutter and John Day.

At Stanford Winters was a student of William Dinsmore Briggs, then chairman of the English department, who was to have a significant influence on the development of his thought. But his relations with the Stanford faculty were not entirely cordial. When an employee of the university, David Lamson, was convicted, as Winters believed unjustly, of murdering his wife, Winters was active in the demand for a retrial. A member of the Stanford School of Medicine had been an expert witness for the prosecution, and Winters was felt to be meddling in affairs about which he knew very little. In 1941 Briggs died. His successor, the Anglo-Saxon scholar A. G. Kennedy, heartily disliked Winters. He informed Winters that his publications were a disgrace to the department; Winters was so upset that he tried to join the army (he was rejected because of his health). When that failed he attempted to move to another university. This incident rankled so deeply that Winters remembered it for the rest of his life and referred to it in an essay first published in 1956, fifteen years after the event.

Despite these upsets Winters did have close friends at Stanford, and certainly his life there was more stable and ordered than it had been in his early twenties. Kennedy was succeeded by Richard Foster Jones, to whom Winters dedicated his *Collected Poems* "with admiration and affection," and Jones's successor, Virgil Whitaker, was also on good terms with Winters. Apart from his academic work at Stanford and the writing of his poetry and criticism, Winters maintained an interest in the little magazines that had first awakened his enthusiasm for contemporary poetry. For a time he was the western editor of *Hound and Horn*, and he briefly (1929) produced a mimeographed magazine of his own, *The Gyroscope*, which contained Katherine Anne Porter's first published story, *Theft*. Throughout most of his career he held fairly junior posts at Stanford. It was only in 1962, four years before his retirement, that he was appointed to a position of any distinction: he was named Albert Guerard Professor of English.

Apart from the quarrel in his early twenties Winters's relations with his father were in general good: Janet Lewis has described her father-in-law as "a charming, gentle, and generous man," and this is borne out by the brief glimpse we are given of him in Winters's poem "On a View of Pasadena from the Hills." Winters's relations with his mother, however, were far more equivocal, and after his father's death (in 1931) the two were estranged for a while. A poem from *Before Disaster* (but not included in Winters's own edition of his *Collected Poems*), "The Werewolf," would seem to refer to his mother. It begins "Wolf-bitch who suckled me," and continues in much the same vein. She seems to have been a difficult woman who quarreled at one time or another with most of her family. She was something of a spiritualist, and her son's pronounced distaste for anything remotely connected with the supernatural, a distaste that seems to have amounted to actual fear, may well be traceable to her occult interests.

Winters had a reputation in academic circles as a pugnacious antagonist, a man quick to defend his views by polemic and sarcasm. His many pupils and friends give a quite different picture—of someone who was charming and unfailingly generous both of his time and of his money. Until a little before his death he was never very well off (when his father died the inheritance passed, with the agreement of Yvor Winters and Janet Lewis, directly to the grandchildren) but he often helped others in financial need. An instance of this is the assistance he gave to Hart Crane when Crane had lost all his possessions in a tropical storm. He was obviously an excellent teacher. The testimony of his students confirms this, but it could have been understood from his criticism, which is rich in the qualities most necessary for a teacher: enthusiasm, clarity of thought, and a profound knowledge and love of his subject. He was clearly a deeply serious man. More than one of his students and friends whom I asked about him made the same remark: "Arthur [the name by which those close to him knew him] had no small talk."

He died, of cancer, in 1968, shortly after completing the manuscript of *Quest for Reality*, an anthology that attempts to define by example the principles of poetry to which his life had been devoted. He was survived by his wife, the poet and novelist Janet Lewis, and two children.

1 The Early Poetry

*In which to be
but not to find*

The protagonist of Winters's first two books, *The Immobile Wind* (1921) and *The Magpie's Shadow* (1922) is on one level the bare landscape of New Mexico in which the poet spent his early twenties; on another it is the mind which perceives that landscape and reads in it, or into it, its own preoccupations. The two fuse in typically romantic fashion. To name these preoccupations is to give us a familiar phrase from the 1920s, Being (in particular Being as an arrested moment of becoming) and Time (which in these early poems, as if in token of its extreme importance to the poet, is almost always capitalized).

But the very first poems which Winters had printed were translations of Ronsard's last sonnets, into strict sonnet form. Though interesting enough in themselves, they are more interesting for what they point to. First, it is significant that Winters's first printed work should be in sonnet form. Almost all of the poetry he published before 1930 was in free, imagist verse, and it has usually been assumed that his interest in traditional form did not appear until after the move to Stanford in late 1927. Second, the works are translations: one of Winters's chief early interests was non-English, specifically Romance, poetry. As he later wrote in the introduction to his *Early Poems*, "By the end of 1927 I knew French literature fairly well and had a passable knowledge of Spanish. My knowledge of English and American literature was very slight." This "very slight" was of course later remedied, but it is true that the great works of the Romance languages, in particular French, remained a standard for him throughout his life. His early familiarity with French poetry had a profound effect on his attitude toward the diction of poetry, and I shall return to this subject later. Third, the subject of the sonnets is a poet's awareness of the imminence of death, seen as a release from pain. We should remember that when Winters made these translations he was gravely ill in a tuberculosis sanatorium, and that at that time the disease was usually fatal. It is common for adolescents, perhaps for adolescent poets in particular, to be preoccupied with death, but Winters's acquaintance with the subject was real, not immature posturing. A great deal of the earnestness which Winters later showed in his criticism when discussing poets' moral or metaphysical attitudes comes, I believe, from this early familiarity with death's imminence, when the reality of what he was later to call the "metaphysical horror" of life and death unsupported by theology came home to him. His impatience with those who have not seen the horror and his respect for those who have, no matter how ill-judged he may have considered their reactions, stayed with him. The attitudes are most trenchantly set out in his essay "The Significance of *The Bridge* by Hart Crane; or, What are we to think of Professor X?" The Ronsard translations, then, are significant both as pointers—to Winters's early interest in traditional form and to the central position Romance and particularly French literature held for him—and for their subject matter, the imminence of death.

Winters's first personal poems, as distinguished from his translations, were collected in *The Immobile Wind*, published in 1921. These poems too were written in the sanatorium at Santa Fe, as were almost all of the poems in *The Magpie's Shadow*, published in 1922. The poems in both volumes, compared with the later work, are slight. *The Immobile Wind* especially is obviously apprentice work: the form is, in the main, unsure, wavering between short, awkwardly rhymed lines and unrhymed, basically iambic lines of varying lengths. There are two poems in heroic couplets. The volume contains fourteen poems and "Two Dramatic Interludes for Puppets." Winters included only two of these poems and parts of three others in his *Collected Poems*, and though a reader may quarrel with some of his exclusions from the later books he will probably feel that here the author has judged his own work correctly. The diction is often received and is reminiscent of a pallid nineties aestheticism. Early Yeats and perhaps early Pound are probable sources. The title poem contains the line "mystic and amorous little hands," which is an extreme example of a general tendency in the book's diction.

As a young man Winters saw himself as an imagist; he wrote an exhaustive essay on the subject, "The Testament of a Stone," first published in 1924. The poems of his first volume reach toward imagism, but the images do not exist purely as evocative description of the visible world. Rather, they function as submerged metaphors. In the second part of the first poem we have,

> Coyote, on delicate mocking feet,
> Hovers down the canyon among the mountains,
> His voice running wild in the wind's valleys.
>
> Listen! Listen! for I enter now your thought.

The coyote is cleanly realized in the opening three lines (with perhaps a suggestion of received diction in the "delicate mocking"), but the last line extends the scope of the poem beyond the purely sensory: the ambiguity of "I" and "your" ("I" could refer to the poet and "your" to the coyote or vice versa) suggests that the poem exists on one level as a metaphor for a thought process—the approach of the coyote is the coming into consciousness of a concept in the mind. We can perceive here, at the very beginning of Winters's imagist phase, the start of that method of writing he was later to define as postsymbolist.

Almost all the poems in this first volume are concerned with extremely delicate, almost unnoticeable, natural phenomena and effects: as well as the coyote that "hovers" we have the turning of a hawk's eye, the wings of a butterfly feeling the wind, feathers that "flicker / like a poplar's crest," "green water seen / through a white rose leaf," a stream "shaken / like a butterfly's antenna"; and this list is not exhaustive. A number of factors meet here. There is certainly the already remarked influence of fin de siècle aestheticism, the concentration on a sensibility that considers the world primarily as a source of exquisite sensation. But two factors are not received and arise from Winters's own mind and situation. There is first what he was himself later to call, in discussing the poetry of Sturge Moore, "the hypersensitivity of convalescence" (*In Defense of Reason*, p. 98), a neurasthenia particularly felt by tuberculosis sufferers (Keats is an obvious precursor) to whom the sensuous details of life become almost oppressively insistent in their minutest manifestations. Second, there is the suggestion of a mind utterly absorbed by the phenomena of the natural world: this absorption begins in mere attention, passes to a trancelike revery, and ends in virtual identification of observer and observed. The coyote entering and perhaps taking over the poet's thought, in the poem quoted above, is a paradigm of this process. This mental absorption in the natural world became one of Winters's major themes. He associated it with a mystical pantheism derived from Emerson, and in his later work wholly condemned it as subversive of the intellect. But in these first poems the trance of the spellbound observer of nature is celebrated, and there can be no doubt that as a young man Winters must have been particularly prone to such self-loss in nature. Writing of two of these poems much later (in 1964) he commented: "'Alone,' like 'The Lie' . . . deals with a kind of solipsistic mysticism. This solipsism was not arrived at by philosophical methods: it struck me as a kind of revelation in early childhood, and stayed with me for some years; I had to think my way *out* of it" ("By Way of Clarification," p. 132). He refers to the same mental state in a later poem, "Summer Commentary":

> When I was young, with sharper sense,
> The farthest insect cry I heard
> Could stay me; through the trees, intense,
> I watched the hunter and the bird.
>
> Where is the meaning that I found?
> Or was it but a state of mind,
> Some old penumbra of the ground,
> In which to be but not to find?

His later rejection of being as against finding must be balanced against the absorption in being evident in his first two books. The main concern of his later poetry is indeed to "think [his] way out" of solipsism, but here he is content to celebrate it. Indeed he tells us that he actively sought the state by "automatic" writing, a process in which the writer attempts to minimize his volition and self-consciousness, to put himself at the mercy of being.

The themes of the early poems are tenuous: the poems seem like the coyote, hovering at the edge of consciousness, eluding precise apprehension. They give the impression of a mind dazed by reality, reaching out tentatively toward particulars that themselves indicate rather than contain truth. But there is no doubt that it is a kind of truth that the poems reach toward: Winters never felt that poetry was "the expression of personality"; it was always a "Quest for Reality." The elusive strangeness of external reality is itself a theme of these poems. The title of the first book, *The Immobile Wind*, indicates Winters's approach to this reality. Immobility is what the perceiving mind must necessarily confer on the flux, the wind, of being, if it is to at all apprehend being. The imagist in particular seeks to catch, to fix like lepidoptera on a pin, the naturally fleeting. Words, in giving permanence to the impermanent, necessarily betray the elusive reality toward which they point. It is this sense of betrayal inherent in language that accounts for the extreme brevity of, for example, the poems of *The Magpie's Shadow*. In these poems Winters is attempting to convey sensation through language, and language, his means of communication, seems to get in the way. His later insistence on words as *concepts*, as mental signs separate from the world, is a direct result of his early attempt to "give" sensation unmediated to the reader. He came to believe that language was irreducibly a matter of the intellect and could not convey pure sensation—the attempt was the pursuit of an ignis fatuus.

One poem in the first book, not a poem included in the *Collected Poems*, is particularly interesting as an early exploration of themes repeatedly referred to throughout his later work.

The Morning

The dragonfly
Is deaf and blind
That burns across
The morning.

And silence dinned
Is but a scream
Of fear until
One turns in dream.

I see my kind
That try to turn:
I see one thin
Man running.

The dragonfly represents natural life, vivid and fleeting, unconscious of its own being. The silence which is a scream (reminiscent of George Eliot's "roar that lies the other side of silence") is the myriad activity of the unseen living world. The scream of fear is the reaction of the mind that perceives the flux of being. (*Scream* is a curiously emotive word for Winters—his diction is usually studiously free of such emotionally weighted words—and when it occurs it is always in this context of a kind of horror of being or nature.) The scream is quietened by dream, the escape into communion with nature, into that undifferentiated Being which Winters sought in his early verse and later condemned. In the last stanza the poet sees mankind—"my kind"—attempting and failing to "turn in dream," that is, to achieve the union of self and the perceived natural world. The poem ends with an image of bewildered fear, the state of man locked out from the dream.

In this early poem we see that nature perceived close to, truly perceived, is a kind of horror: the silence of the natural world, the fact that its activities and sounds *mean* nothing but simply *are*, without even knowing that they are, terrifies the poet. In the early poems Winters believes that the horror can be stilled in tranced communion with nature, in that state of solipsistic revery that he claims pervaded his adolescence. He shares, or wishes to share, the nature mysticism of writers like Wordsworth and Emerson. But the scream is alien to these writers, and it is the horror that finally predominates in Winters's work, not the dream. But we should emphasize *finally*: long after he had consciously rejected the possibility of the dream as a rational goal, he still felt very strongly the attraction of the romantic desire to merge oneself with the natural world: we can see the two sides of him, the nature mystic and the rationalist, wrestling with each other in some of his later prose, for example, the essay on Jones Very.

The poems of *The Magpie's Shadow* are reduced to a bare linguistic minimum. They are prefaced by an epigraph from Rimbaud—"*O saisons, ô châteaux!*"—whose poetry Winters had recently discovered, but direct influence is undiscernible. The poems are as slight as possible and have none of the rhetoric, passion, and confusion of the French poet. Each poem is a single-line image, normally of six syllables; occasionally when the last syllable is weak there are seven. The poems are divided into three groups—In Winter, In Spring, In Summer and Autumn. Each image attempts to indicate an aspect of the described season. The *châteaux* of the epigraph are absent, unless they are the poems themselves in so far as they give a "home" to the seasons: the poems are entirely concerned with the natural world, and the single reference to a manmade object is to a "doorframe."

The avowed influences on these severely reduced poems are translations, from Japanese and more particularly from American Indian poems. The title of the book is a gloss on an Indian poem translated by Washington Matthews and mentioned by Winters in his essay "The Indian in English" (1928).

The poems are in the main tenuous evocations of the minutiae of life in a barely hinted landscape. As in *The Immobile Wind*, the aspects of life selected for attention are usually fragile or tiny—leaves, bees, eyelids, flowers. Certain of the poems seem to have been reduced virtually out of existence and convey little. But the best of the group work in two directions: they indicate both an aspect of the natural world and the bemused, almost frightened, wonder of the observer. The sense of wonder before natural phenomena is a well-documented and frequently discussed feature of American literature, and in its imagist version has received its most famous expression in the early work of William Carlos Williams. In his early twenties Winters greatly admired Williams's verse, and it is likely that he was influenced by Williams. The tone of his poetry, however, even when it is closest to Williams in content, is quite noticeably not that of Williams's verse. It is altogether more rapt and intense, and it has at times a devout quality that is quite alien to Williams's robust naturalism.

The neurasthenic sensitivity of the convalescent, mentioned above, plays as large a part in these poems as any general national characteristic, or the influence of specific writers. Here is one of the poems, one Winters chose to include in his *Collected Poems* (he included two out of a total of twenty-eight):

The Aspen's Song

The summer holds me here.

The point of this is the tremulous ever-shifting movement of an aspen leaf, which seems perpetually about to detach itself from the tree, and which of course will detach itself when the summer ends. A whole tree of such leaves is a myriad shimmering, even in the stillest air. The tremulousness of the aspen, held for the tiniest segment of time, is an image of the fleetingness of all natural phenomena. The poem is a reference to the theme of *The Immobile Wind*—the attempt to fix the wholly evanescent, to isolate being from the time in which it has its existence.

Here is another of the poems (one not included in the *Collected Poems*):

Sunrise

Pale bees! O whither now?

The pallor of the bees is taken from the thin dawn light; the "O whither now" suggests the first tentative circlings as the bees begin the day's search for pollen, but it also suggests, particularly in the faintly religiose word *whither*, the tentative reachings out of a mind reawakening to the world. And the first poem of the collection gives the same suggestion of hesitant renewal:

Myself

Pale mornings, and
    I rise.

The separate placing of "I rise" after the run-on line ending "and" conveys an impression of cautious expectancy; the mood is here referred specifically to the poet, but it pervades the whole collection. It is not too much, I believe, to see in the wonder and sense of renewal of these slight but curiously rapt poems the grateful returning to life of the young convalescent. In Adelaide Crapsey's poems written while she was suffering from tuberculosis there is the same coincidence of the demands of imagist fashion and of the "hypersensitivity of convalescence." Crapsey's poems lack the hope of Winters's, but they share a recognizable tone; her poems were highly praised by Winters, largely, I suspect, because he had shared the sensibility they refer to and was able to confirm their authenticity from his own experience. It is as if the febrile mind is seeking to ration the sensations that threaten to overwhelm it. In *The Immobile Wind* there is a poem called "Where My Sight Goes"; after a list of images (blossom, children, leaves) the poem ends,

> And all these things would take
> My life from me.

The mind seems drunk with the richness of the world; the restrictions of such poetry are partly a deepened focus of attention, partly a warding off of too potent sensation.

It is in the volume *The Bare Hills*, published in 1927, that we find the major poetry of Winters's early period. Though his poetry was to change radically shortly after the publication of this volume, many themes persist from the earlier period into the later; we have already seen an example of this in his treatment of nature which seems both dream and horror. But there is one theme which occurs extensively only in the early work. Its existence has already been suggested in the poems of *The Magpie's Shadow*, but it receives its most thorough treatment in *The Bare Hills* and *Fire Sequence* (also published in 1927). This is the theme of renewal, and in these two volumes it is presented specifically as resurrection, in either a literal or metaphorical sense, that is, a renewal after death. Again I feel the psychological source for this is Winters's "return to life" after tuberculosis, which must have seemed a kind of living death, particularly when we recall Winters's own description of the treatment he was given—long periods of enforced immobility.

The Bare Hills begins with a poem describing a burial and is followed by four poems describing the slow approach of spring; the second one of these four is called "Resurrection" and refers back to the man Jesus Leal whose burial is the subject of the first poem. A similar though more complex pattern is discernible in *Fire Sequence*, which begins with a poem about coal as an image of stored potential (analogous to the committing to earth of the dead man in *The Bare Hills*) and proceeds through a love poem, a poem about spring, and poems concerned with the lives of the miners of the Santa Fe area, to describe life's violent release of stored energy.

The poems of *The Bare Hills* are still fairly minimal by most standards—they are short, composed of short lines, and the vocabulary is severely limited—but in comparison with the single-line verses of *The Magpie's Shadow* they are rich and discursive. There is still a pervading sense of the shaping sensibility having only a tenuous grasp on reality, as it were trembling in wonder before its subject matter; but the poems are much tougher than those already discussed, and the poet's sensibility is much less in the forefront of either the poet's or the reader's mind. Winters was obviously aiming at an absolute clarity and simplicity (by far the most often repeated words in the early poems are *air* and *stone*; their persistence gives the poems an aura of elemental, prehuman authority), and this he achieved. What is perceived is a bare, hard, but curiously lovely landscape in which the simple facts of death and spring are focused by a clean, self-effacing technique. The poet almost never comments or overtly suggests an emotional response to the scenes he describes, but the constant tone, apart from wonder, is of the pathos of the infrequent manifestations of life in the wide, still landscape:

> Goatherds inevitable as stones
> And rare
> As stones observed.

The "observed" has us realize how common stones are in this landscape, so common as to be almost unnoticeable, and the young boys who herd the goats have become almost indistinguishable from the barren landscape. Again,

> A man,
>
> Heavy and iron-black,
> Alone in sun,
> Threading the grass.
> The cold,
>
> Coming again
> As Spring
> Came up the valley,
> But to stay
>
> Rooted deep in the land.

And again,

> The stallion
> Stood like water
> In cold shade
> On riven soil.

The man and the stallion, though distinct from the land, have become so much part of its processes, partake of its life so deeply, that they seem virtually its attributes rather than separate existences. The things chosen to describe the stallion in the landscape are themselves taken from the landscape, so that the animal seems hardly to separate itself out from its background. The anonymity of such lives, the sense of the poignance and beauty of obscure life persisting in bare, almost lifeless landscapes, pervades many of the poems of *The Bare Hills, Fire Sequence,* and *The Proof* (1928) and reappears in the great poems in heroic couplets of Winters's maturity.

It is in certain of the poems of *The Bare Hills* that Winters first allows specific features of his own biography to enter his poetry; in previous poems the poet had existed purely as an observing sensibility. Poem 5 of part 1 begins

> My mother
> Foresaw deaths

which, according to Thomas Parkinson, the editor of Hart Crane's letters to Winters, was literally true. "His mother correctly predicted the death of some twenty people and when he was very young dragged him off to séances" (Parkinson, *Crane and Winters,* p. 133). The poem begins with this reference to death and continues with an image of the young poet struggling clear of his morbid past. Significantly, he attempts to leave the occult world, suggested at the poem's opening, by study—that is, by an exercise of the intellect, which was to be Winters's typical reaction to the darker areas of human experience. Paradoxically, his self-denying study returns him to the world:

> My very breath
> Disowned in nights of study,
> And page by page
> I came on spring.

The rest of the poem invokes and celebrates different kinds of beginnings: the writing of a poem, the cock-crow of dawn, the appearance of love, Christ as an image of resurrection, and the spring itself are all brought together in eight short lines, but with no sense of crowding or strained rhetoric. Rather the lines are themselves an example of the desolate, bare beauty they celebrate. The poem ends with the line, "And spring, the sleep of the dead," which returns us to the opening motif of death, but subdued by the word *sleep,* implying the awakening of spring and resurrection.

In this poem Winters writes of "The Christ, eternal / In the scented cold." Christ is used as an image of life, which, as if miraculously, re-awakens every spring, but there is no sense of a transcendental or specifically religious meaning being given to the concept. Christ appears fairly often in the early poems, usually, as here, as a token of earthly resurrection. The word is absent from the later poems (that is, those written after the publication of *The Proof*, 1930) though "Jesus of Nazareth" does appear: here the implications are of Jesus' ethical beliefs and the ethics based by others on his teaching or example. The Christ of the early poems is a much more directly experiential concept, suggesting a vivid force in nature: Jesus of Nazareth, by contrast, suggests an ethical system, an intellectual construction. This shift of emphasis, within a particular complex of ideas, from the immediate to the mediated, from experience to interpretation, is typical of the general direction of Winters's development.

The word *God* in his work has a different meaning again. It occurs in both early and later work; its implications vary somewhat, but at no point is there a suggestion of belief in a personal God like that of Christianity. He remained a religious skeptic throughout his life, but he was strongly attracted to what may be loosely termed the religious edge of metaphysics. He had, as we shall see, a particularly high regard for the metaphysics of Roman Catholicism. We can discern in his work, especially in the later work, an intense concern with the problems of absolutes and authority. Even the earliest work manifests a strong drive towards independence of judgment and practice which probably effectively debarred him from committing himself to any institution such as the Catholic church, but equally evident is an almost obsessive desire for certainty, for a knowledge that admitted of no doubt or ambiguity. He had a particular taste for poetry that treats of man's metaphysical ignorance, of an unanswered desire for certitude, and his strongest dislike was reserved for poets who, he considered, blurred such issues, either by tawdry ideas or by self-deception.

The metaphysical subject that interests Winters most in *The Bare Hills* is Time and its relation to Being. The interaction of these two imponderables is seen at its most vivid in life, particularly in those brief minutiae of life that dominate the pages of *The Immobile Wind* and *The Magpie's Shadow*. But though life exists as process in time, the mind which observes life, itself a product of that process, seems to be able to abstract itself and to exist in some sense outside of time. This notion was to become particularly important to Winters. In his early poems the existence of the thoughts of the past in literature and philosophy functions as an example of how time may be evaded or overcome, and there are frequent references to print, pages, books, and the like, as evidences of thought born from the processes of life but now standing aside from them. Again we may suggest Winters's early awareness of death, because of his illness, as a source both for his minute apprehension of time passing and for his desire to in some way transcend it. In a review of *The Bare Hills* Agnes Lee Freer referred to the notion of time in the book as "almost a physical sensation of pain to him" (quoted in Parkinson, *Crane and Winters*, p. 117).

"The Crystal Sun," poem 6 of part 1 of *The Bare Hills*, is yet another work concerned with spring. The poem opens with a description of "a living tide of green," and, as in "The Morning," the response of the observer is an ambiguous scream, as if possessed by ecstatic fear. In the second stanza an entranced communion with nature, an intimation of pantheistic oneness, is celebrated:

> The stones
> That held the hills,
> The sun that held the
> Sky with all its
> Spreading rays, were of one
> Substance
>   and my God
> Lay at my feet
> And spoke from out
> My shadow, eyed me
> From the bees:
> And he was not, or
> Else I—none could
> Say.

The sense of radiant unity conveyed by the image of the sun's rays (a common image in mystical literature) is certainly ecstatic in implication, but the loss of personal separateness reinforces that edge of panic suggested by the first stanza's "I screamed." The next stanza lists specifics of local life as if the poet is clutching hold of particulars to convince himself of the world's reality. (The specifics mentioned are admittedly peculiar, but their peculiarity is probably incidental and I do not think they are meant to signify anything other than a return to the mundane. The literary source for their strangeness is probably the dandyish particulars of some of Wallace Stevens's early poetry, which Winters greatly admired.) There follows this stanza:

> What wonder, then,
> That I went mad
> Amid the cloudy stone
> And looked at
> Print.

Returning from the trance, and from the slightly bizarre details of life about him, the poet feels "that way madness lies." The stone is cloudy not only because of its color but because it seems to disintegrate in the mystic's apprehension. This sense of the lack of solidity of the world as mystically experienced was reinforced by Winters's reading of the physics of his time, which was breaking down subatomic particles into electrical charges: this is the subject of "The Vigil," a poem from *The Proof* (1930). Mystic and physicist joined forces in declaring substantial matter to be illusory. In fear of madness the poet turns to "print," the written wisdom of the past, in hope of finding something abiding. And it is print, the repository of thought, which helps him regain his mental balance, so that once again

> The earth took form
> In my place
>   at my feet.

The poem records a loss of a sense of reality through mystical experience, and the regaining of this sense through print, that is, conceptual thought rather than unmediated experience. In this it is indicative of the later developments in Winters's poetry.

The edge of terror present in this poem is almost absent from the remainder of part 1 of *The Bare Hills*. This section, which had begun with the passage of time manifested in spring, reawakening, and growth, ends with the same passage manifested in autumn and intimations of decay. It thus repeats the seasonal structure of *The Magpie's Shadow*. The aspens of that book reappear as emblems of evanescence—

> The fainter aspens
> Thin to air

—and in "The Upper Meadows" there is this fine moment recording time passing:

> Grass laid low by what comes,
> Feet or air—
> But motion, aging.

In two of the poems there is expressed a desire for some kind of epiphany or savior, but the desire even as it is expressed is tempered with a recognition of its vanity; in "The Moonlight"

> . . . no guardian
>
> Strides through distance upon distance,
> His eyes a web of sleep.

And in "The Impalpable Void" the poet's representative is a latter-day Adam,

> But no beast comes
> Golden and silent,
> A rest for the hand.

The lonely protagonist of this poem is brought out of his tranced communion:

> his vision
> Drifts from the place
> Where the lawn was,
> Where dew was the sea.

(How well rhythm and the image of the last line indicate the rapt depth of vision.) Bereaved of grace, he senses not only the approach of the year's winter, but of a winter of the mind:

> The leaves will be fainter than rain
> Ere he senses the void
> High on air.

Part 2 of *The Bare Hills* is divided into seven sections; the most typical, in the sense of being closest to Winters's other early work, are the poems of sections 1, 5, and 6. The sections which point towards the poems of Winters's maturity are 2 (most of which he included in the *Collected Poems*) and 7. The poems of the first section introduce the themes treated throughout part 2.

The first poem, "Genesis," uses the image of a door as a metaphor for introspection and its sterility. The second poem, continuing the biblical analogy, is called "Exodus" and shows us man "pursuing the slow monsters of the brain." The exodus involved seems to be an escape from the self. In the third poem the mind confronts the external world in the shape of a "wrinkled tree," gnarled, persistent life at its least obviously vital.

The fourth poem, "Moonrise," is about a dog possessed by the moon. The moon occurs frequently in Winters's poetry, usually with a suggestion of dark and uncontrollable aspects of life, fecund but terrifying and not subject to the conscious will. And the fifth poem continues this suggestion, being an invocation to Hecate. This short sequence traces, albeit obscurely, a movement out of the self towards a force associated with night and the moon; the force invoked is itself obscure, but using the evidence of Winters's later poetry we can guess that it is the imagination as a source of hidden truth.

The first poem of section 2 is "The Cold." The tentativeness of Winters's early rhythms is here used with brilliant effect to describe ice slowly taking hold on a landscape; the poet watches in fascinated horror, his brain held in a numbness analogous to his body's. What moves the poet is the bare clarity of the scene and the certainty of the stars' course above it—they are given their ancient names as if to emphasize their persistence. Again landscape is used to suggest a mental state and here, as elsewhere in the early poems, the later postsymbolist method is adumbrated.

Bareness, clarity, and certainty are the qualities Winters was to continue to value throughout his career as a poet. There is a direct relation between the kind of scene, landscape, or incident he chose to delineate in his verse—bare landscapes in clear air, incidents purged of moral confusion where choice is difficult but necessary, and ethical judgment not in doubt—and the stylistic qualities he sought to cultivate in his own work and looked for in the work of others: honesty before the chosen theme, complete clarity of purpose and expression, the excision of blurring rhetoric.

The second poem of this section is one more example of a poem beginning with an image of death, which slowly expands into a celebration of early spring. It ends with the lines,

> and the pale and small
> children that run shrieking
> through March doorways
> burst like bubbles
> on the cold twigs
> block on block away.

The children are like the young goatherds who appear in many of the early poems, embodying the tough, persistent innocence of the landscape.

Poem 3, the last of this section, is one of the best known of the early poems, "Quod tegit omnia," and is probably the finest expression of the themes which preoccupied him during his twenties. The poem opens with a confused, rich image (which the later Winters would probably not have countenanced). A suggestion of earth's parturition produces a bear; immediately, in apposition to the bear, the poet shifts his ground to the human mind, which

> stored with
> magnificence, proceeds into
> the mystery of time, now
> certain of its choice of
> passion, but uncertain of the
> passion's end.

The bear represents the mind, powerful, heavy with passion, but ignorant, foraying into reality. The specific passion evoked is the passion of the intellect, our need to know. Again the rhythm of the poetry is a major factor in our apprehension of the phenomenon described—the verse reaches forward with the slow, hypnotic concentration of the bear-mind. The second stanza is concerned with Plato, and through the shorthand of his name the chief concepts associated with him—unchanging Truth subsisting in a pure realm divorced from the quotidian. The poet is obscurely moved by the Platonic vision, but in the next stanza returns to the temporal, to Time, "the sine-pondere," "an excellence at which one / sighs." In its excellence, its imperturbability, it seems paradoxically to partake of the eternal and unchanging. But in the last stanza the poet declares unequivocally that his place is the temporal, immediate world,

> Adventurer in
> living fact, the poet
> mounts into the spring,
> upon his tongue the taste of
> air becoming body: is
> embedded in this crystalline
> precipitate of time.

Time in the previous stanza had been capitalized as if in recognition of its abstract and absolute status; here the lower case brings the concept down to earth as it were—it is time as lived process rather than as an object for abstract contemplation. The poem is a statement of Winters's early belief that the material of the poet is the immediate and specific rather than the conceptual and ideal world of Plato. The poet's realm is "living fact."

Section 3 of part 2 of *The Bare Hills* consists of five love poems. As if to emphasize the poet's choice of the quotidian and physical as his proper realm, the poems are dense with a half-articulate, violently adumbrated physical passion. Four of the five poems describe night scenes (the events of the other poem could also take place at night—there is no indication of time) and the force of passion is conveyed not only by evocations of awesome darkness (darkness in Winters's verse tends to suggest loss of spiritual control) but by the traditional and universal prop of violent weather:

> cold rain hovers
> in the air and
> breaks, and drenches
> shoulders, hair, and
> legs

and

> The wind came
> down the gulley
> buffeting the earth like a
> great rock—
>   I
> trembled in the wind

The most interesting poem of this section is poem 4, "Under Rain," which begins with a description of a house that seems about to be swept away in a violent storm. Winters returned to this theme later, most clearly in the sonnet "Phasellus ille." In the early love poem we are only given to understand that the house is not in fact swept away: the violence of the weather is assimilated to the lovers' passion, which is the main focus of the poem's interest. But in the later sonnet the emotional emphasis is on the house's staunch resistance to the storm. That is, Winters's vision did not change radically, but his emphasis did. In both poems the house clearly represents the poet's mind almost swept away by instinct, passion, the flood of immediate experience (this is not to deny, of course, that it also simply represents a house!), but in the youthful love poem Winters is content to leave it at that, and our chief impression is of violent force. In the later poem it is not the passion that is celebrated but the house's, the mind's, resistance to it.

Section 4 is rather derivative of Wallace Stevens's early work, familiar to Winters since his school days. The first poem in particular could easily have come from the opening pages of *Harmonium*. Another influence, mentioned previously, is William Carlos Williams; it is clearest in the charming imagist vignette of a young goat, "April." This is the poem in full:

> The little goat
> crops
> new grass lying down
> leaps up eight inches
> into air and
> lands on four feet.
> Not a tremor—
> solid in the
> spring and serious
> he walks away.

The fifth section is a return to the minimal verse of *The Magpie's Shadow*; it comprises three single-line poems. Two of the three work very well, given the extreme limitation of the form. Number 2 is "Love Song," which consists of the line "What have I said of thee?" with the implication that anything said must fall short of the beloved's excellence; here the brevity is made part of the compliment. Poem 3, "Sleep," is the line "O living pine, be still!" The restless flickering of the pine needles that is implied reminds us of the aspen tree in the previous volume. The movement presumably refers to the kaleidoscopic activity of the dreaming mind, desiring oblivion but unable to achieve it.

In the sixth section the poet's horizon suddenly widens: the minimal and self-involved verse of the earlier sections (in which there are no people except the poet himself, an anonymous lover and the occasional unindividualized goatherd) is followed by a poetry concerned with the lives of the poor in a bare, desolate landscape. These poems are intimately connected with the subject of Winters's only short story, *The Brink of Darkness*, and I shall discuss them together with that story in Chapter 3.

The last section of part 2 is a summation of foregoing themes, arranged as a spiritual odyssey. The language is, particularly in the first poem of the group, "The Streets," much looser, more discursive than anything Winters had so far published. "The Streets" deals with the literal and spiritual wanderings of the poet, or his persona, in search of epiphany or spiritual enlightenment. It is the first poem (of the very few) in which Winters attempted to deal with a modern urban landscape; the randomness of such a landscape functions as an analogy to the randomness of the poet's wanderings and experiences; the fact that the epiphany is elusive implies a condemnation of the disordered life described. The poem does not altogether escape what Winters later called "the fallacy of imitative form"—the doctrine that a poem must be chaotic to describe chaos, or confusing to describe confusion. It is wordily obscure in parts, though the general direction is clear. A short opening stanza suggests the strangeness of external reality, "the algebra of miracles," as if the commonest features of the world, cold, air, and sun, withheld some arcane meaning. This prompts the speaker to set out on his quest for enlightenment. The obvious source of such enlightenment for a young man is the religion in which he has grown up, and the second stanza deals with the speaker's "quarrel" with Christianity. He rejects it, though without rancor. In stanza 3, intimations of a pantheistic absorption in nature, such as we have already remarked in previous poems, invite the poet, but he hesitates in awed wonder; again ecstasy is balanced by fear:

> The terror in the taste
> and sound of the unseen has
> overwhelmed me; I am on the
> mythical and smokey soil at last.

In the fourth stanza we enter the city and acedia sets in: the poet is disgusted with his own vapidity; the quotidian is merely banal. There are still intimations of divinity in even the most commonplace surroundings (the "God in the streetcar" of this last stanza is probably an emblem for the mining poor, for the wretchedness of whose lives Winters felt great sympathy at this time, as is evident from *Fire Sequence*), and the poem ends in irritated exhaustion:

> black streets like
> unlit windows, coffee hour by hour,
> and chilling sleep.

The second poem of the section, "The Rows of Cold Trees," begins like a direct continuation of "The Streets." It is the most substantial of the early poems Winters chose to include in his *Collected Poems* and was a particular favorite of Allen Tate. We have left the amorphous confusion of the previous poem and are back with the solitary consciousness facing reality without aid. The poem opens with the phrase "To be my own Messiah to the / burning end." This is the task of the romantic poet who rejects the revelations of religious dogma, seeing himself as a vatic interpreter of the natural world, somewhat in the manner of Wordsworth.

But the phrase, given the normal meaning of *Messiah*, draws attention to the apparent impossibility of the task and is an indication that Winters was already uneasy with such attitudes. The first stanza gives us the poet in his room, studying, meditating on reality, at the edge of madness with the magnitude of his task. In the second stanza we have him again walking the streets in lonely meditation (such passages in Winters's poetry recall similar moments in Frost and Hardy, though, for me at least, the "metaphysical cramp," the sheer wonder and terror before reality, are more urgently conveyed in Winters's poems than in the work of either Frost or Hardy). The third stanza continues the image of the poet's wanderings, now "among the tombs" where

> —the rushing of the air
> in the rich pines above my head is that which
> ceaseth not nor stirreth whence it is:

The wind seethes and is constant, it is the "immobile wind" of the first volume. In its constancy and power it is offered as a manifestation of absolute reality, and the archaic definition of "that which ceaseth not nor stirreth whence it is," which reads as a mystical definition of God, attempts to confer on the emblem the authority of the language of revelation. It is possible that the stanza also implies a metaphoric reference to the "living dead," the philosophers and poets of the past, whose work sustains the author in his quest; read in the context of Winters's later poetry, this concept seems to hover at the edge of the stanza's meaning. However, it contradicts the opening emphatic statement of a wholly unaided quest.

In the last stanza the poet refers to the "madness of my youth that left me with / this cold eye for the fact." In 1964 Winters explained this phrase as a reference to his "very intense" adolescent solipsism, in which the boundaries between the self and the world seemed dissolved in trance. The poem ends with a repetition of the essential loneliness of the quest. In his later explication of the poem Winters wrote, "The poem is the poem of a very desperate young man." In its confrontation of the isolated human consciousness and the alien, absolute power manifested in "that which ceaseth not nor stirreth whence it is," it represents a quest to find meaning where there is in fact only being, the insentient natural world. It is interesting that in this struggle to wrest meaning from what the poet perceives as essentially alien and meaningless, the verse approaches the traditional form of English meditative poetry and closes on an iambic pentameter. This is despite the fact that the poem was written during the time Winters was "doing my most radical experimenting" ("By Way of Clarification," p. 130). The attempt to articulate meaning and mental process, rather than the transmission of pure imagist sensation, was already associated in the poet's mind with traditional form.

Poem 3 of this section is "Prayer beside a Lamp." One of Winters's favorite poems of the seventeenth century was later to be Vaughan's "The Lamp," and there are similarities between the two poems. However, the first mention of Vaughan in Winters's prose is in a review dated 1927, the date before which Winters claimed he knew little English poetry, and it is likely that the Vaughan poem was not known to him when he wrote his own exploration of the same theme. If this is so it may well be that one of the reasons for his later admiration for the Vaughan poem was its confirmation to him of the ideas he had set out in his own verse.

The poem begins with a theme we have already met—a house resisting an onslaught of wind. In line 4 the poet seems to shift ground:

> The mind that lives on
> print becomes too savage.

One statement is a metaphor for the other—the house resisting the wind is like the print-trained mind that abstracts and organizes reality, resisting the wind of experience. The poem seems at first like a self-admonition to be more open to the flux of reality, curiously un-Wintersian advice. There is a kind of compromise suggested at the end of the first stanza: "my house is built of bone that bends." By bending one both retains identity and responds to the wind. The second stanza is a series of questions which are basically one question: the poet rhetorically asks the reader (or himself) if he can truly face the alien strangeness of the universe—its vastness, violence and incomprehensibility.

In the last stanza we have the lamp ("the humming oil drives back the / darkness") representing the working intellect, but not the intellect engaged with the vastness of the universe, which would be as futile as expecting the lamp to illuminate the whole night. Rather the mind is busy with those restricted areas of reality it can comprehend. A sense that vast areas of reality are incomprehensible, and that to attempt to understand them is at best folly and at worst to court madness, gradually emerges from Winters's poetry. It is a position curiously similar to that of certain philosophical schools then emerging that attempted, for quite other reasons, to simply not ask the larger metaphysical questions.

The final poem of this section is "Man Regards Eternity in Aging." The poem is concerned with autumn, in which "rotting Time again leaves bare the god." "The god," as the following lines make clear, is the earth itself—ultimate reality is thus for Winters still wholly immanent in the world. The autumn of the season is linked to the poem's speaker, who is "aging," in the autumn of his own life. In the second half of the poem he addresses a "youth of the village," who stands "glassyeyed . . . haunter of the rigid silences," an example of the solipsistically absorbed adolescent Winters described himself as having been. The poem can be seen as a farewell to this tranced state of youthful revery—the youth is regarded from outside, the speaker is "aging"—but it offers no other suggestions of meaning or coherence apart from the nature in which the youth had been absorbed—"the god" is the world.

Part 3 of *The Bare Hills* consists of two short prose passages descriptive of Winters's school-teaching life. What speaks to us in these descriptions is the loneliness and privation of the life, a loneliness that seems to have an almost hallucinatory effect, and his sense of impotent compassion for the anonymous brutal lives of the miners and their children. One sentence—"Then I withdrew to an empty room I shared with an indeterminate consciousness"—hints at a theme later to be of great importance in Winters's work, that of demonic possession. From the evidence of the short story *The Brink of Darkness* we can surmise that this notion gradually became important to him while he was living alone in the more isolated parts of the country he knew in his early twenties, and that he fell a prey to it because of his solitude and hypersensitivity. This theme was to be an extremely important factor in Winters's later turning away from the blurred and unexplained toward what is precise and amenable to reason.

In 1927 Winters published in *American Caravan* a group of poems of which he had high hopes, *Fire Sequence*. Hart Crane had said that he intended *The Bridge* to be an alternative to the lax pessimism of Eliot's *The Waste Land*, and Winters wrote that he felt his poem to be trying for something similar. To quote Thomas Parkinson, "The 'Fire Sequence' and 'The Bridge' were parallel if not competing works. On September 15 of 1928, Winters wrote to Tate that the 'Fire Sequence' had attempted a synthesis of more diverse materials than 'The Bridge,' and that if it fell short of Crane's work, that was because of Crane's genius" (Parkinson, *Crane and Winters*, p. 72).

The sequence must, I think, be judged an ambitious failure. Winters here further extends the range of his language to include colloquial speech, and his subject matter includes not only the vignettes of natural life and meditations on spring and death, with all of which he felt more or less at home, but the random violence of the miners' lives. This ambitious range of subject matter and language is not sufficiently focused and the sequence as a whole sprawls disjointedly. Winters was obviously dissatisfied with the narrow concentration of his work hitherto and was groping to find a new language and a wider subject matter. This temporary loss of direction continued with most of *The Proof* and was not resolved until Winters's commitment to traditional form and meter. The poems of *Fire Sequence* and *The Proof* are in general inferior to many of the poems of *The Bare Hills* (which contains the majority of his most impressive early poems). *Fire Sequence* is best regarded as a false start, an attempt to think his way out of his early imagism, but along a path that was not particularly congenial to his talent.

Fire Sequence is truly a cycle, beginning with a poem on coal as an example of inert stored potential energy, taking the reader through different manifestations of such energy, and ending with a poem on death, the return to the ground that is the home of the opening poem's coal.

The first three poems celebrate the release of potency; after the opening verses on coal, the second item is a love poem in which the beloved is

> freed from death
> now twisting a
> slow course in Time

and love is seen, traditionally, as a way to evade the years, to triumph over time and death. The third poem returns to Winters's most persistent subject in his early work, the release of natural forces in spring. But in this poem the landscape is that of a small mining township, such as those where Winters had taught in his early twenties, and the spring celebrated is not that of the kids and goatherds we have found hitherto, but of "the dances dripping blood."

Poems 4, 5 and 6, named "Bill," "The Vanquished," and "The Victor," deal with a fight. In poem 4 the defeated person speaks in truculent defiance. In poem 5 the poet observes the defeated and places him in a general context of brutal poverty and failure; the poem ends with a comparison of the beaten miner to Christ, or rather an assimilation of his being to that of Christ, which suggests, in terms of the associations of the word in Winters's poetry, a future resurrection of the defeated:

> stiff ruts lay black and heavy
> Christ lay

>   drunk among them in a
>   gully stones were white in dark He
>   shuddered into sleep.

In the sixth poem the victor of the fight is celebrated—Winters's compassion for the defeated does not preclude a fascination with violent independence, or, remembering his boxing interests, a good fighter. The winner of the fight is seen as a personification of the ruthless energies of spring:

>   The Slav stood in the
>   door the green light hung a
>   mist about his black hair
>   forehead shadowed like the hills
>   above the valley.

There is a momentary suggestion in these poems concerned with the fight of the tough Hemingwayesque pose adopted by many American writers at this time. The seventh poem is about a burial, apparently of the Slav of poem 6. As he represented in some degree the energies of the spring, the poem makes explicit the theme of the whole sequence—the storing, release and re-storing of energy:

>   now let the granite
>   press you into
>   coal black rich
>   with heat.

Poem 8, "Vacant Lot," is an image of winter sterility; after the explosion of energy in the fight and the burial, the year has passed into a purely potential state again. In poem 9, "Tragic Love," the suicide of a girl in winter is described. The central section describes vicariously the girl's experience, her wonder and terror, which are clearly similar to the poet's own experiences as described in other poems. A short coda to the poem describes a species of resurrection; again the cycle of death and return is emphasized:

>   Then between her thighs
>   the seeded grasses
>   of airy summer—
>   the slow hairlike flame.

Poem 10 is an invocation to Christ, and though it is called "To the Crucified" it is Christ as an emblem of resurrection who is invoked. The first half of the poem is about a fire, which is both a literal fire, an image of released energy, and a metaphor for Christ as a force that has apparently "died"—like coal—but is able to flare out in illumination. As in many of Winters's early poems (for example, the second of "Two Songs of Advent" from *The Immobile Wind*) it is difficult to say which part of the metaphor (in this case, that of the coyote) is vehicle and which is tenor. Is the poem about a fire incidentally compared to Christ, or about Christ compared to a fire? Both aspects of the metaphor are subjects of the poem, and the focus alternatively shifts from one to the other.

The next poem is an invocation to the force that is able to draw out the earth's potency, so beginning the process that will result in the future stored energy of coal:

> O Sun who make
> the earth sweat
> shadowy and acid
> life for whom the
> black pines grip
> and tear the living
> rock

and the poem continues with a mixture of the natural manifestations of this power, and of man's artifacts, which are seen as "blasphemies" against it.

Poems 12 and 13 are concerned with themes by now familiar to us: lovers in a house threatened by violent storm (12) and the mystery of earth's slow changes in early spring (13).

Poem 14, "The Bitter Moon," is Winters's first significant exploration of a complex of ideas to which he was later to return frequently. This is the notion of the moon and moonlight as symbols of the poetic imagination and of a world in which experience is presented with the clarity of hallucination but with suggestions of an inexplicable authority that threatens to undermine the poet's mental balance. He explored this theme at regular intervals throughout his poetic career, most notably in the long sequence *Theseus: A Trilogy*, and in "Moonlight Alert." Winters's poems on moonlight and the imagination have the authority of personal conviction, but it is possible that a literary source, or at least confirmation, of one aspect of this symbolism, was the poetry of Wallace Stevens. As R. P. Blackmur wrote in *Language as Gesture*, "Moonlight for Mr. Stevens is mental, fictive, related to the imagination and meaning of things." The supposition is given further weight by the fact that Winters used other symbols in a manner very reminiscent of Stevens's work, most notably the sea. However, the edge of hallucinatory fear (of madness or possession) that is present in Winters's treatment of this theme is wholly and typically his own.

The opening of the poem reads like a particularly desperate form of love poetry, with the beloved addressed as a possible salvation from the poet's predicament:

> Should I believe
> in this your body, take it
> at its word? I have believed
> in nothing.

But it becomes apparent as the poem proceeds that the "you" is the "Bitter Moon" of the title. The second stanza opens with the signal word of Winters's early poetry, *scream*, suggesting that metaphysical terror that pervades *The Bare Hills*. Connected with this is a theme that was to assume a central place in Winters's work, that of "The voices / of the dead," which "still vibrate." These are the "living dead," the great minds of the past whose example and achievement draws the young poet away from the quotidian. In this poem the imagination (moonlight) is hardly distinguished from the world of the "living dead," that is, the life of the mind, and in particular of the rational will, guided by the wisdom of the past. In his later work they were to be sharply distinguished, and indeed came to represent almost opposite extremes of mental life. Here they are seen together as an alternative to the metaphysical impasse in which the poet found himself. This impasse was the result of an attempt to go beyond pure, unmediated sensation, to apprehend meaning where only Being had hitherto seemed accessible: the attempt had resulted in the terror repeatedly signaled in the early work by the uncharacteristically emotive word *scream*. This poem is a declaration of allegiance to the life of the mind, of interpretation and evaluation, and an implicit rejection of the life of tranced absorption in sensation that had been the subject of his first two books.

Fire Sequence ends with a poem in which Winters draws together the themes of death and resurrection, and the new theme of the surviving intellect:

> Old concentrate of thought, ironveined and slow,
> that willed itself and labored out of earth,
> man grinds his plough through corrugated rock
> and draws a wake that lasts a thousand years.

The poem is called "The Deep: A Service for All the Dead." The images of coal and resurrection have been developed beyond the notion of mere stored energy into a metaphor for mental achievement that survives beyond death. The sequence is not a turning away from life, though it does move from the brutal insistence of the fight in poems 4, 5, and 6 to the realm of the intellect in poems 14 and 15; it is rather an attempt to gain a perspective on life, to move beyond sensation to meaning. Winters has here begun to "think his way out" of the solipsistic dream of youth, a dream that had at times seemed close to nightmare, towards the more intellectually coherent poetry of his maturity.

The Proof, published in 1930, is a transitional volume of poetry, containing both imagist, free-verse poems and poems written in traditional meters. A number of the latter are included in the *Collected Poems*, and as they mark the beginning of Winters's mature style, I consider them, together with the later poems, in chapter 4. Here I am mainly concerned with the poems written in the earlier manner.

The language of the poems of *The Proof*, compared with that of the first three books, continues the move toward a more hectic and violent vocabulary noticeable in parts of *Fire Sequence*. In "To the Painter Polelomena" the following verbs occur: *wring, seize, crush, smelt, temper, drives, bursts, cracks*. All suggest a struggle with reality rather than the mere observation of it. There are only four relatively neutral verbs in the piece (*lasts, is, lives, blows*). In a poem like "See Los Angeles First" the reader is bombarded with heterogeneous and incongruous images; as in "The Streets" (from *The Bare Hills*) there is a suggestion of what Winters later called "the fallacy of imitative form," the attempt to convey confusion by writing confusing poetry. The predominant season of the volume is high summer rather than the spring of the previous books, and again the language used to describe the season suggests violent extremes of experience:

> now incest burns
> the very shade
> hate rains about me
> in the red light
> through the trees
>
> July!
>   ("The Red Month")

The themes of the poems are in general those already established, but they are given a blurred urgency that is alien to the atmosphere of the earliest work. The poetry still seems eccentric to everyday human experience, but it is nervous or angry rather than neurasthenic. One theme that becomes important in this book is that of a kind of spiritual ascent. We perceive it metaphorically in "Sunflower," where the lines

> Hold fast
> to what you are, in spite of
> the wormseething loam,
> the boiling land

though addressed to the flower, read as self-admonition, in "Satyric Complaint," and in "Communion." "Satyric Complaint" contains the following lines:

> The earth became wood, wood was
> flesh, flesh beauty, beauty mind. Mind
> became agony to glare
> from gray eyes knowing
> its end rooted in its feet.

The significance of these transitions of form is suggested by the title—the satyr is part human, part beast, and in his dual nature suggests the human dualism of mind and body. Winters's poetry had hitherto dealt mainly with sensation presented in uninterpreted images, but, as we have seen, his poetry had by the end of the 1920s begun to move toward a more mediated and abstract account of reality. It is this struggle that is expressed in "Satyric Complaint": the end of the quoted passage is significant—"its end rooted in its feet"; the feet of the satyr are of course cloven, the feet of a goat. They are evidence of the bestial side of the satyr's being and therefore represent in the scheme of the poem the sensations of the phenomenal world, which are the source of our mental life. Winters later adopted a line from his wife's poetry—"tangled with earth all ways we move"—as an epigraph for one of his poems, and the line expresses a similar awareness: that the mind's activity, which attempts to transcend the phenomenal and immediate life of sensation, is unavoidably rooted in that life.

In "Communion" we have a description of the same struggle to free the mind from quotidian sensation so that it can participate in a more abstract life. In this it is reminiscent of poem 14 ("The Bitter Moon") of *Fire Sequence*: the two are a distinct change of attitude from the atmosphere of "Quod tegit omnia" (written before 1925), where the poet had rejected such conceptions, preferring to remain as "Adventurer in / living fact." "Quod tegit omnia" had rejected Platonism, and it is perhaps indicative of Winters's changing attitude that the transition from flesh to beauty and from beauty to mind (in "Satyric Complaint") is a Platonic formulation. In "Communion" the mind is able to participate in "death-less will," a far more abstract communion than that celebrated in the ear-liest poems with their tranced absorption in natural phenomena. The poem suggests (albeit weakly; Winters did not reprint it) a participation in that life of the mind invoked in the last two poems of *Fire Sequence*.

Winters's early poems show three related kinds of development: from sensory images to abstractions, from the minimal to the discursive, and from the particular to the general. These three trends, already evident in the work of his twenties, were to intensify throughout his poetic career. The earliest work is concerned with discrete, specific sense impressions; however, these are usually presented as emblems of an epiphany in which observer and observed are felt to merge their identities in a Words-worthian "privileged moment," rather than as mere things for them-selves in the manner of most of Williams's verse. The epiphany was deliberately sought by Winters, as the theoretical writings of his twenties make plain. However this sense of communion with nature is accom-panied in many of the poems by an atavistic fear ("the terror in the taste / and sound of the unseen") which is quite alien to the similar quest which we find in, for example, Wordsworth or Emerson. Winters's ap-prehension of nature or Being as a horrifying flux into which the con-templative spirit seemed to be ineluctably drawn was deepened by his reading of the physicists of his time (see "The Vigil"). The sense of con-stant flux was further reinforced by his hypersensitivity to the passage of time and to the fact of death—a hypersensitivity that probably derived from his illness and convalescence. This convalescence is also the likely root cause of the very substantial number of poems on spring, the re-newal of life, and resurrection.

From *The Bare Hills* onward, an atmosphere of metaphysical tension, which sometimes approaches hysteria, is apparent in the poems. Far from being attracted to the numinous specifics of *The Immobile Wind* and *The Magpie's Shadow*, the protagonist of these poems wishes to move be-yond particular sensation to a life of the intellect. The struggle is ex-pressed in violent and indeed desperate language. The satyr of "Satyric Complaint" is like an emblem of Winters himself—unable to transcend the physical world but desperately desiring to do so.

The language of the earliest poems is extremely simple. It is largely composed of words that have an unambiguous sensory (rather than abstract) referent, and it is very largely monosyllabic. The rhythm is usually hesitant, leading the reader on as if in rapt expectancy. Winters has a particular preference in these early poems for ending a line with a word that offers no resting place for the reader (he frequently ends lines with the definite article, which gives the effect both of leading the reader on and also, in the slight pause of the line end, of hesitating before the following noun). These imagist poems are written with a tentative delicacy that is extremely beguiling in itself and that is admirably suited to conveying the minutiae of life that Winters was then attempting to record. Abstract and polysyllabic words are rare in the early poems: their appearance is often a signal of the hysteria already referred to, as in phrases like "blackthrobbing blasphemies" ("The Sun") and "electric / apertures to Hell" ("Remembered Spring"). Often their appearance is unsuccessful and Winters seems to be searching for a way to accommodate a more complex language to what is still essentially a simple form. When such words appear successfully we seem to see the mind visibly raising itself to the concept, as with the word *humility* in this extract from "Simplex munditiis":

> The goat nips yellow blossoms
> shaken loose from rain—
> with neck extended
> lifts a twitching flower
> high into wet air. Hard
> humility the lot of man
> to crouch beside
> this creature in the dusk
> and hold the mind clear.

But Winters became dissatisfied with the extremely limited subject matter and range of effects that could be incorporated into such poetry: "It was becoming increasingly obvious to me that the poets whom I most admired were Baudelaire and Valéry, and Hardy, Bridges, and Stevens in a few poems each, and that I could never hope to approach the quality of their work by the method which I was using" (*Collected Poems of Yvor Winters*, p. 15).

Also, and equally importantly, he was becoming suspicious of the presuppositions that had led him to adopt his imagist technique. As he himself was to demonstrate in his later criticism, imagism, as he had practiced it, involved an idea of the value of the unique sensory moment as an epiphany in itself, and a corresponding notion of the poet's tranced absorption in the phenomena of the natural world as a self-evident good. Both these concepts he came not only to doubt but actually to fear. He gradually began to "think himself out" of imagism and its attendant philosophy. But the process was difficult; in the sudden widening of his aspirations, and under the influence of the metaphysical fear that pervades *The Bare Hills* and *The Proof* (a fear that will be discussed more fully in Chapter 3) Winters occasionally lost his bearings. The more ambitious of the poems of these two books and of *Fire Sequence* are often less satisfactory than the admittedly simpler images of *The Magpie's Shadow*. It was only with the poems in traditional meters that he was able to regain his spiritual and poetic balance. However, these early poems are often extremely fine in their expression of wonder before the natural phenomena of the world, in their bare clarity, and in their clear perception of the pathos and vivid strength of the lives they celebrate. This is nowhere more apparent than in the poem "Simplex munditiis," partly quoted above. Here is the poem in full:

Simplex munditiis

The goat nips yellow blossoms
shaken loose from rain—
with neck extended
lifts a twitching flower
high into wet air. Hard
humility the lot of man
to crouch beside
this creature in the dusk
and hold the mind clear;
to turn the sod,
to face the sod beside his door,
and wound it as his own flesh.
In the spring the blossoms
drown the air with joy,
the heart with sorrow.
One must think of this
in quiet. One must
bow his head and take
with roughened hands
sweet milk at dusk,
the classic gift of earth.

2 The Early Prose

A poem is . . . a permanent gateway
to waking oblivion.

    I have indicated in the previous chapter that during his late twenties Winters radically rethought his position on the nature of poetry and its relations with reality. There is little prose from before this period: one could claim that in his early twenties he was a more or less spontaneous poet who had no conscious system of poetics, and that it was only when his poetry became problematic to him that he attempted to work out for himself a conscious theoretical position. There is some small truth in this, but Winters's early interest in the nature of poetry is evident from his most substantial piece of early prose, the essay "The Testament of a Stone," published in April 1924 and later incorporated into his M.A. thesis. The essay is a survey of the nature of imagism.

    The first prose piece Winters published was a highly favorable review of *The Collected Poems of Edwin Arlington Robinson* (1922). Readers of his later criticism will be aware of his high regard for Robinson's poetry, but it may come as a surprise to find the twenty-one-year-old author of the minimal images of *The Magpie's Shadow* praising work so alien to his own. A further surprise, for those familiar with Winters's later likes and dislikes, is that the review opens with a quotation from Emerson. Though Emerson is described as "a sentimental philosopher," it is certain that the young Winters admired his work: he himself cited Emerson as the model for the last line of his "The Rows of Cold Trees," (see "By Way of Clarification," p. 131), and the quotation from Emerson included in the essay on Robinson contains the phrase "diadems and faggots," under which title Winters had published his first translations. The rest of the essay offers a curious mixture of names, some of whom, like Emily Dickinson and Robert Frost, Winters continued to praise throughout his life (often in a very qualified way), and others for whose work he later had little patience (such as D. H. Lawrence and Robert Browning). His notorious contempt for Poe and Whitman is already evident. But most noticeable is his awareness of his older contemporaries and of the importance of the poetry then being published; he mentions with approval Stevens, Eliot, Pound, H. D., and Marianne Moore. Stevens he calls "this greatest of living and of American poets"—a supremely confident, and correct, assertion from a twenty-one-year-old living in intellectual isolation in New Mexico, writing the year *before* Stevens's first volume of verse, *Harmonium*, was published.

Two points from this essay stand out as interesting when we consider Winters's later beliefs. First there is his consideration of philosophy and general concepts, on which he was to change his mind. He writes, "To those to whom philosophy is comprehensible it is not a matter of the first importance." A little further in the same paragraph we have: "When he [the poet] becomes more interested in the possible effects of his belief upon others, and expounds or persuades, he begins to deal with generalities, concepts . . . and becomes a philosopher, or more likely a preacher, a mere peddler . . . it is only the particular, the perception, that is perpetually startling. The generality, or concept, can be pigeon-holed, and absorbed, and forgotten."

It would be possible to claim that neither quotation contradicts the letter of any of Winters's later statements, but they certainly contradict the spirit. Winters shows himself in this early review to be aware of philosophy (though he later admitted he had read very little of it at this stage), but he considers it peripheral and probably inferior to poetry. At twenty-one he considers the stuff of poetry to be "the particular, the perception" and not "the generality, the concept." Though it is perhaps impossible for poetry to wholly transcend the particular, and though Winters always recognized this, nevertheless his later work gives far more prominence to "the generality, the concept," and can show an impatient irritation with those whose poetry rests solely in "the particular, the perception."

The second point of interest is the statement of a position from which Winters never moved, and it is surprising to see it explicitly set out in such an early essay. Winters praises Robinson because he focuses his "mind upon the object of the instant, makes it one with that object, and eliminates practically all individual 'personality' or self-consciousness. The so-called personal touch is reduced to a minimum of technical habit." The only phrase here to which the later Winters would probably have taken exception is "makes it one with that object." It would be possible to read this description of the poet's function as a plea for the imagism which Winters himself was then practicing, but the fact that he is describing Robinson in these terms shows us that this is not his main purpose. He is considering poetry as an attempt to come to terms with an external truth, and he is distinguishing good poetry from that kind of writing which is chiefly concerned with the expression of personality. The medium is like a lens through which the poet peers, and the clearer the lens the better. A distorting lens, a conspicuously eccentric manner, may be interesting if one is searching for eccentric personalities but not if one is concerned with external truth. This, of course, presupposes that there *is* an external truth, and Winters's later prose acknowledges this. The Robinson review continues with qualified praise for Browning, qualified because Browning "was so curious of the quirks with which he could approach an object, that he forgot the object in admiring, and ex-pecting admiration for, himself." Robinson is praised for keeping his eye on his subject; Browning is condemned for keeping his eye on himself.

The essay is somewhat brash in its scattering of names—the author is very insistently presenting his credentials as a man of taste—and in its ex cathedra tone. We might ascribe the tone to the author's youth, and no doubt this would be partially true; nevertheless, it did not noticeably mellow with time. I suspect that this mannerism, which has alienated many of Winters's readers, became a habit during the relatively lonely years in New Mexico. As there were few people living near him who can have shared his interests he was forced to come to his conclusions largely by his own unaided efforts. In his later criticism he often drew attention to the intellectual isolation of poets he admired (particularly American poets), and his remarks read like the sympathy of a fellow sufferer. His literary judgments frequently have the assertiveness that we associate with the autodidact.

A further mannerism that remained with Winters is the grading of poets, often by unstated criteria: for example, "She [Emily Dickinson] was greater than Emerson, was one of the greatest poets in our lan-guage." Winters very often uses words like *great* in such a context, and the reader is left to take it or leave it with no explanation. Even when the reader agrees, he would like to know how Winters had reached this con-clusion, and though constraints of space can be pleaded in a review, this is not always so. There is also the curious mixture of high praise and flat contempt meted out to the same poet and often in the same sentence. Two phrases about Emerson illustrate this: "a sentimental philosopher with a genius for a sudden twisted hardness of words" and "He was slight enough but at his best a master." Of course it is possible to defend these judgments—what is strange, and characteristic of Winters's prose, is to find words like *sentimental* and *genius* juxtaposed and referring to the same writer. Anyone who has read extensively in Winters's critical works will be able to multiply examples at will.

Winters always attempted to separate out the constituents of a work and to consider them in isolation. The tendency to consider a poet's work in its entirety, as a complex in which one aspect is always dependent upon others and is indeed a manifestation of them, is quite alien to Winters's method. He labeled certain elements of a given oeuvre as acceptable and others as unacceptable. In part this is a reaction againt the personality cult of romantic art; Winters's interest was in artifacts rather than in the personality of the artist, and facets of the personality, though they might *explain* aspects of a work of art, could not justify them. What Winters would not accept was that the "good" may be intimately and inseparably bound up with the "bad," so that an excision of one would destroy the other. In his desire for clarity Winters could not allow that a poet's triumphs may in fact be dependent on his faults, and that without the latter we could not have been given the former. This is especially noticeable in his discussions of Hart Crane's poetry. Winters later came to admire the writings of Aquinas very highly, and there is a passage in Aquinas, on Plato, that is curiously suggestive of Winters's critical technique. Aquinas wrote, "We should remember that for Plato whatever is separated in thought is in reality also separated" (*De veritate*, q.21.a.4,c). However, this reification of universals by the mind, so that whatever the mind can distinguish can also be distinguished in reality, though it was certainly available to Winters after his late twenties and though it is a conspicuous strategy of his later critical method, was probably not available to him at the stage when he wrote the essay on Robinson. The most plausible outside source for the stylistic mannerisms of the early essays is the criticism of Ezra Pound, and this is considered, together with Pound's influence on his later writings, in Chapter 5.

The other significant early essays are favorable reviews of books by William Carlos Williams, Marianne Moore, and Hart Crane (with whom he was at this time carrying on an amicable correspondence), and two essays on the American Indian. The first of these last is a very funny (and very angry) mockery of a fake Indian festival held in Santa Fe; the second is a review of the then-available translations of Indian poetry into English. Winters thought very highly of the translations, and reading his review it is immediately apparent why he was attracted to these poems; they are remarkably similar, in many ways, to his own early work. They are in the main short evocative images imbued with a sense of expectant wonder. A poem like "Song of Spring"—

> As my eyes
> search
> the prairie
> I feel the summer in the spring.

—or a line like "The snowy earth comes gliding, the snowy earth comes gliding" could well be by Winters himself, and such poems were an influence on the development of his own early verse. In his review he coins an image almost as fine as the poems he is discussing, and very much in their tradition, "These poems, so minute in appearance, shrill as the voice of a gnat dying out past the ear." Toward the end of the piece there is the expression of a nostalgia Winters was later to discuss in connection with writers like Frederick Goddard Tuckerman: he draws attention to "a sense of the unity of both the race and the individual with the physical (which is also the spiritual as there is only one) universe, which gives to all phenomena, personal or objective, an immediacy to the perceiver and a vastness of emotional implication, which our own culture, with all its ramifications of causes, explanations and mystical dualisms, has lost, and which only the occasional artist . . . can regain for us." This desire for a "sense of unity . . . with the physical universe" is kin to the nature mysticism of Winters's own early verse, a goal he later felt obliged to repudiate. The view of the artist in this quotation is close to Hart Crane's Medicine-man, who is conjured to "lie to us,—dance us back the tribal morn!"—again a goal he repudiated as self-deluding and indeed insane.

"The Testament of a Stone" was the first piece of prose in which Winters wrote directly of his own preoccupations and beliefs, free from the constraints of a review. The essay, subtitled "Being Notes on the Mechanics of the Poetic Image," proceeds by way of a series of axioms, definitions, and taxonomic subdivisions of the possible types of images. The extremely methodical discussion of the possibilities of a subject, which was to become a characteristic method of Winters's criticism, is already evident. The aim is a logical, clear, even lapidary discussion of imagism. In so far as it has a model, that model is again, from internal evidence, the early criticism of Pound, but it lacks both the aggressive colloquialisms and the arbitrariness of judgment that characterize Pound's prose.

The essay does allow itself a moment or two of rhetoric, not surprising when we remember the author's age. A significant moment occurs near the opening: "A poem is . . . a stasis in a world of flux and indecision, a permanent gateway to waking oblivion, which is the only infinity and the only rest." The claim that the poem is "a stasis in a world of flux" will come as no surprise to those familiar with Winters's imagist verse—one is reminded of his poems on the subject of a house withstanding a storm and of his first book's title, *The Immobile Wind*. What does sound strange from Winters, particularly to those more familiar with his later work, is the "gateway to waking oblivion." This is an expression of Winters's nature mysticism, the desire to merge oneself with a more authentic reality. It is an oblivion because the poet or reader is lifted out of himself, it is waking in contradistinction to quotidian life, which is seen as a sleep of the faculties. Despite the romantic mysticism inherent in this notion, a mysticism that goes back at least as far as Coleridge, as Grosvenor Powell demonstrates (*Language as Being in the Poetry of Yvor Winters*, p. 100), the philosophy behind the essay is ultimately one of aestheticism.

Traditional religion is ignored, but the poet is left with a desire for some kind of epiphany. The epiphany is vouchsafed through art, the poem is the "gateway" to revelation. The intensest revelation is given not by "generalities and concepts" but by precisely apprehended images. Winters does allow a place for "intellectual correlations that are not evident to the simple senses," and he calls such correlations antiimages, but it is apparent that his preference is for the concrete rather than the abstract particular, and certainly for the particular, concrete or abstract, rather than the general. A great deal of the essay is taken up with a painstaking analysis of the different types of image and antiimage available to the poet. Rhythm is included as a function of the image, and the discussion of the ways in which rhythm can effect the total impression given by a poem is often very acute, as in this extract on Laforgue: "A rhythm that has traditional associations or one that has acquired such associations in the given poem . . . may comment upon its meaning-content either by contrast or augmentation. Laforgue achieves this . . . by putting a ridiculous fact into a traditionally plaintive metre, or by putting a sentimental or tragic fact into a ridiculous metre, or by various shadings between these two extremes." The essay ends with a list of the different ways in which a poem can be constructed; this section was to be considerably developed in Winters's later criticism.

Though the form and tone of the essay owe something to Pound, the content owes a certain amount to T. S. Eliot, particularly to his famous analogy of the chemical catalyst and poetic "fusion" worked out in "Tradition and the Individual Talent," an essay Winters quotes and acknowledges. However, the essay is typically far more radical in its conclusions, and more thoroughgoingly clearheaded, than the work of either of its models.

Winters's next direct statement on the nature of poetry appeared in 1929, in two articles written for his own magazine, *Gyroscope*, and in the long essay "The Extension and Re-integration of the Human Spirit through the Poetry Mainly French and American since Poe and Baudelaire," published in the *New American Caravan*. In these three essays the ideas associated with Winters's later criticism are first fully set out: the last of the three, in particular, is of crucial importance in understanding Winters's change of poetic direction from the experimental to the traditional.

3 The Change of Direction

Le regard du démon embusqué
dans les ténèbres . . .—BAUDELAIRE

A comparison of Winters's opinions, from the early and late 1920s, on the nature of poetry and the importance of philosophy, indicates the extent to which he changed his mind on these issues.

In 1924 he had described a poem as "a permanent gateway to waking oblivion"; in 1929 he wrote, in defence of traditional poetic form: "Technique then . . . is . . . created by the spirit to make its boundaries more precisely . . . to differentiate itself a little more distinctly from the remainder of the universe, from 'nature,' from that which will eventually absorb and destroy it. Technique so understood not only has a place in the moral system, but is the ultimate development of the moral system; it is the outer boundary of consciousness" ("The Extension and Reintegration of the Human Spirit," p. 245).

In 1922, in connection with Edwin Arlington Robinson, he had written, "To those to whom philosophy is comprehensible it is not a matter of the first importance"; in 1929, reviewing a book by Louise Bogan, he wrote, "The poet of the present age, in order to free himself from the handicap of the philosophical misconceptions of the age, has, I believe, to turn metaphysician in a profound and serious way" (*Uncollected Essays and Reviews*, p. 58).

That is, in 1924 he had seen poetry as a way toward communion with nature, as a kind of spell to induce a sense of oneness with the universe; in 1929 he saw it as the spirit's chief strategy in its attempt to disentangle itself from the general mass of Being—the "nature" which absorbs does so by destruction. His emphasis has shifted from oblivion to definition, and it has also taken on a moral dimension. In 1922 he had seen philosophy as a perhaps interesting but basically trivial ancillary to the poet's needs; by 1929 he was demanding that the poet "turn metaphysician." I have indicated that we can discern three related lines of development in Winters's early poetry: from sensory images to abstractions, from the minimal to the discursive, and from the particular to the general. The move from sensory images to abstractions can be seen as the outward manifestation of his attempt to move, in the words of his poem "Summer Commentary," from being to finding, from the mystical intuition of real-

48

ity to categories of meaning. The verse he admired and wrote in his early twenties was arational, minimal, and concrete; his later work is rational, discursive, and, to a large degree, abstract. The above quotations document a phase of this development: we can see the shift from the arational and mystical to the rational in his remarks on form and the nature of poetry, and we can see the increased importance which he began to give to at least preliminary abstract thought. The shift from the minimal to the discursive is a natural result of the other two developments—rational abstract process cannot be represented by curt, unglossed images of the physical universe. The year in which Winters gave expression to these changes in his beliefs, changes which had been maturing for some time, was, as the quotations indicate, 1929.

Before considering Winters's personal changes of belief it is perhaps important to point out that he was not alone in his attempt to "think himself out" of his youthful solipsism. The solipsism he felt as an adolescent may have come to him as a revelation, as he later claimed, but it was something very much in the intellectual air at the time. Though it is beyond the scope of a study of Winters's work, it would not be difficult to demonstrate that an impressionist subjectivism, in which the barriers between the self and the external world were dissolved or ignored, pervaded intellectual and artistic life at the end of the nineteenth century in both Europe and America; that this was equally true in literature philosophy and music; that this tradition felt itself to be exhausted and inauthentic by, say, the 1920s; and that there were various attempts to move out of this solipsistic atmosphere into a more objective world and to restate a belief in external traditions that did not depend upon the individual's psyche. The self, which had threatened to reach out and engulf all external reality under romanticism, had become a vast prison from which artist and philosopher sought escape. Late-nineteenth-century poetry is notoriously will-less, vague, and self-involved, the sensibility it exhibits exists merely as the recipient of sensation. The mists of Tennyson, the clouds of Ruskin, and the fogs of Dickens seemed to have spread like a miasma over the whole plain of fin de siècle literature, rendering everything insubstantial and indefinite. The same was true of philosophy: Hegel, who had the highest reputation of any philosopher at the end of the nineteenth century, is the most elusive of thinkers, and his emphasis on Mind as the ultimate reality renders the physical universe wholly impalpable; the main work of his chief rival during this period, Schopenhauer, opens with the words, "The world is my representation." This subjectivism, in which external truth existing independently of the observer, once the supposed goal of philosophy, recedes so far that it seems not to exist, had been implicit in European philosophy since Descartes and had become central since the epistemological doubts of Hume and Kant's belief that the thing-in-itself is unknowable. The intellectual climate of the nineteenth century, particularly in its later decades, was one of subjective relativism, together with a pining for lost objective certainty, preferably in the form of religion.

We can trace an analogous attempt (to Winters's) to break out of the subjectivity of the intellectual tradition of his youth in the work of T. S. Eliot with his conversion to the external tradition of Anglo-Catholicism. There is an even closer parallel in the career of Wittgenstein, who, like Winters, exhibits an excessively hermetic and quasi-mystical apprehension of reality in his earlier work, only to reject this in favor of the more public truth of an external tradition, in his case that of everyday language. Eliot, Winters, and Wittgenstein all attempted to break out of the extreme subjectivity bequeathed them by the tradition in which they grew up, Eliot by taking the nineteenth-century road of religious conversion, Wittgenstein and Winters by attempting to align themselves with a public mode of discourse with recognized rules. To use a theological metaphor, they attempted to stop being saints looking for a personal revelation and, like Eliot, to accept the authority of a church. The difficulty is, of course, that a church too is based finally on a revelation, if not one's own someone else's: Winters chose the "church" of Aristotelean reason, as being the one with the least suspicious premises; Wittgenstein chose "normal" language ("Let the use of words teach you their meaning" [*Philosophical Investigations*, p. 220]; "An expression has meaning only in the stream of life" [Norman Malcolm, *Ludwig Wittgenstein, A Memoir*, p. 93]), which led to the later gibes about the "Koranic status" of the *OED*. Both were attempting to ally themselves with what they took to be a strategy for arriving at a public, shared truth, and both turned away from the hermeticism of their early work.

But to return to the specific details of Winters's situation. In 1966, in the introduction to his *Early Poems*, he wrote that he had particularly admired the work of a few poets (Baudelaire, Valéry, Hardy, Bridges, Stevens), "and that I could never hope to approach the quality of their work by the method I was using" (*Collected Poems*, p. 15). Though this was written in 1966, almost forty years after the event, there is no reason to doubt the author's word. But an examination of the texts he produced immediately before and after the change of direction, and of the circumstances of his life at this time, suggests that other, more personal concerns were also significant in his decision. Winters, in his later criticism, was quick to point out the ways in which poetic technique is frequently an indication of the moral and philosophical presuppositions of the poet; it would therefore be surprising if he himself had changed his technique for purely technical, rather than spiritual, reasons.

We here enter the uncertain terrain of the relations between an author's life and his published work. It is, of course, possible to see the approach as illegitimate, and Winters himself was hardly an advocate of such ventures. However, experience and published work center on the same individual, and it would be incredible if they did not interpenetrate. Further, despite his general distaste for the procedure, we have Winters's example as a precedent, in his criticism of, for example, the work of Jones Very, Edwin Arlington Robinson, and Gerard Manley Hopkins.

In his essay on Hopkins he wrote, "As to . . . biographical reasons, we can merely surmise, and although I confess to some distaste for biographical surmises, which are invariably both inascertainable and in the nature of arguments *ad hominem*, nevertheless certain guesses are hard to lay aside" (*The Function of Criticism*, p. 136). In Winters's case too, "certain guesses are hard to lay aside." Curiously, the passage continues: "Whatever the reasons may have been, Hopkins in his later years passed through a period of psychological crisis in which his mental balance, if he really preserved it at all times, was precarious. The reasons for this crisis are hard to guess, and perhaps are not important, but the crisis appears to have been real." If we substitute for "Hopkins in his later years" the phrase "Winters in his mid twenties" we have the guess which it is "hard to lay aside"—that the author "passed through a period of psychological crisis" and that this is the fundamental reason for his renunciation of imagism and its attendant, as Winters perceived, philosophical notions. The evidence is discernible in his poetry, in the nature of his life during this period, in his single published short story, *The Brink of Darkness*, and in his criticism. Taken singly, each of these may not amount to much, but together they indicate a pattern of evidence that is difficult to discount.

I take the short story first. *The Brink of Darkness* was published in 1932; it describes the experience of a teacher (who keeps Airedales, as Winters did) living as a lodger in a remote part of the country. The wife of the family with whom he is staying dies, the house is sold, and the narrator has to move. The story ends, "In a month I should be leaving for Colorado. I would never return." Between 1921 and the spring of 1923 (when he "left for the University of Colorado"—*Collected Poems*, p. 14), Winters lived, as a teacher, in the remote township of Madrid, near Santa Fe.

The landscape of the story may owe more to Winters's later stay in Moscow, Idaho, but it is similar to that described in *The Bare Hills*—wide, desolate emptinesses sparsely populated by the rural poor. The story is certainly substantially autobiographical, and Grosvenor Powell treats it as such in his study of Winters's poetry (*Language as Being*, pp. 93–94). It is extremely interesting as evidence of Winters's state of mind during his early twenties, or at the least as that state of mind appeared to him after an interval of a few years.

His own prefatory comment to the story reads as follows: "This story is a study of the hypothetical possibility of a hostile supernatural world and of the effect on the perceptions of a consideration of this possibility." From another writer this might suggest that the work is some kind of science fiction, but given Winters's view of art as a "Quest for Reality" we cannot seriously entertain the idea. The story is meant as a serious attempt to explore reality. Whether this means that Winters actually believed, at least for a part of his life, in the existence of a "hostile supernatural world" would be difficult to ascertain: what is apparent is that he felt there were phenomena that eluded rational apprehension, and that they were terrifying and possibly malevolent. This intuition, that the uncharted areas of reality are a repository of vague, destructive, and horrifying forces, seems astonishing from a man who called his major critical work *In Defense of Reason* and who became famous as an advocate of logic and clarity. But there is no paradox. It was precisely this apprehension that the darkness beyond the illuminated circle of reason may be rapaciously destructive that led Winters to mistrust those who foray blithely into the dark, and to insistently proclaim the values of logic and clarity. His insistence on clarity does not spring, as some critics have implied, from a blindness to those areas of experience unillumined by reason, but from a too-present awareness of them.

The story opens with a description of a snow storm which begins tentatively, "as if exploring the terrain," and increases in violence until the "air was an unbroken sheet of snow through which one could hardly move." The protagonist goes skiing over the landscape: "The clouds were a soft even gray, and they seemed to have no lower edges, so that the sky had no identity, there was merely the soft air. The snow merged into the air from below with no visible dividing line. Often I should not have known whether I was going uphill or down, had it not been for the pull of gravity and the visible inclination of the skis." The setting of the opening indicates a blurring of identities (snow, air, clouds) in which the narrator loses his sense of direction and almost of reality. Readers familiar with Winters's work will recognize this as a warning sign—when distinction is lost and the mind cannot define or separate out the constituents of reality it becomes defenseless, open to possession by the undefined and inchoate. We are reminded of the opening of one of Winters's favorite poems, Fulke Greville's "In night when colours all to black are cast":

> In night when colours all to black are cast,
> Distinction lost, or gone down with the light.

We may easily substitute the snow of Winters's story for Greville's darkness. The end of the poem, in which the alarmed soul "tells news of devils / Which but expressions be of inward evils," is also apposite to a discussion of the story.

The narrative continues with the death of Mrs. Stone, with whom the narrator lodges. There is a lengthy description of the preparations for the funeral, in which the narrator plays the part of a sympathetic and helpful outsider. After the funeral he is left alone in the house and is slowly invaded by a diffuse terror born of loneliness and the apprehension of death. He spends as much time as he can in his room upstairs, away from the place where the corpse had lain, with his two dogs. Then the dogs disappear and he is completely alone in the house. He reads and watches the mice that scamper unmolested around him.

One night after I had been watching the mice without moving for nearly an hour, I got up suddenly and went downstairs for a glass of water. The sound of my feet rang out with tremendous volume as I descended the stair; as I crossed the glare of the front room, the echo seemed to resound from the room above, as if I were walking up there. I stood still to quiet the noise. I was alone and erect, a few feet from the broad window, bright emptiness behind me. The light from the window fell on the snow outside. It had been warm enough at noon for a slight glaze to form. The shape of the light on the glaze was sharp-edged and clear. Only, at the upper left-hand corner of the window there was a darkness, a tangle of withered vines outside. I stared at the smooth surface of the snow thus suddenly revealed to me, like a new meaning not divisible into any terms I knew. Again I had the illusion of seeing myself in the empty room, in the same light, frozen to my footprints, cold and unmeaning. A slight motion caught my eye, and I glanced up at the darkened corner of the window to be fixed with horror. There, standing on the air outside the window, translucent, a few lines merely, and scarcely visible, was a face, my face, the eyes fixed upon my own. I moved on quickly to the kitchen; the reflection started and vanished.

The next day he hears of the death, in horrible circumstances, of a child with meningitis. There is another funeral, and after four days one of his dogs returns

emaciated and limping, her head and throat, inside and out, completely covered with quills, her mouth forced open with the mass of them, her tongue hanging out, swollen, and white with quills as far back as I could see.

He pulls out the porcupine quills with great difficulty, the other dog returns, and with their recovery his life slowly moves free of the aura of violence and horror that had surrounded it throughout the winter. The story ends with the advent of spring, and thus repeats the structure of so many of Winters's early poems and poem sequences, from death and terror to the resurrection of spring.

Throughout the story there is the repeated image of a surface which hides something indistinctly perceived; the first instance is the snow that falls at the opening, obscuring the landscape, then there is the face of the dead woman. "The skin was preternaturally and evenly white, and in the wrinkles there seemed a trace as of an underlying darkness"; there is also the curtain that hides the body, and then the flowers that hide the casket. The meaning of these images is made explicit at the end of the story:

It was as if there were darkness evenly underlying the brightness of the air, underlying everything, as if I might slip into it at any instant, and as if I held myself where I was by an act of the will from moment to moment.

This passage could be taken as an epigraph for a great deal of Winters's later poetry, and it indicates an important aspect of the ideas which inform his criticism. A vision of individual integrity maintained, precariously, by the conscious will against the impersonality of a nature perceived as a devouring void rather than as the pantheist's beatitude underlies verse and prose alike.

The protagonist, whom we may take to be Winters himself, interprets his experience thus:

I remembered that I had read somewhere of a kind of Eastern demon who gains power over one only in proportion as one recognizes and fears him. I felt I had been the victim of a deliberate and
malevolent invasion, an invasion utilizing and augmenting to appalling and shadowy proportions all the most elusive accidents of
my life. . . . Finally . . . I had begun to recover the limits of my
old identity. I had begun this recovery at the time of the immersion
in the brute blood of the bitch.

This last sentence refers to his pulling the quills from his injured dog, a
messy process graphically described; his recovery "at the time of the immersion in the brute blood" is a result of his baptism in the forces of natural life that give him strength to resist the supernatural.

The notion of demonism and demonic possession is one to which Winters frequently returned, and the nature of the demon here described is
significant. The demon gains power over one as it is recognized—the
mind confers strength on its adversary by its own concern. In this trope
we can perceive Winters's compelling need, in his later work, to occupy
himself with definition and clarity; to examine the darkness is to give
it power over one. For whatever personal psychological reasons, and
we can only guess as to the nature of the crisis *Brink of Darkness* perhaps
metaphorically, perhaps directly, records, Winters found it necessary to
turn away from those areas of experience that were unamenable to reason. The unknown and the indefinable became for him a source of barely
evaded terror. It is perhaps apposite to repeat here the information already quoted from Thomas Parkinson's book: "His mother correctly
predicted the death of some twenty people, and when he was young
dragged him off to séances." The correct prediction of death by one's
mother, on such a grand scale, would render most people somewhat
wary of the supernatural, particularly if they had been made as conscious
of their own mortality as Winters had been during his tuberculosis.

The experiences described in *The Brink of Darkness* are also the source
of the poems in section 6 of part 2 of *The Bare Hills*. The first poem,
"The Cold Room," hints at the theme of an undefined presence, and the
second refers to the reflection of the face that had so horrified the narrator
of the short story:

> and went upstairs
> to meet the monstrous
> nakedness of

his own face
with unchanged step.

The third and fourth poems refer to the bereaved family, the woman's corpse regarded by her husband,

> condensed in
> grief the old man
> walks beside the bed or
> lifts the flamepure sheet
>
> to see this
> woman

and the husband confronting the fact of his own approaching death:

> this old man
> wrinkled in
> the fear of Hell.

The external circumstances of Winters's life during his twenties would have encouraged the development we can discern in his work from the brief quasi-mystical, intensely private early poems to the discursive later writings with their emphasis on the public tradition of reason. His late teens and early twenties were spent in illness and convalescence, in an isolation that was more than merely intellectual, and in environments (the sanatorium, the mining towns where he worked as a teacher) that must have put a considerable strain on his mental resilience. His circumstances began to improve with his marriage in the summer of 1926 to Janet Lewis; in the following summer he entered Stanford University as a graduate student. We may presume that his marriage went some way towards mitigating his sense of isolation, a mitigation confirmed by his status as a graduate student in a reputable university (despite some later spectacular tussles with certain of its staff). Particularly important was Winters's meeting with William Dinsmore Briggs.

Briggs had become chairman of the English department at Stanford in 1926. He took a personal interest in Winters and became something of a mentor and model for him. His influence on Winters was highly important in at least three ways: first, he was a Renaissance scholar, and it was under his tutelage that Winters first read Jonson, Gascoigne, Googe, and Herrick (Winters's particularly high regard for Jonson may be connected with the fact that Briggs's scholastic work had been largely on an edition of Jonson); second, Briggs encouraged his students to read widely in philosophy, and it was at his suggestion that Winters first read Aquinas; third, Briggs turned Winters's attention from modernist imagist poetry to the literature of the past, and in particular to the literature of the American nineteenth century, where Winters later believed that he found the conceptions out of which the poetry of his own generation had grown. Briggs was for his student the kind of father figure, cautious, scholarly, precise, "a skeptic with a strong sense of order" (Parkinson, *Crane and Winters*, p. 158) that Winters himself was later to be to a younger generation of poets who, in J. V. Cunningham's words, "made the pilgrimage to Palo Alto," where he settled. Winters wrote three poems either to Briggs or inspired by him, and the nature of his debt may be gauged from this stanza taken from "Dedication for a Book of Criticism":

> In the motions of your thought
> I a plan and model sought;
> My deficiencies but gauge
> My own talents and the age;
> What is good from you I took:
> Then, in justice, take my book.

By the age of twenty-eight Winters had begun his successful, lifelong marriage, moved to the university and the landscape with which he would be associated for the rest of his life, and met a teacher whose traditional learning he could admire and hope to emulate. We may also assume that the "hypersensitivity of convalescence" had begun to fade by this time, and that the world was taking on a more quotidian aspect. This release into a broader, more social and more learned world after the illness, isolation and vicarious brutality of the time spent in New Mexico, gave Winters, at the least, a greater stake in quotidian reality. It is at this time that, from the evidence of his poetry, Winters ceased to consider himself as an ahistorical, intuitive and isolated sensibility, and instead began to see his task as involved with a tradition of rational thought that he saw stretching, with many falterings, from Aristotle to the present day. The tinge of the ineffable never finally left his poetry, but it does fade appreciably as one proceeds through the *Collected Poems*, and the emphasis is more and more on the shared strategies of reason.

The prose of Winters's late twenties corroborates the evidence of his life and poetry. The two most significant pieces of writing from this period are the "Statement of Purpose" and an extended critical essay, "The Extension and Reintegration of the Human Spirit through the Poetry Mainly French and American since Poe and Baudelaire."

"Statement of Purpose" was, as its name indicates, a kind of manifesto, in this case for the first issue of Winters's mimeographed magazine, *The Gyroscope*. Winters's first epigraph (to *The Magpie's Shadow*, 1922) had been from Rimbaud; the "Statement of Purpose" (1929) is prefaced by a quotation from Baudelaire, and if we consider his view of these two poets, the guardian presence of their names at the head of his own work is a sign of the journey he has traveled. Rimbaud he saw as a poet "destroyed by a metaphysical vision," Baudelaire as someone "to whom the metaphysical experience is the central experience coloring and involving everything else" (*Uncollected Essays and Reviews*, pp. 54, 242), but whose "spiritual discipline" enabled him to "outstare" the horror he perceived. The hallucinatory quality of Rimbaud's poetry was something Winters had admired and perhaps attempted to reproduce in his own early verse, but he had come to see such derangements of consciousness as destructive, as a surrender to that devouring void adumbrated in *The Brink of Darkness*. His emphasis turned from absorption—which had promised beatitude but revealed itself as a source of terror—to resistance. That reality, clearly perceived, was a "metaphysical horror" had become a truism for Winters by his late twenties. Rimbaud is swallowed by the horror, Baudelaire outstares it. We are reminded of Winters's poems on a building battered by a storm: in the early treatments of the theme the emphasis is on the violence of the storm that threatens destruction; in the later "Phasellus ille" it is on the building's staunch resistance.

The "Statement of Purpose" is extremely short: the aim of the journal was an attempt to "fix in literary terms some approximation of a classical state of mind." This "classical state" is then defined, at first by formulations, in Winters's typically taxonomic manner, of what it is not. It is not "emotional . . . or religious expansionism," the "expression" of a time or place, or "emotional receptivism." *Emotional* is quite clearly used pejoratively in these phrases. Opposed to the emotional is "the intellect, the core of conscious existence," which is seen as a self-evident good. Art is considered as "the only satisfactory means of evaluating the phenomena of life"; within art, "stylistic precision is merely the ultimate manifestation of spiritual precision and strength" (an indication, if one were necessary, that Winters's own change of poetic technique was not merely a technical affair).

In his new concern with precision and strength, in his distrust of the emotional and indefinite, and in his concept of art as evaluation, we can see the theoretical analogue of his rejection of the hermetic epiphanies of imagism. Imagism, as Winters had practiced it, had attempted to break down the barriers between the self and the external universe in order to assert and experience a state of numinous absorption in nature. For whatever personal reasons, he experienced this absorption as terror, an intimation of the dissolution of death. Absorption in phenomena, the loss of conscious control in a surrender either to the external numinous power of nature or to the interior realm of the subconscious, came to be seen by Winters as a crossing of the "brink of darkness," a courting of spiritual (if not literal and physical) death. The "Statement of Purpose" is thus a rejection of the goal of "waking oblivion" that Winters had advocated in 1924. His new ideal is one of clear and precise understanding that leads to "evaluation" rather than "delirium" or "receptivism." Again it should be emphasized that the ideal sprang from an abiding awareness of how much of experience is not amenable to such treatment. The new values were largely defensive, and it is not chance that his major critical work bears the title "In Defense of Reason"; the view of the mind we gain from his later writing is of conscious clarity beleaguered by mindless confusion, of an ever-present darkness beneath the surface, like the darkness perceived in the wrinkles of the dead woman's face in his short story. This posture of defense makes him particularly contemptuous of "emotional receptivism," and he cites "Mr. Eliot and Mr. Macleish, who employ despair as a drug and a luxury, and who, therefore, may be justly suspected of never having actually experienced it." The unpleasant arrogance of the implication (reminiscent of certain confessional poets' claims to have had more interesting nervous breakdowns than each other) is explicable only in terms of Winters's fear of despair, his conviction of the necessity of the "*exercice de la volonté*" of his epigraph from Baudelaire.

Baudelaire and the "*exercice de la volonté*" dominate the foreword of "The Extension and Reintegration of the Human Spirit" (1929). The essay reads as a credo for Winters's new beliefs and has an emphatically personal tone, particularly in its opening and closing sections, that distinguishes it from most of his later criticism. Winters did not reprint it (probably because of this personal, even passionate, tone of commitment); nevertheless it is a singularly interesting document as it sets out the presuppositions of his later critical writings particularly cogently.

The essay is a discussion of the nature of poetic form, and in the foreword formal excellence is seen as a manifestation of "discipline spiritual and literary." Winters cites authors whose work he admires—Baudelaire, Shakespeare, Hardy, Dickinson, Racine—and comments, "It is not what is said that weighs so heavily; but one feels behind the line, in all that is *omitted*, a life-time of monstrous discipline, from which is born the power of absolute wisdom without additional effort" (*Uncollected Essays and Reviews*, p. 226).

This emphasis on discipline is a new note in Winters's work; its origin is the apprehension he had developed in his late twenties of the occasions for that despair noted above:

> The facts of life are at best disheartening; the vision of life which man has little by little constructed (or perhaps one should say stripped bare) is all but crushing. To evade the facts and attempt bluff vigor, as Browning often seems to do, is not convincing to a man who has experienced the imaginative facts. The artist who is actually ignorant of the metaphysical horror of modern thought or who cannot feel it imaginatively—and there are many such—is of only a limited, a more or less decorative, value. But the artist who can feel the full horror, organize it into a dynamic attitude or state of mind, asserting by that very act his own life and the strength and value of his own life, and who can leave that state of mind completed behind him for others to enter, has performed the greatest spiritual service that can be performed. [*Uncollected Essays and Reviews*, p. 226]

Winters obviously considers himself as one who has "experienced the imaginative facts": the discipline is necessary as a means to resist the "metaphysical horror of modern thought," and the passage continues with a discussion of the will, taken from Baudelaire, as a means of such resistance. "Discipline," "dynamism," "the will" indicate a repudiation of that passivity of mind so evident in Winters's early imagist poetry. There the poet had sought to dissolve the barriers between the self and the world; in the later work the self arms its integrity against external reality.

The phrase "metaphysical horror" is disconcertingly vague but can be interpreted in the light of what we already know of Winters's concerns at this time. A page further on in the essay he writes of T. S. Eliot, whose "sense of time in an incomprehensible universe leaves him gasping." In fact the phrase would be more apposite as a description of Winters's own early poems (in which *Time* is almost invariably capitalized) than of Eliot's work. Linked to his sense of time passing was his vivid apprehen-

sion of death. The modernity alluded to is probably a reference to Whitehead, whose work Winters read in his late twenties. One or two of the
earlier poems (most notably "The Vigil") refer to the modern physicists'
dissolving of substance into energy, and the theme takes on an almost
manic note in the poems of *The Proof* (1930). Winters's characteristic notion of reality by the end of his twenties was of a horrifying, mindless
flux which threatened to destroy the individual consciousness, particularly if that consciousness were to passively acquiesce in a surrender of its
integrity, or even to actively seek annihilation. It is this notion that constitutes the "horror" he is bent on resisting.

The essay continues with a discussion of Baudelaire's poem "Le Goût
du néant." Winters is clearly deeply interested in the subject of the poem,
which is an aspect of those problems which, as we have seen, were then
troubling him. What impresses him is Baudelaire's extremely tight—
"disciplined"—technical mastery, which in its persistent and rigorous
structural control represents a kind of spiritual victory over the nullity it
addresses, or as Winters expresses the notion, "a negation of the idea-
tional material it contains" (*Uncollected Essays and Reviews*, p. 228). The
discussion of the poem is prefaced by a quotation from Baudelaire on another writer: "*Il ne recontrera que le vice inévitable, c'est à dire le regard du
démon embusqué dans les ténèbres.*" This is of course very close to Winters's
own preoccupation with the demonic, and when he comments, "Baudelaire, having himself felt those same eyes in the dark, was strong enough
and skilful enough to stare till he could find them and face them," we
are aware that he considers that he too has "felt those same eyes in
the dark."

He is at pains to point out that the technical control of "Le Goût du
néant" is "a part of what is said, a subtle and powerful manifestation of
the spirit" (*Uncollected Essays and Reviews*, p. 231). The technique is a visible equivalent of the spiritual stance. The poem is a perfect illustration of
Winters's new theory of poetry: it is concerned with the "metaphysical
horror" that all but obsessed him, it faces the horror directly and does not
attempt to mitigate it by gestures either toward dogmatic religion or toward the comforts of a vague Emersonian pantheism, and its technique is
a clear paradigm of the author's embattled consciousness.

At the opening of the essay Winters had cited a number of poets whose
work he admired—Shakespeare, Baudelaire, Hardy, Dickinson, Racine.
He is concerned with technical mastery as a means of conveying "wisdom," but, as we have seen, he considers technical matters as the outward manifestation of a spiritual stance. If we leave aside Shakespeare,
whose conceptions of reality are notoriously elusive, we find a fairly

close spiritual agreement among the writers listed. Hardy, professing agnosticism if not atheism, nevertheless expends a great deal of energy in inveighing against God and his indifference or malevolence; Emily Dickinson hovers between willed belief and the despair of one who feels herself abandoned by the divine; Baudelaire writes in a French tradition of revolt against God, a revolt carried out entirely in religious terms (Genet is a modern representative of the tradition); and, perhaps most interesting of all from Winters's point of view, Racine believes in a quite inaccessible God—the celebrated *Dieu Caché*—who imposes absolute moral imperatives which worldly emotion attempts, usually successfully, to subvert. All four writers quarrel with the divine; each one is aware of a distance between the human and the divine which seems to preclude benevolence or aid, coupled with a sense of the superlative authority of the divine over human affairs. Humanity cannot call on God for aid, but it equally cannot escape from the divine will. The authors further share the feeling, amounting at times to anguish, that the nature of this divine will is hidden from humanity, which must operate in ignorance of the nature of the absolutes it is called on to obey.

Winters frequently reveals in his later criticism a preference for literature, especially poetry, that presents just such a version of man's relations with the divine; it is indeed impossible to avoid the conclusion that he promoted poetry that accorded with this view and found it difficult to sympathize with poetry that contradicted it. Because of his own belief in the interdependence of technical and spiritual matters it would be surprising if there were not a certain homogeneity of metaphysical outlook in those poems he found technically fine, and this is so. He liked poems that take account of the *néant* of the world, but that nevertheless resist it, usually by the invocation, implicit or explicit, of absolute values from an undefined, or barely adumbrated, divine source.

The second, and longest, section of the essay, "The Mechanics of the Mood," is an examination of four different methods of structuring a poem. These are the scattered method, the logical method, the narrative method, and the psychological method. It is apparent, both from the amount of space allotted and from the tone of the discussion, that Winters is mainly interested in methods 2 and 4, the logical and the psychological.

The scattered method is dealt with quickly. It consists of a list of details—images or statements—that "converge upon a common center," or serve as illustrations of the poem's theme: Nashe's "Adieu, Farewell Earth's Bliss" is given as an example. The logical method is here largely identified with the work of the seventeenth-century metaphysical poets; though Winters indicates that the method existed prior to the seventeenth century, he does not develop the suggestion. He defines it as follows: "The important fact about the logical method is that, as its name implies, each statement follows clearly out of the last through an apparently inevitable logical sequence" (*Uncollected Essays and Reviews*, p. 234). and adduces Marvell's "To His Coy Mistress" as an example. He then interestingly mentions a poem, Rimbaud's "Larme," to which he was frequently to return as an example of a ne plus ultra of coherence, a point beyond which it is impossible to proceed and remain comprehensible. He points out that the poem is not at all logical; he would find it "difficult to say" whether the poem is weakened by its lack of logic. I have indicated that the general movement of his mind was from an early interest in arational mental states toward the clarity of reason and logic: we see him here hesitating, already more at home with the logical but unable to relinquish an alogical poem that in his youth had struck him as masterly.

He offers as an example of the logical method Vaughan's "The Lamp," "a frankly didactic poem of great beauty." In his discussion of the poem he remarks on how the metaphysical poets' metaphors sometimes resulted in "elaborate absurdities": "This occurred mainly when the poet started with an external object and tried to draw similitudes from it, as in 'The Weeper,' and seldom when, as in the greater portion of Donne, he began with an abstract concept and proceeded into the field of concrete experience." Again we see him on the edge of a change of emphasis. Parallel with the movement from the arational to the rational there developed a related movement from the concrete to the abstract: here Donne is praised for beginning "with an abstract concept," and it is suggested that the absurdities of Crashaw's poem arise from his starting "with an external object." Both types of metaphor involve both concrete and abstract elements, but Winters finds the metaphor that is concerned primarily with the abstract notion, and only secondarily with concrete phenomena, preferable to the metaphor that begins with the concrete and proceeds to the abstract. This is a reversal of the notions expressed in his anatomy of imagism, "The Testament of a Stone" (1924).

Mention of the metaphysical poets leads Winters to acknowledge Eliot's criticism on the subject, which it would be "an impertinence to attempt to improve upon" (an opinion he later revised), and this in turn leads him to examine the claim, much bruited at the time, that Eliot's own poetry was in some way metaphysical. The idea is emphatically rejected. Winters quotes two passages of rather flaccid verse from Fletcher (on which he comments, "the imprecision of thought results in a corre-sponding imprecision of metre"; again he is concerned to point out the link between conceptual and metrical clarity) and suggests that this kind of Elizabethan writing—"the blurring out, the decadence"—is Eliot's model, rather than Donne. The passage closes with a relatively brusque dismissal of *The Waste Land*, in which "the writing is looser [than in 'Gerontion'], the metre more lax and the organization of the whole very slight" (*Uncollected Essays and Reviews*, pp. 239–40). Winters's dislike of Eliot's poetry brought him some notoriety; his main objection is indi-cated by the remark on Fletcher's verse quoted above—he perceived an imprecision of thought behind the "lax" meter. If we remember that Winters and Eliot were at this time attempting a comparable commit-ment to an external tradition of thought, Winters's objection becomes clearer: Eliot's capitulation to dogma rather than reason appeared to Win-ters as a relatively easy option, a "lax" rather than disciplined develop-ment. The section closes with the suggestion that the true metaphysical poems of the time were being written by Allen Tate and Wallace Stevens.

The third method, the narrative, like the first, is dealt with shortly. Much of the brief discussion is concerned with prose fiction rather than verse. Winters's chief caveat concerning the method is that it "frequently tends to concentrate too exclusively upon external data" (*Uncollected Es-says and Reviews*, p. 242)—again we see his turning away from the specif-ics of concrete phenomena. He praises James's novels highly, but objects to their absorption in the quotidian, and especially to the mediocrity of the characters presented: "The metaphysical experience is almost com-pletely eliminated, and for the reader—let us say a Donne or a Baude-laire—to whom the metaphysical experience is the central experience, colouring and involving everything else, such a novel as *The Golden Bowl* can be little more than a luxury, exquisite, marvellous, but not necessary or enormously important as a spiritual experience, and on the whole a trifle exasperating" (p. 242).

It could be objected that James's "metaphysical experience" is as sharp as Baudelaire's, that his perception of "*le néant*" was as acute, but the di-rection of Winters's thought is clear. Again we see the subject matter of the work—in this case the inclusion or exclusion of the "metaphysical experience"—used as a criterion of value. (Winters later recorded that he read *The Golden Bowl* while he was a schoolmaster in the mining towns of New Mexico, and one can imagine that in such circumstances it would appear "a trifle exasperating.")

The discussion of the psychological method is the longest and most detailed of the essay. Much of it reads as a preliminary exposition of ideas more fully developed in Winters's book-length study of contemporary poetry, *Primitivism and Decadence* (1937). The method is more commonly called the "stream of consciousness," and, unlike the other techniques discussed, is confined to the late nineteenth and twentieth centuries. Winters defines it thus: "It consists of a lowering of the connections between the parts of the poem . . . to or below the threshold of consciousness, so that the progression from place to place, from event to event, from idea to idea, or from sense-perception to sense-perception, is similar to the method of change in dream or revery." He takes as an example of a poem written according to these principles a work already mentioned, Rimbaud's "Larme," which "comes near to being the most profound and magnificent expression of the imprecise, wandering and frequently terrible feeling attendant upon dream, revery and insanity, that I have ever read" (*Uncollected Essays and Reviews*, p. 243). The progressions in this sentence are highly significant; "imprecise, wandering . . . terrible," "dream, revery . . . insanity"—imprecision leads to the terrible and dream proceeds ineluctably to insanity. Of the end of the poem he writes, "the protagonist is suddenly sucked deeper in the direction of complete unconsciousness, and the terror becomes more profound," and we are reminded of that dark void that threatened his own protagonist in *The Brink of Darkness*, "as if I might suddenly slip into it at any instant, as if I held myself where I was by an act of the will from moment to moment." Though it is apparent that Winters admires Rimbaud's poem, it is also apparent that he regards it as a warning rather than an invitation, that the "terror" evoked is definitely something to be avoided rather than sought. He associates the psychological method with a suspension of the will, with a deliberate courting of revery and thus, in his terms, of insanity and the annihilation of judgment.

The essay continues with other examples of the method, taken from Mallarmé, Hart Crane, and Joyce (a passage from *Finnegans Wake*). Winters gives the method its due; indeed he seems to be fascinated by the effects that can be achieved by it, and he is particularly impressed by Crane's "Repose of Rivers," in which "the words are constantly balancing on, almost slipping from, the outermost edge of their possible meaning" (p. 247). But his final attitude is that this flirtation with chaos and dream is "wasteful and subversive." Quoting an apologist of the modernist movement, a Mr. Jolas, he sums up the arguments as "a belief that it is desirable to submerge the conscious in the subconscious" and comments, "One enters [the subconscious] . . . only by departing from the center of consciousness and only in so far as one departs from that center of consciousness; that is, in so far as one approaches unconsciousness complete or death. In cultivating the subconscious for itself one's point of approach, or ideal, therefore remains annihilation" (p. 250). The surrender of the conscious will by now meant for Winters not beatitude or even revelation but annihilation.

Two further sections follow, called "The Alternation of Method" and "The Alternation of Mood," the first setting out ways in which the four methods already discussed may be combined in a single work, and the second demonstrating how a poem may use one of the above methods but vary in mood. This section ends with a sympathetic discussion of the techniques of the drama, a sympathy that was to wane considerably in Winters's later writings. The last section of the essay, apart from a concluding summary, returns defensively to imagism, a movement with which Winters had been associated but which, as we have seen, was already ceasing to interest him.

This essay, "The Extension and Reintegration of the Human Spirit," is an extremely interesting, and at times confused, exposition of Winters's theories of poetry during his late twenties. It was clearly written with some emotional intensity and lacks the cooly objective mastery of material that characterizes most of his later criticism. But its very intensity is a mark of the importance of its themes to Winters at this time. And its themes are: the importance of the "metaphysical horror" for modern poets; the necessity for discipline and will in the face of such horror; the superiority of the logical method of poetry; the correspondence between clarity of thought and metrical excellence; the function of technique as an "outer boundary of consciousness"; and a dislike, amounting to fear, of literary revery, which is seen as the prelude to terror and insanity.

The "Notes on Contemporary Criticism" (1929), which appeared in Winters's magazine *The Gyroscope*, read as a postscript to the longer essay. The notes are curiously named because they are concerned almost entirely with questions of religious and ethical belief—another indication that Winters at this time tended to consider literary questions in terms of the author's metaphysical inclinations.

It is in these notes that, having declared his inability to accept religious revelation as a source of truth, he first announces an allegiance that was to remain with him for the rest of his life—to the rational ethics of Roman Catholicism. There can be little doubt that this was as a result of reading Aquinas at the instigation of W. D. Briggs. Winters was of course aware that there is something of a paradox in accepting Catholic ethics and rejecting Catholic dogma (he was later to condemn as "parasitic" such dependencies in other writers, for example, Emerson's rejection of Protestant theology and acceptance of its ethical system), and he attempts to resolve the paradox by the claim that the system is common to Aristotle and the Stoics as well as to Catholicism, and that it is ascertainable by reason alone. Aquinas's division of the paths of reason and faith enables Winters to accept the reason and reject the faith.

His commitment to reason raises the problem of emotion, traditionally considered, in classical and Catholic psychology, as opposed to reason. About this he is unequivocal:

> The basis of Evil is in emotion; Good rests in the power of rational selection in action, as a preliminary to which the emotion in any situation must be as far as possible eliminated, and, in so far as it cannot be eliminated, understood. I say "as far as possible" advisedly, for such an elimination can never be complete; and the irreducible emotion, if properly evaluated, may even function on the side of Good. . . . If it be objected that I propose no end for which a man should reduce his emotion to a minimum and then, if need be, thwart that minimum, I answer with the Stoics that the end is a controlled and harmonious life. [*Uncollected Essays and Reviews*, p. 221]

That "a controlled and harmonious life" is desirable is taken as self-evident. Winters is clear that emotion is "irreducible" and it is this irreducible emotion that is the occasion for art. But art's function is not to indulge this residue but to enable us to "understand" it. His new emphasis is on understanding, judgment, evaluation, rather than on participation or identification.

The idea that emotion is the basis of evil is a clear reference to the Socratic belief that man will, all things being equal, choose the good, and that the unequalizing factor which so often makes him choose evil is emotion, which blurs his perception and persuades him that a lesser good (for example, the satisfaction of his own desire) is greater than an in fact greater good (for example, honesty). Such a theory involves an objective hierarchy of values (according to which one good *is* "in fact" greater than another), and this leads to a belief in absolutes. Winters found himself holding such a belief, almost without realizing it, as he acknowledged. To anticipate, in the foreword to *In Defense of Reason* (1947) he wrote, "If experience appears to indicate that absolute truths exist, that we are able

to work toward an approximate apprehension of them and that our apprehension is seldom and perhaps never perfect, then there is only one
place in which those truths may be located, and I see no way to escape
this conclusion" (p. 14). This "one place" is clearly God, and in the same
passage Winters described himself as a "theist." The passage bears the
clear mark of Aquinas's influence—it is in essence Aquinas's fourth proof
(in *Summa theologiae*, 1.q.2,a.3) of the existence of God.

Among the most cogent pieces of evidence for the change in Winters's
position during his late twenties are the three essays he wrote on the poetry of Hart Crane. These date from 1927, 1930, and 1947 and were
therefore written just before the change, just after it, and at a distance of
some eighteen years or so, by which time the sense of personal anxiety
that informs the writings of his late twenties had given way to a clear and
settled intellectual position.

    Winters and Crane exchanged letters from October 1926 until January
1930: the correspondence was terminated by Crane after Winters's predominantly hostile review of *The Bridge*. Crane's letters to Winters sur-
vive, and they show that in general the two men had a warm respect for
each other, and that Winters was often, especially in the earlier stages of
their correspondence, very enthusiastic about Crane's poetry. Until Winters's hostile review the only hiccough in the otherwise friendly relationship seems to have occurred when Winters somewhat tactlessly offered
Crane moral advice—probably, as far as one can infer from Crane's angry
reply, connected with his homosexuality. The two men met during the
Christmas week of 1927; the meetings seem to have been wholly amicable and Winters refers to them with evident emotion in his 1947 essay.

    On 27 April 1932 Crane was drowned at sea; almost certainly his death
was suicide. Crane's presumed suicide had a profound effect on Winters.
Crane represented in his poetry the type of romantic pantheism which
Winters considered to be most subversive of the intellect, indeed a form
of mental suicide after which literal suicide seemed the only logical step.
He had written, in "The Extension and Reintegration of the Human
Spirit," of a Mr. Jolas, who held more or less the same views as Crane
about poetry: "Mr. Jolas, being a poet, has so far as I am able to discern
but one choice, could he penetrate the haze of his own style and actually
see what he is talking about; the abandonment of his doctrine or the suicide of a gentleman" (*Uncollected Essays and Reviews*, p. 250). And in
1930, reviewing *Dear Judas* by Robinson Jeffers, he was even more explicit: "Union with God, oblivion, the complete extinction of one's hu-

manity, is the only good he is able to discover. . . . For Mr. Jeffers a simple and mechanical device lies always ready: namely, suicide, a device to which he has not resorted" (*Uncollected Essays and Reviews*, p. 65).

Winters's contempt for Jolas and Jeffers is clear; he believed they were merely playing with concepts they could not follow through or perhaps even understand. But his characterization of Jeffers's poetry is very similar to what he believed Crane was attempting in, for example, the "Pocohontas" section of *The Bridge*, "oblivion," a merging of the self with a greater reality, here the "Being" of America. His ironic recommendation of suicide to Jolas and Jeffers must have seemed chillingly prophetic when the serious disciple of the ideas that informed their work—Crane—actually did commit suicide. Indeed, Winters's belief that emotional "expansionism," the ecstatic identification of the perceiving mind with the perceived universe, if seriously believed in, *could* only lead to suicide, was more than confirmed by Crane's death. He honored Crane for the courage of his convictions, for "the suicide of a gentleman," but this death was specific proof, if he needed it, that his suspicion of enthusiastic pantheism of the Whitman-Emerson variety as a destructive delusion was well founded.

Winters's first published opinion of Crane's poetry was the 1927 review of *White Buildings*, which appeared in the magazine *Poetry*. The review is almost wholly laudatory. He agrees with the introduction to the volume, by Allen Tate, calling the poems "more or less imagistic," details a couple of minor shortcomings, and continues: "The greatest poems, for me, are 'Repose of Rivers,' 'For the Marriage of Faustus and Helen,' 'Recitative' and 'Voyages' II and V. They maintain almost throughout a level of intensity that seems to me a maximum, and place Mr. Crane—in my own opinion—among the five or six greatest poets writing in English" (*Uncollected Essays and Reviews*, p. 49). At this stage, then, Crane's beliefs did not prevent Winters from admiring and praising his poetry very highly.

But in the 1930 review we find an attitude similar to that shown towards Rimbaud in "The Extension and Reintegration of the Human Spirit"—Winters's new beliefs will not accommodate poetry whose premises contradict those beliefs, but he still feels the power of the work he rejects. He both rejects and praises Crane's work. The review exhibits to an extreme degree a characteristic of Winters's criticism that has already been mentioned: the tendency to damn and praise the same author in almost the same breath. It is not that he damns with faint praise: rather he attempts to separate out aspects of the work he is considering into good and bad constituents, and his positive reaction to the good seems as hyperbolic as his negative reaction to the bad. The tone seems emotional, even angry, almost as if Winters felt betrayed by someone he wished to trust. This hyperbolic praise and blame is often an indication that the author under discussion is one whom Winters has been initially attracted to (usually because of a mastery of language) and then repelled by (usually because of his, to Winters, inadequate metaphysics).

The 1930 review (of *The Bridge*), published in *Poetry* like its predecessor, begins, in Winters's typically taxonomic style, with an attempt to classify the poems according to genre. He decides that the book is "a collection of lyrics" and that "the model, in so far as there is one, is obviously Whitman, whom the author proclaims in this book as a master" (*Uncollected Essays and Reviews*, p. 73). Winters had a low opinion of Whitman's verse, and an even lower opinion of his ideas, and the review becomes more hostile as it proceeds. At one point Winters leaves Crane aside and for a lengthy paragraph castigates Whitman's idea of the epic. There follows a passage of extravagant praise ("extraordinary poetry," "genius of the highest order," "a brilliant performance," "worthy of Racine") for isolated sections of the book. The praise is in the main for the manner in which particulars are realized in the language, for the poet's rhetorical skill; the blame is for the ideas, derived from Whitman, on which the poem is based. Winters sees Crane's linguistic talents as great, but his poetry as vitiated by shoddy metaphysics (in essence this is his objection to almost all the best-known poets of the twentieth century, including Williams, Pound, Eliot, Yeats, and the later Stevens). Winters's review was a shock to Crane and their relationship ceased forthwith. There was no contact between them from this time on, and in 1932 Crane was drowned.

"The Significance of *The Bridge* by Hart Crane; or, What Are We to Think of Professor X" begins by briefly establishing Winters's personal relations with Crane: "Crane and I began publishing poems in the same magazines about 1919; I started quarreling with Harriet Monroe about 1925 to get Crane's poems into *Poetry: A Magazine of Verse*; Crane and I started corresponding shortly thereafter; I spent a few evenings talking to Crane during the Christmas holidays of 1927; our correspondence ended as a result of my review of *The Bridge* in 1930; and about two and a half years later Crane committed suicide" (*In Defense of Reason*, p. 577). I suspect that this bald statement hides a strong sense of personal involvement with Crane and his fate; there is even a slight suggestion of guilt in the juxtaposition of his review with Crane's suicide, though the two events were separated by "about two and a half years." Further evidence of Winters's feelings about Crane and his death are the two poems "Orpheus: In Memory of Hart Crane" and "The Anniversary" (perhaps, as Parkinson points out, the anniversary of Crane's death), which ends,

> Crane is dead at sea. The year
> Dwindles to a purer fear.

The essay continues with a lengthy exposition of the ideas of Emerson and Whitman, whom Winters takes to be Crane's mentors. The exposition ends with the sentence, "The ignorance of philosophy and theology exhibited in such ideas is sufficient to strike one with terror." It is not merely the ignorance which strikes Winters with terror; it is the ideas themselves—those notions of pantheistic beatitude, of union with undifferentiated Being, which, as I have indicated, did indeed fill Winters with terror. Remarks reminiscent of those previously made in connection with Jolas and Jeffers follow: "The doctrine of Emerson and Whitman, if really put into practice, should naturally lead to suicide: in the first place if the impulses are indulged systematically and passionately, they can lead only to madness; in the second place, death, according to the doctrine, is not only a release from suffering but is also and inevitably the way to beatitude" (*In Defense of Reason*, p. 590). Crane's suicide is seen therefore as a direct result of his having taken seriously an inadequate philosophy: "We have, it would seem, a poet of great genius, who ruined his life and his talent by living and writing as the two greatest religious teachers of our nation [that is, Emerson and Whitman] recommended. Is it possible to shrug this off?"

The Professor X of the essay's title is a portrait compounded of traits Winters found particularly exasperating among literary academics—a sentimental romantic who does not take his professed ideas seriously enough to actually live by them. His appearance in the essay is not gratuitous; by apparently believing in the same notions as Crane did, and by leading a humdrum life with no hint of suicidal mania, he may be taken as living proof that such theories do not inevitably lead to self-destruction. Winters argues that Professor X survives because he pays only lip service to such notions, and he points out that in periods—such as the end of the eighteenth century—when literary theory actively encourages the surrender to impulse, a great many of those poets who take their vocation seriously end their lives insane.

Significantly Winters discusses Crane's absorption in Emersonian and romantic ideas in terms of demonic possession, a by now familiar trope

(perhaps not merely a trope) in his writing. The importance of this notion, which received its primary impulse from Winters's own psychological experiences and which was later defined by him, using Aquinas's
theory of evil, as privation, cannot, I think, be overestimated. It accounts
not only for his view of what happened to Crane's mind—that it was
"possessed" by an evil doctrine—but also for his own increasing suspicion of the undefined and uncharted areas of human experience, particularly the subconscious.

Winters is adamant that Crane had great literary gifts, and that he was
destroyed by a serious belief in romantic notions of the surrender to impulse and the desirability of some form of pantheistic identification of the
self with the universe. He separates the two aspects of Crane's poetry,
praising the one and condemning the other. He believed that there was
nothing inevitable about the ideas we live by, and as we have seen he
changed his own considerably. There is an implication that Crane need
not have submitted to the notions that destroyed him. What Winters does
not discuss is how far these two aspects of Crane's talent were interdependent: as Winters himself emphasized in his discussion of Baudelaire, a
rhetorical technique is often intimately connected with the author's philosophical presuppositions, and Winters's own poetry is a further clear
example of this. Winters writes that Rimbaud was "destroyed by a metaphysical vision," but an equally cogent explanation for his later silence is
that his adolescent world-view simply collapsed and that without it his
rhetoric failed; Hoffmannsthal is an analogous case. The suggestion that
Crane's rhetoric was somehow detachable from the romantic notions it
expressed is therefore suspect. Crane, for Winters, was a warning of
where such notions could lead, but he was also, clearly, a brilliant poet;
Winters wished, in his own life, to reject Crane's theories, but he also saw
himself primarily as a poet. He could not allow himself to believe that
Crane's shoddy philosophical notions and brilliant poetic talent might be
inextricably linked while he himself was attempting to develop as a poet
but to reject those same ideas.

The essay ends by honoring Crane for at least taking his, in Winters's
view, mistaken ideas seriously, unlike Professor X: "Crane had the absolute seriousness which goes with genius and sanctity; one might describe
him as a saint of the wrong religion." After the appearance of this essay,
in 1947, he mentioned Crane less and less and there are none of Crane's
poems in *Quest for Reality*, the anthology intended to demonstrate by example his theories of poetic excellence, made shortly before his death.
But it is perhaps significant that Winters destroyed, or ordered to be de-

stroyed, all letters to him from other poets, except those of Crane, which he preserved. Crane was for Winters an example of the pernicious effects of the theories he rejected in his later twenties, and a comparison of his three essays on Crane's work clearly charts his admiration, suspicion, and final turning away from these theories.

4 The Later Poetry

*Ocean and forest are
the mind's device.*

The reader who turns from *The Early Poems of Yvor Winters,
1920–1928* to his later work, for example, the poems on the David Lamson murder trial, will be struck not only by the formal shape of the later as compared to the earlier poems, but also by a noticeable shift in the nature of the language employed. Discussing the imagist work of his early twenties, I remarked on the preponderance of monosyllabic words—words like *cold, wind, stone*. This was due partly to his imagist ambitions—to render the visible world directly and with a minimum of authorial comment—and partly to his instinct for clarity and simplicity (the instinct that told him ambiguity is usually an obfuscation or evasion), to a desire for the undeniable and irreducible, cleansed of the dross of consciousness.

To some extent the mature work continues this concern, and a great deal of the monosyllabic vocabulary is retained. But it is joined by a preponderantly polysyllabic and abstract vocabulary of evaluation, largely derived from Greek and Latin. In the first "traditional" poem of *The Collected Poems*, the sonnet "The Moralists," we have the words *dicta, hypothesis, formulate, existence, mathematic, unmitigated*. Despite this accession of a new area of vocabulary, the reader of Winters's poems will miss large categories of language normally associated with poetry, and this limitation is accentuated by Winters's tendency to repeat certain words which take on an aura of particular meaning in the context of his work (examples are *pure, wrinkled, crumble* (and its derivatives), *steady*). The vocabulary of his poetry remained fairly small, and certain areas of language are almost completely excluded.

For example, words whose chief function is to direct the reader's emotional response are very rare. Adjectives with a clear emotional implication—*sad, gloomy, happy, desperate, ecstatic*, and the rest—almost never appear. With few exceptions the later poems do not invite or celebrate emotional empathy. The implicit questions they ask are not, How do I feel? but What is happening? or What is true? Emotion is strongly present in the poems—given Winters's view of reality it would be surprising if the emotions of, at the least, loss and fear did not figure in his work—but it is there as a residuum of comprehension, as an implication of tone, rather than as the explicit raison d'être of the work. To the same end Winters is sparing of adjectives which denote a simple observable fact but have specific emotional connotations, such as *wan* and *pallid*.

Further, in keeping with the development from the concrete to the abstract already noted in Winters's writing, there is little attempt in the later poems to present the reader with details of sensuous reality. The poems are frequently located in a specific landscape, and this is cleanly presented, but the landscape never exists in these poems for itself; it is there to present the context or evidence for an act of moral evaluation, and a minute description of particulars would draw attention away from Winters's purpose. That feature so beloved of certain schools of literary criticism, the specific fact evoked by "concrete" language, is virtually absent. A line like "The lacy fronds of carrots in the spring" stands out in the mature poems as an almost shocking example of sensuous description.

Winters's feelings about the natural world were clearly ambivalent. His interest in Aquinas, and his increasing tendency to consider universals and abstractions as the proper focus of intellectual concern, led him to a profound suspicion of nominalism as a philosophical position. Literature that lists specifics, or that dwells on their particularity rather than on those features held in common, seems to tacitly endorse nominalism, the theory that reality *is* merely discrete particulars, each existing only in terms of itself. Writing on Joyce in *The Function of Criticism* Winters says, "The world is teeming with such particularity, and as we grow older we become less interested in details and more interested in such conclusions as can be drawn from details" (p. 37). The word *conclusions* indicates his main interest: comprehension of what is generally valid, rather than the evocation of what is local and various. Then there is his feeling about the natural world in general (rather than his impatience with literature concerned solely with particulars), about nature as it exists distinct from man's mind. On the one hand we have the evidence of his own life—a man who kept goats, bred dogs, and cultivated a large vegetable garden—all of which seems to indicate a sympathy for and ease of being with natural phenomena. On the other hand we have the ambiguous evidence of his poetry. There is the rapt trance of the early work and the suspicion of nature of the later work, where nature frequently appears as something beguiling, fascinating, perhaps innocent, but for the human observer potentially destructive. The best poems keep in view both aspects of nature—its fascination and its potential for destruction. The less successful poems attempt to exclude, to annihilate by rhetoric, the fascination.

If there is something of the Manichee about many of Winters's poems concerned with the natural world—that it is the source of evil against which the spirit must maintain vigilance—in his most moving poems there is also something of that converted Manichee Saint Augustine when he prayed, "Make me chaste, Lord, but not yet." If the poet would ultimately withdraw from sensuous reality, he is still fascinated by its charm and power, and though he seems to condemn this fascination he cannot elude it. This tension in the apprehension of nature (the sense of charm a survival of his youthful nature-mysticism, the turning away a complex reaction compounded of psychological, intellectual, and purely literary motives) informs most of his best mature poems. When the tension between the claims of the world and the claims of the mind dissipates, the poems tend toward formula and tautology. A line like "He who understands is wise" can only be read as a cliché. Though one may accept on trust the mental struggle that lies behind the line, the engagement with reality that led the poet to this startlingly obvious truth is absent from the poem's language.

However, the high incidence in Winters's later poetry of Latinate words, often denoting abstractions, is not due solely to the author's turning away from the sensuous and particular toward a more consciously intellectual apprehension of reality. A contributory and perhaps decisive factor is that Winters's earliest formal studies were not of English literature at all, but of the Romance literatures. As he himself wrote, for most of his twenties he was more familiar with the traditional literatures of Spanish and French than with the English poetry of the past (his interest in literature written in English was largely confined to the poetry of his contemporaries and immediate elders). And as we have seen, his first published attempts to write traditional poetry were translations of sonnets by Ronsard; he returned to traditional forms, after his experimental phase, by way of translations of French and Spanish poems, many of them sonnets. His first substantial group of poems in traditional forms, after his change of direction, were also sonnets, and a formal influence is therefore likely. We should remember too that in the essay which more than any other articulates the turning away from his earlier manner, "The Extension and Reintegration of the Human Spirit," his chief apologist (the term is Winters's own) is Baudelaire. From what we know of his reading, and from the evidence of his own writings (both his translations and criticism), it is apparent that he considered traditional verse, at least during the period when he was working towards the style of his later poetry, largely in terms of Romance (chiefly French) models.

Now Winters's knowledge of French and Spanish during his late twenties was confined to an ability to read and perhaps write these languages. He could not, at this stage, speak them with any confidence, and it is, indeed, unlikely that he would have had much opportunity to hear fluent colloquial French spoken—the French priest in Santa Fe who gave him his first French lessons was probably his sole native source. His knowledge of these languages, particularly of French, whose authors he looked to much more than those of Spanish, was thus largely a passive knowledge of the literary language. Such a knowledge can often involve, despite a highly developed sensitivity to meaning, an uncertainty over linguistic register or tone.

The crude but workable distinction that exists in English between the more sensuously immediate German-derived vocabulary and the more abstract Latin-derived vocabulary cannot, of course, obtain in French or Spanish, where almost all words, whether concrete or abstract in their referents, derive from Latin. There is a further connotation in English that a Latin-derived vocabulary often carries with it a more learned dignity, an implication of scholasticism or classicism, that is lacking in the homely Saxon equivalent. If we compare words like *aqueous* and *watery* or *umbrageous* and *shadowy*, we immediately see that the Germanic word is the more familiar and that the Latinate word has the more learned air, though the words are synonymous. What I am postulating is that Winters perceived a dignity and classical strength in certain Romance works (by, for example, Baudelaire or Racine) which he attempted to reproduce in his own English poetry by adopting the English vocabulary that was closest to his French and Spanish models—that is, a largely Latin-derived vocabulary. He does not unduly exaggerate the role of Latinate words, but he often eschews the immediacy available in the more homely Germanic vocabulary of English. The simple Germanic words which constantly reappear in his poems—*cold, wind, stone,* and the like—had been there from the first; the new element is largely Latinate. This is as it should be, because abstractions in English are largely derived from the classical languages, and it was abstractions that more and more engaged his attention. Though this new language is entirely appropriate, given the structure of English and the new direction of his verse toward evaluation and comprehension rather than empathy and immediacy, the force of such a vocabulary was probably suggested to him by his reading of Ro-

mance literatures. In a Romance literature a Latinate vocabulary cannot
have this connotation of intellectual abstraction, because the whole language is Latinate, but it could *appear* to have such connotations to a non-
native speaker alive to the different implications of *watery* and *aqueous* or
shadowy and *umbrageous* in English. Winters's Latinate vocabulary is in
part a form of "translationese," an attempt to reproduce in English effects
he had perceived in French and Spanish.

To his models in French poetry must also be added his new conception
of the status and function of poetry. If in his youth he had seen poetry as a
means of participation in Being, he now saw it as a means of distinguishing the self from reality, and he referred to technique as "the outer
boundary of consciousness." Language that maintains its distance from
its subject (that seeks a perspective on reality from which the mind may
understand and evaluate, rather than emotional identification) was therefore appropriate to his new aim, and the formality of his later poetry is
directed to this end. Connected with such a concern is his sense of language as the repository of thought which stands back from the flux of
reality and whose truths should be valid beyond the exigencies of a particular time; this notion naturally led him to attempt a lapidary, even pa-
trician, style removed from local and temporal idiosyncrasies of diction.

The Sonnets from *The Proof*

The first significant poems in traditional forms which Winters wrote after his experimental phase were the sonnets included in his
1930 volume *The Proof.* The seven sonnets he retained and included in his
Collected Poems are concerned with one theme, the mind's attempts to apprehend reality. Two of them deal with intellectual categories for reality,
those of the moralists in the poem of that name, and of the physical scientists in "The Invaders." "To William Dinsmore Briggs Conducting His
Seminar" is concerned with the scholar's reconstruction of the past and
"To Emily Dickinson" with a poet's relation to the absolute. Two approach the subject through myth ("The Castle of Thorns" and "Apollo
and Daphne"), and one records the impact of death (and by implication that spiritual void which death evoked for Winters) on an observer's mind.

This latter poem is one of the few by Winters that have found their
way into anthologies. This is unfortunate, because it is not one of his best

mature poems and it is certainly less successful than all but perhaps one of the other sonnets with which it is grouped. Parts of the poem share the almost hysterical language of certain of the free-verse poems of *The Proof* and of the rejected sonnets (especially "The Fact That Offers neither Cause nor Gain") from the same volume.

The first line establishes the tone and theme of the octave: "Death. Nothing is simpler. One is dead." The abrupt rhythm and syntax and the simplicity of diction are similar in purpose to the suspended images of Winters's earliest poetry—they are an attempt to convey reality unmediated by the intellect. This purpose was part of a theory of solipsistic beatitude in the early work; here it is an indication of the intellect's impotence before the fact of death. The poem moves to a consideration of the soul, which, it states, "is mortal, nothing," but it immediately draws back from the thought:

> But thought clings flat
> To this, since it can never follow that
> Where no precision of the mind is bred.

"This" refers to the body, "the clay . . . on the bed," "that" to the void which has absorbed the personality or soul of the dead person. This void is unthinkable and the mind recoils from it: dead matter is to some extent knowable, but the nature of the personality or soul after death is unknowable and to speculate on it is to forgo all "precision of the mind." The end of the octave hovers on the "brink of darkness," the mind hesitating before the void opened before it by death.

The sestet of the sonnet records the "view" from the brink, as if the mind had chosen to ignore its own warnings and stare into the darkness. The language mimes the intellect's fear:

> Nothing to think of between you and All!
> Screaming processionals of infinite
> Logic are grinding down receding cold!
> O fool! Madness again!

We have seen how in the early poems the word *scream* and its derivatives are associated with a metaphysical terror, a terror which is here explicitly linked to the "infinite," the indefinable. The meaning squirms free, and the lines do not seem to be wholly paraphrasable, though the experience to which they refer is vividly presented. Many of the poems of *The Proof* contain such an unparaphrasable residue, which appears to be the result of the metaphysical uncertainty, indeed terror, of the years when Winters was rethinking his poetic and philosophical position. Though this residue can seem a virtue (in, for example, "The Castle of Thorns"), a dreamlike promise of undisclosed significance, Winters was soon to renounce such strategies as barely legitimate, a courting of the void rather than a definition of the intellect's limits. If the protagonist of *The Brink of Darkness* was held "by an act of will from moment to moment" on that brink, in this poem the speaker seems momentarily to lose his balance.

The poem ends with the mind admonishing itself to return from the void to the particulars of the immediate world. But even quotidian reality now takes on the lineaments of fear. The speaker's own mortality has been made real to him—"Quick! You are old!"—but old here also implies age that includes comprehension as well as nearness to death. The realization of the reality of death both confirms age (as mortality) and brings it (as comprehension). But in this sonnet that calm stoicism of comprehension toward which so many of Winters's later poems move is hardly given time to establish itself. The prevailing tone of the poem's close is still one of barely controlled fear; the mind has not been able to formulate and contain its insight but has been almost unhinged by it.

Of his sonnet "The Invaders" Winters wrote, in a note to *The Collected Poems* (1960), "The Invaders are the modern physical scientists, of whom I would not write in quite the same terms today." Here is the poem:

> They have won out at last and laid us bare,
> The demons of the meaning of the dead,
> Stripped us with wheel and flame. Oh, where they tread,
> Dissolves our heritage of earth and air!
> Till as a locomotive plunges through
> Distance that has no meaning and no bound
> Thundering some interminable sound
> To inward metal where its motion grew—
>
> Grew and contracted down through infinite
> And sub-atomic roar of Time on Time
> Toward meaning that its changing cannot find;
> So, stripped of color of an earth, and lit
> With motion only of some inner rime,
> The naked passion of the human mind.

In its tendency toward hyperbole the sonnet's language is reminiscent of that of the opening of the sestet of "The Realization," and the vision of an endless and appalling void is also similar. There is the same pivotal use of the word *infinite* (in both poems isolated at the end of a line) and the concepts associated with infinity—concepts that always indicate fear in Winters's later poetry—are very close; "no precision" and "Blurring a definition" in "The Realization," "no bound" and "no meaning" in "The Invaders." The infinite, which eludes our understanding, rouses in the poet a fearful fascination: in "The Realization" the brute fact of death, in "The Invaders" the whirlwind of the "sub-atomic roar" (the dissolving theories of contemporary physics to which Winters had already referred in similar terms in "The Vigil") threaten to draw the poet's consciousness into a vortex in which the intellect is powerless.

"They," of the poem's opening, are the physical scientists who by the comfortless vision of reality which they offer have "laid us bare," rendered us naked and homeless in the world. Significantly, they are spoken of as "demons," a word which—as we have seen—had a particularly potent connotation of evil for Winters. He defines the demon as a being who partially exists but who "at the same time may have achieved an extraordinary degree of actuality in the regions in which he does exist" (*In Defense of Reason*, p. 601). The vision of science is seen as partial and obsessive, persuasive in its authority, demonic in its implications: the "earth and air," the natural habitation of man, become alien to him, their Being becomes problematic and "dead." ("The dead" refers not to the dead of humanity but to matter regarded as the scientist regards it— "the meaning of the dead" is thus the significance of a wholly material universe).

"Wheel and flame" (line 3) at first seem to refer both to the scientist's tools and to the artifacts which become possible through scientific knowledge, but their appearance leads to the long trope of the locomotive which dominates most of the poem. This trope is extraordinarily varied and powerful in its implications. The syntactical shape of the simile, which it is easy to lose sight of, is, "as a locomotive plunges . . . So . . . The naked passion of the human mind." The final line is in apposition to the locomotive, so that the verb *plunges* (and all the subsequent activity attributed to the locomotive) also refers to the mind.

The first result of this comparison, indicated by words like *plunges*, *thundering*, is to impress on the reader the all but unrestrainable power of the mind. Secondly the locomotive "plunges through / Distance that has no meaning and no bound"—the immensity of the vista open to the intellect seems endless, but in place of the sense of triumph which we may expect at this celebration of the mind's power we perceive that edge of horror always associated in Winters's work with the infinite and meaningless. (The distance has "no meaning" because it is the "dead" infinity of physics, an infinity to which human values cannot apply.)

The poem then concentrates on the sound of the locomotive, which thunders "to inward metal where its motion grew." As so often in these sonnets (and this distinguishes them from most of Winters's subsequent poems), the meaning blurs slightly. But it is clear that the metaphor functions on three levels: the sound of the engine's all-pervading roar is compared to the equally all-pervading "sub-atomic" roar of the matter of modern physics, and it is also, if we remember that the locomotive represents the mind (specifically the scientific mind), a reference to the obsessional vision of a consciousness focused wholly on categories of its own making. As the locomotive moves through infinitely receding distance, so the subatomic roar can be traced in infinite regress; there is no point of stasis for the searching mind. In the last three lines the alien strangeness of the locomotive plunging through vast spaces (we should perhaps visualize the spaces of the American Midwest if we are to share Winters's conception) is likened to the alien quest of the scientific mind, which follows only its own laws (the "motion . . . of some inner rime"). There is an implicit suggestion that the laws are like railway tracks—leading the mind through immense vistas but narrowly directing it so that its perception of the reality through which it passes is dogmatically partial.

Though the vision of reality implied by this sonnet is remarkably similar to the vision of "The Realization"—an infinite void through which the mind plunges in vertiginous horror—and though both poems are concerned with death, either literally or with a vision that renders reality as "dead," the strategies they examine are opposed. In "The Realization" the intellect is powerless to categorize or understand the experience which confronts it; in "The Invaders" the intellect, by following its own laws, "plunges through" reality, violates it. The poems refer to opposing (and equally feared) extremes—the mind is overwhelmed or attempts to overwhelm. A great many of Winters's mature poems are concerned with finding a just balance between mind and reality, in which neither invades the other, so that a just tact informs their relationship. The locomotive, as an image of hubristic arrogance, represents one extreme, as repugnant as the opposite extreme of "The Realization."

Like "The Invaders," "The Moralists" is also a poem concerned with formulation, with dogma that interferes with perception. The octave of the poem is concerned with such attempts to "formulate our passion," and though the tense rhetoric of the stanza indicates the poet's sympathy with the moralists' struggle, its closing lines clearly state that the mind cannot in fact reduce experience to its formulae:

> In some harsh moment nowise of the mind
> Lie the old meanings your advance has packed.

("Packed" I take to mean "covered over," "obliterated.") The "harsh moment nowise of the mind" can be interpreted as a moment of direct confrontation with reality when reason quails at the immensity of its task. Such moments of arational, existential terror are typical of Winters's poems at this period and account for a great deal of their wrenched syntax and vocabulary. The poem's sestet rejects the possibility that the mind can "hold existence," encompass and thus subdue it—though again it offers a kind of despairing respect to the heroism of the attempt. The sonnet ends with the poet's claim to

> Have faced with old unmitigated dread
> The hard familiar wrinkles of the earth.

"The hard familiar wrinkles" are Winters's shorthand for the ineluctable and ultimately incomprehensible facts of existence. The word *wrinkles* is a recurrent one at such moments in his poetry; it carries its usual connotations of experience and suffering, but clearly there is a deeper implication, of an enduring strangeness that inheres in reality, of its undeniable but also unknowable being. Though Winters's later work invests its hope in reason, the poet is obviously conscious that reason seems somehow to glance off the world, to be unable to penetrate into the quiddity of things. The world and the mind remain separate, and the mind's schemes remain self-contained: finally they have nothing to say about "the hard familiar wrinkles of the earth," which abide in uninterpretable strangeness. In a later poem, "Chiron," Winters has the centaur speak of "studying my long defeat," and it is partially this defeat to which he refers—the mind's defeat in its struggle to know reality.

The sonnet "To William Dinsmore Briggs Conducting His Seminar" is a tribute to Winters's mentor at Stanford. Here we are concerned with the scholar's strategies to reclaim the reality of the past from oblivion. The poem records and to some extent enacts those values of rational skepticism and passionate regard for objective truth which were, apparently, Brigg's distinctive characteristics and which Winters hoped to emulate. Briggs was wont to use the complexities of the Overbury murder trial as an example for the necessity for accurate scholarship. The separation of truth from gossip and innuendo was particularly hazardous in this case: Overbury was poisoned in the Tower of London in 1613, probably by the Countess of Essex; the case involved some of the most important families in Jacobean England and it has remained a scandalous mystery.

In common with other poems of this period, the poem contains some very obscure moments, but these clarify somewhat if we assume that the subject of the seminar discussed is the Overbury murder, or some similar historical event, rather than a literary text.

The poem opens with the "redefinition" of "some crime" from the past—the particulars are rescued from oblivion and the irrelevant. The closing four lines of the octave record one of Winters's preoccupations of this period, and they do so with that obscurity already mentioned:

> Your fingers spin the pages into Time;
> And in between, moments of darkness pass
> Like undiscovered instants in the glass,
> Amid the image, where the demons climb.

The lines refer to the way reality escapes our categories and evaluation, despite the scholar's activity, and how this indefinable darkness threatens our integrity—not only, it would appear from the tone, our intellectual certainty, but also our emotional and spiritual security. It has been suggested that "the glass" refers to an hourglass, in which the sifting sand measures instants inseparable from each other in the same way that evil and the indefinite are here inextricably involved with what is true and definable. The interpretation is ingenious and possible, but, given the subject of the four lines and the presence of the (for Winters) key word *demons*, I prefer to consider "the glass" as some kind of mirror or window in which "the image" (of that truth the scholar seeks) is reflected. The trope of reflection accompanied by a sense of evil and the undefined recalls that moment in *The Brink of Darkness* when the protagonist momentarily sees his own "image" in the "glass" of the window: the metaphor was clearly associated by Winters with an apprehension of unformulable evil, and its implications are thus suitable for the subject of this sonnet.

The sestet continues the theme of the demons that "mean" yet do not "emerge"—their meaning remains as an inapprehensible and oppressive potency. The emphasis then shifts from the unknowable to the mind that desires to know, to the scholar who embodies the "definitive and final stare," "the hard book" of what we can and cannot know. The sonnet is similar to "The Moralists" and "The Invaders" in that it is concerned with the intellect's strategies to apprehend reality, but its tone carries none of the implications of disapproval which we find in the other two poems: the moralists and the invaders (scientists) attempt to impose an order on reality, to violate its separateness by their schemes—the scholar attempts to elicit truth from data, and he accepts that truth ultimately escapes him. His method is an example of that tact (neither abasement nor arrogance) before the world which Winters was to celebrate in many of his later poems. The sonnet also concerns itself with a theme that was of great importance to Winters at this time: the links which he perceived between the undefined and evil. In making the subject of the seminar a crime (possibly the murder of Overbury) Winters is able to demonstrate the intimacy of the two—but the wider implications of the sonnet, and of a great deal of Winters's later poetry, are that the undefined is per se demonic, even if no crime were involved. The sonnet is therefore something of a sleight of hand, as well as a fine tribute to Winters's teacher.

If "To William Dinsmore Briggs" deals with the scholar's quest for truth, "To Emily Dickinson" is concerned with the poet's quest—this particular poet's, but by implication that of all poets true to their vocation and thus also (he would hope) Winters himself.

The poem opens with a declaration of the writer's sympathetic response to an oeuvre which by its own austerity seems to forbid any maudlin display of pity:

> Dear Emily, my tears would burn your page,
> But for the fire-dry line that makes them burn—
> Burning my eyes, my fingers, while I turn
> Singly the words that crease my heart with age.

The lack of self-pity in the best of her work and the honesty it evinces in its understanding of her predicament are themselves beyond the comfort of tears, and they forbid that indulgence in the observer. The poem begins with a conventional expression of sympathy (no less moving for its convention), which is seen as irrelevant before the "fire-dry" austerity of her vision. In the phrase, "I turn / Singly the words" we have a fine indication of the way the reader is forced to read Emily Dickinson's poems. The phrase could, of course, apply to the careful reading of any poet's work, but it suits with a particular aptness that wary tentativeness with which we thread our way through an Emily Dickinson poem. Her eccentric vocabulary, and the way that she can juxtapose items of quite different registers, make individual words especially prominent in their contexts, so that we do indeed turn them singly, pondering their idiosyncratic implications. It is such moments of "burning" vision that "crease the heart with age"—that is, bring home to the reader the nature of his own being and mortality. In the second half of the octave the poet wishes that he could "kneel before you as you found your tomb." There is the implication of the wisdom traditionally glimpsed by those about to die, and Winters says that if he could receive this extremity of vision, an extreme towards which Emily Dickinson moved with rare purpose and self-consciousness (from the evidence of her poetry she lived as if perpetually aware of her own mortality, as Winters seems to have done for much of his twenties), then he "might rise to face my heritage," and he would be able to comprehend the wisdom of the past and perhaps take his own place in its tradition.

In the sestet it is not this suggestion of a heritage that is developed, but the nature of Emily Dickinson's extreme and lonely vision:

> Yours was an empty upland solitude
> Bleached to the powder of a dying name;
> The mind, lost in a word's lost certitude
> That faded as the fading footsteps came
> To trace an epilogue to words grown odd
> In that hard argument which led to God.

The "upland solitude" suggests, as well as loneliness, a kind of spiritual preeminence, but it also implies, and the implication is augmented by the eeriness of the following line, the lifeless desolation that visits the spirit so far advanced in its quest. We recognize this desolation as that lack of faith of a mind constitutionally anxious to secure faith, a species of the dark night of the soul. The strangeness of language alluded to is not only the strangeness of her own language in her poems, which is a kind of evidence of mental pressure and stress (and perhaps a model for Winters's own waywardnesses of diction during this period), nor even the peculiar unreality that language takes on to a person almost constantly alone; it is that radical disjunction between language and reality which troubles mystic and poet alike. The "word's lost certitude" and the "words grown odd" are symptoms of the poet's dependence on and suspicion of words which seem altogether unable to embody truth. The words have their own peculiar reality, a reality reinforced by solitary meditation on their meanings, which seems quite separate from the truths of experience. The concept is similar to that expressed in "The Moralists," where the mind's formulations of the world glance off reality and have nothing to say about "the hard familiar wrinkles" of experience. Winters utilizes and augments this sense of disjunction, of verbal evasion, by his line "That faded as the fading footsteps came." What fades in the first use of the verb is the certainties of language. The "fading footsteps" are primarily the weakening pace of Emily Dickinson herself approaching the end of her quest, but the whole phrase "the fading footsteps came" suggests a paradox, as of the simultaneous approach and retreat of some personage or truth, as if what she approached remained constantly elusive. What she approaches, as the last line indicates, is God, and this paradox of nearness and distance is one traditionally applied to God.

It will be noticed that the poet's quest is seen as one toward the absolute and is concerned with what Winters called "metaphysical" truths—the nature of mortality and God. It is a quest away from the vivid multiplicity of quotidian life toward "an empty . . . solitude." Winters's conception of the nature of poetry has modified considerably from the position set out in "Quod tegit omnia," with its rejection of the notion of absolute truths existing beyond the quotidian, or at least the rejection of such truths as being relevant to poetry. This latter notion, the notion of Winters's twenties, is of course a much commoner theory of poetry in the twentieth century than his later impatience with the contingent, and in abandoning it he cut himself off from the main current of modernist poetical theory.

We may also note in passing that the last three sonnets discussed contain the word *hard* in the last line:

> The hard familiar wrinkles of the earth. ["The Moralists"]

> And that hard book will now contain this wrong. ["To William Dinsmore Briggs"]

> In that hard argument which led to God. ["To Emily Dickinson"]

There is an attempt, in each case, to have the sonnet come to rest in some lapidary certainty: the poem is seen as a movement towards what is incontrovertible and persistent, even though the subject of the sonnets is the elusive strangeness of reality. It is largely this tension between the quest for certainty (for "hardness," what I referred to at the opening of this chapter as Winters's desire for the undeniable and irreducible), and the poet's acknowledgment of the shifting and indefinable nature of that reality he anatomizes that gives these poems their distinctive tone.

The remaining two sonnets in this group of seven included in *The Collected Poems* reinforce the suggestion, already noticed, that such definitive certainty is impossible, that reality cannot be contained by the mind's categories, nor by its instrument, language. We have the feeling that the mind as it forays into reality (as the active agent of moralist, scientist, scholar, or poet) is doomed to failure, but that its failure is necessary, even heroic—an expression of resistance to chaos and the undefined. The sonnets "Apollo and Daphne" and "The Castle of Thorns" seem to me to be two of Winters's finest poems. Both work by allegory (this is more obvious in "Apollo and Daphne"), and in both there is a residuum of meaning that remains unexplained by the allegorical details. Both have a power which, like the elusive reality that is their subject, evades precise definition. This lack of definition within the poems is not due to an auto-telic symbolism; it is not that the symbols "mean themselves" and remain untranslatable; rather, they have external significance (bluntly, Apollo equals the mind, Daphne equals the world), but this significance does not exhaust their evocative power. Winters's objection to imprecision of symbolism in other poet's work is an objection to symbols that do not *even* refer to something beyond themselves, not to an undefined power above and beyond their translatable reference to reality. I mention this only to make plain that I am not accusing Winters of what he saw as a fault in other writers. Nevertheless he did gradually come to distrust such indefinite significance more and more, and its place diminishes in his poems.

In "The Extension and Reintegration of the Human Spirit" (published in 1929; *The Proof*, from which the sonnets are taken, was published in 1930) Winters wrote apropos of Crane's "Repose of Rivers":

> The symbolic value of the details however is not so precisely deter-
> minable—they are details not of the life of man nor even directly
> referable to the life of man, but are living and marvellous details of
> a river's course, with strange intellectual and emotional overtones
> of their own. Mr. Robert Penn Warren has remarked that the life of
> an allegorical poem resides precisely in that margin of meaning that
> cannot be interpreted allegorically. As in the poem of Mallarmé,
> the words are constantly balancing on, almost slipping from, the
> outermost edge of their possible meaning. [*Uncollected Essays and
> Reviews*, p. 247]

At this period, then, Winters did not deny the power of imprecision in allegorical poetry, and in the two sonnets under discussion this impreci-sion is an important part of their sense of compelling revery, of a dream-significance not quite apprehended. In his later allegorical poems, "Hera-cles," for example, the relationship between symbol and referent was to be much more one to one, and for this reason they often lack the rapt visionary quality of these two sonnets.

"Apollo and Daphne" is the clearer of the two. Here is the poem:

> Deep in the leafy fierceness of the wood,
> Sunlight, the cellular and creeping pyre,

Increased more slowly than aetherial fire:
But it increased and touched her where she stood.
The god had seized her, but the powers of good
Struck deep into her veins; with rending flesh
She fled all ways into the grasses' mesh
And burned more quickly than the sunlight could.

And all her heart broke stiff in leafy flame
That neither rose nor fell, but stood aghast;
And she, rooted in Time's slow agony,
Stirred dully, hard-edged laurel, in the past;
And, like a cloud of silence or a name,
The god withdrew into eternity.

Apollo, the god of light and poetry, represents poetic genius, the aesthetic principle as an amoral power. Daphne represents experience or the world, and the sonnet is thus an allegory of the poet's attempts to know and subdue or seduce reality. It differs from the Emily Dickinson sonnet in that it is less concerned with the absolute than with immediate experience: the "failure" of Apollo is bound up with this concern.

As Daphne evades the grasp, the attempted rape, of Apollo, so reality evades the grasp of the mind, it becomes inapprehensibly other. In Daphne's metamorphosis into vegetation there is the suggestion that the mind can never know the world-in-itself. When approached Daphne changes and evades the god's grasp; Apollo cannot change as she does—world and mind remain irreducibly separate (there is here an implicit rejection of Winters's earlier near-pantheism). The distance between the conceptual world of the mind and the actual world of external reality is indicated by the two capitalized words of the poem—Time and Eternity. The world (Daphne) flees into Time to escape the grasp of the mind (Eternity/Apollo). As in the previous poems of the group the implication is clear: quotidian reality evades the mind's strategies to apprehend it.

In the octave of the poem two kinds of light are contrasted—"sunlight" (that is, Apollo) and "aetherial fire," equated with "the powers of good," which effect the metamorphosis and snatch the goddess from Apollo's grasp. The "aetherial fire" which saves the goddess is something alien and uncanny, a force obviously beyond the power of simple sunlight: it is itself the inapprehensibility of the world, the force that removes reality from our mental grasp. It is significant that the "aetherial fire" is equated with "the powers of good." This at first might seem to contradict Winters's usual version of things, where it is the mind that is more usually associated with good. What upsets the normal Wintersian equation is a Heraclitean belief in a natural balance, in forces not straying beyond their proper limits. Just as the *surrender* of the mind to the chthonic powers of nature is seen as evil, so the attempt to subdue nature by the mind is also seen as an evil. Winters is endorsing a respectful demarcation between the mind and the world. This sense of things in their just places is an important constituent of Winters's instinct for order, and the anger that is evident in many of the later poems (for example, on California history) often springs from the feeling that this natural justice has been outraged. One would expect the poet to be sympathetic to the mind in its attempts to know the world, but in this poem Winters is unequivocally on the side of the world. His choice of the Apollo and Daphne myth as the vehicle for the poem, where Daphne rather than Apollo engages the reader's sympathy, indicates this. The octave ends with Daphne's metamorphosis, her flight into a form beyond Apollo's power.

The sestet of the poem is perhaps one of the most beautiful stanzas Winters wrote. The metaphor of the fire is continued in the phrase "leafy flame," which at the same time indicates the metamorphosis into laurel. The flame—the leaves—does not stir; an indication that Daphne is no longer the evanescent goddess, but the slower, duller, and more profoundly strange being of the leaves, "rooted in Time's slow agony," substance caught in the ineluctable process of time. The metaphor brilliantly conveys the contrast between the mind's conceptions of reality, and the way that reality itself, when approached, retreats into an intractable strangeness—as alien as the being of vegetative nature is to the being of the god. The mind, balked of its prey, retreats from Time, the province of external reality, to Eternity, its own province (particularly in Winters's later poetry, in which the mind is frequently associated with notions of eternity).

There is a suggestion that the mind suffers deprivation by being unable to truly enter into the province of external reality: reality is caught in time and that is its pathos, but the mind excluded from any true intimacy with reality has its own pathos. The phrase "like a cloud of silence or a name" can suggest the numinous aura of the god, but it also conveys the impotence of defeat, the vague sadness of a mind isolated from the world. There is the final irony that the laurel, into which Daphne transforms herself, evokes the poet's crown and is a symbol of poetic excellence. This symbol is almost an intimation of defeat: Apollo desires Daphne but touches laurel, the poet desires truth but achieves poetry, a concinnity derived from truth but lacking its evanescent numinousness. The sexual metaphor that underlies the poem, the attempted rape, was to be used by Winters in other poems in order to express this concept of the mind's frustrated and violent relations with inapprehensible experience.

"The Castle of Thorns" is perhaps the most obscure of the sonnets at first reading. However, Winters added a note to it, and this, together with a slight knowledge of Winters's concerns imported from other poems, dispels most of the difficulty. The note reads: "In medieval romance, which is for the most part a refurbishing of ancient folklore, the Robber Knight commonly represents Death. In taking his victim to his castle, which is normally surrounded by a wood of thorn, he must in some way cross or dive under water, which is the most ancient symbol of the barrier between the two worlds" (*Collected Poems*, p. 189). The sonnet is therefore clearly concerned with death. It is also, like the other sonnets of the group, concerned with what we can and cannot know. It opens with the poet drawing water (to give to his goats) into an iron pail. The water in the pail is like a tangible example of that power (the "aetherial fire" of "Apollo and Daphne") that withdraws the world from our grasp. The verse has a hallucinatory quality very reminiscent of Winters's earliest free verse:

> Through autumn evening, water whirls thin blue,
> From iron to iron pail—old, lined, and pure;
> Beneath, the iron is indistinct, secure,
> In revery that cannot reach to you.

This barrier between the mind and the world reminds him of the myth to which the note alludes and thus, by association, of the barrier between the living and the dead and also between immediate experience and meaning:

> Water it was that always lay between
> The mind of man and that harsh wall of thorn,
> Of stone impenetrable, where the horn
> Hung like the key to what it all might mean.

These three oppositions—world-mind, life-death, experience-meaning— are frequently associated in Winters's work.

The sestet then moves to the goats for whom the water had been drawn. The goats represent "a strong tradition that has not grown old," and from this tradition the poet draws a relative peace, though a peace gained within the consciousness of death. What is this tradition? It would be tempting to see it as the traditional learning that Winters was at this time investigating as a result of his contact with Briggs, but nothing in the poem supports such a notion, and it is a little absurd to see the goats as representing Aristotle and Aquinas. It is rather, I suggest, that tradition of the antique, pastoral world (which goats might naturally call to a poet's mind), in which man lived within his natural experience with a tact and intimacy that he has since forfeited. His modern alienation from this world leads him to attempt either the subjugation of nature and experience ("The Invaders," "The Moralists") or a self-destructive submission of his own being to an undefined pantheist All. Winters would reject both these extremes in favor of a classical poise and understanding. The tradition is that of the "gardens bare and Greek" of the later poem "By the Road to the Air-Base," or of the opening stanzas of "John Sutter," or even, to give it another application, of his definition of poetry as "laurel, archaic, rude."

These sonnets form an introduction to Winters's mature poetry. Their chief theme is that "quest for reality" which he always considered to be the poet's main task. The theme leads to a consideration of the various means by which the mind attempts to know reality and of the dangers involved in these means. His ideal is of an intimacy of tact and understanding—an ideal that is threatened both by man's hubristic arrogance and by his delirious self-abasement before the otherness of experience. The main representative of such otherness for Winters was death. In the technique of the last two sonnets discussed, "Apollo and Daphne" and "The Castle of Thorns," we see indications of that form of modified allegory which was to be his most constant poetic strategy.

It is not my intention to work chronologically through all of Winters's collected poems explicating each one. Rather I shall divide them into groups which often cut across the chronological order and consider in detail what I take to be the most important poems of each group. The division is necessarily somewhat arbitrary, and some poems straddle more than one group, but I hope this scheme will in general clarify rather than obscure Winters's preoccupations.

I have postulated five groups of poems, as follows: (1) poems concerned with the explicit opposition of the mind and reality, and with reality's potentially destructive effect on the mind; (2) poems in which nature is seen as at least partially benign, and the typical mood is one of nostalgic revery; (3) poems concerned with time, mortality, eternity, and the idea

of God—a subdivision of this section is concerned with poems on scholarship and the intellect, themes which Winters usually treats in terms of
time and the eternal; (4) poems with subjects drawn from Greek myths;
and (5) occasional and public poems dealing either with the poet's own
family or themes such as the Lamson trial, politics, and war.

The Opposition between the Mind and Reality

The most important poems that are included in this group
are "The Slow Pacific Swell" and "Sir Gawaine and the Green Knight."
But the theme is adumbrated in "The Fable," a poem from *The Proof* and
therefore written towards the end of the poet's twenties. Here is the
poem in its later, shorter version, as it appears in *The Collected Poems*:

> Beneath the steady rock the steady sea,
> In movement more immovable than station,
> Gathers and washes and is gone. It comes,
> A slow obscure metonymy of motion,
> Crumbling the inner barriers of the brain.
> But the crossed rock braces the hills and makes
> A steady quiet of the steady music,
> Massive with peace.
>   And listen, now:
> The foam receding down the sand silvers
> Between the grains, thin, pure as virgin words,
> Lending a sheen to Nothing, whispering.

The poem shares the hypnotized quality of Winters's early work, which
had approved, and attempted to induce, the merging of consciousness
with the observed object. But it lacks the tense fixity of, for example, the
poems of *The Bare Hills*. The wash of the sea suggests passivity at the
edge of oblivion rather than the rapt intensity of the earliest poems. The
sense of hypnosis is conveyed more by the benumbing rhythm than by
imagist concentration of focus. In the first three lines we have the repetition of "steady," then the paradox that seems like repetition, the concepts
as it were returning on themselves, "in movement more immovable than
station," and in the third line there is a similar effect produced by the pat-

tern of the verbs. But there is in the poem a tacit acknowledgment of the presence of the poet, which had been missing from much of the earlier work.

The poem is clearly not only concerned with natural phenomena—its title indicates its metaphoric status—and we realize in the fifth line, "Crumbling the inner barriers of the brain," that it deals with one of Winters's constant themes: the invasion of the mind by the natural world, or, to view the process from the other side, the surrender of the mind to the mindless. Winters frequently refers in his criticism to the potency of the sea as a symbol for unstructured, chaotic experience. This passage, from his essay on Wallace Stevens, is typical: "The first part of the poem deals with Crispin's encounter with the sea, that is, with his realization of a universe, vast, chaotic, and impersonal beyond his power of formulation or imagination and rendering him contemptible by contrast" (*In Defense of Reason*, p. 440). There are very similar passages in the essay on Melville.

Bearing such passages in mind, we understand (an understanding confirmed by the symbolism of "The Slow Pacific Swell") that the opposition of the rock and the sea which we perceive in this poem indicates the opposition of intellect and experience. The "crossed rock" that "braces the hills," the solid land that resists the erosions of the sea, becomes at least potentially a symbol of the rational mind resisting the flux of experience. And it is the rock that "makes / A steady quiet of the steady music / Massive with peace"—the mind harmonizes experience—from the otherwise destructive sea. But the poem ends with a return to the hypnotic vision of the opening lines: the image of the foam receding

> Between the grains, thin, pure as virgin words,
> Lending a sheen to Nothing, whispering.

is almost mystical in its implications, as if suggesting that experience itself is merely a "sheen to Nothing," inapprehensible by the intellect, a retreating strangeness we cannot formulate. The poem occupies a position halfway between the arational early poems, with their implied intuition of Being, and the later work committed to reason's categories and methods. Its halfway status is indicated by its form—blank verse, a traditional form associated by Winters with the traditional disciplines of reasoned discourse, but a blank verse curiously benumbed by its repetitions and somniferous rhythm, inviting revery rather than analysis. In the same way the use of the sea-land opposition indicates that opposition between the mind and reality which we associate with Winters's later work, but the opening and closing passages of dreamlike revery recall, albeit in a different form, the tranced states of the earlier imagist work. "December Eclogue," a rejected poem in heroic couplets from *The Journey* (1931), occupies a similar transitional position. The poem opens with images very similar to those of Winters's first books, but they are dismissed by the line "These are not signals and I go my way." The rest of the poem turns from the opening's sensuous particulars and concentrates on academic and intellectual matters; such a shift from the sensuous to the abstract is wholly typical of Winters's development.

"The Slow Pacific Swell" is one of a group of poems written in heroic couplets and included in *The Journey*. Like Schumann, Winters tended to stay with one form until he felt he had at least temporarily exhausted its potential for himself. The sonnets from *The Proof* form a definite group, and the poems in heroic couplets of *The Journey* are another such group. He was particularly impressed by the possibilities of the heroic couplet, and in *Primitivism and Decadence* (1937) he wrote, "The heroic couplet must have certain qualities which enable the poet employing it to pass easily from description to lyricism, to didacticism, to satire, and so on, or even at times to combine several of these qualities at a single stroke" (*In Defense of Reason*, p. 141).

It is *The Journey* which marks the real emergence of Winters's mature style, if we except one or two of the more successful sonnets from *The Proof*. The mature work can be easily distinguished from the earlier poems by certain obvious features: traditional form, a discursive and fully grammatical syntax rather than the presentation of suspended images, the shift from intuition to reason as a guide to the interpretation of reality. What distinguishes these poems from the intermediary work of *The Proof* can best be indicated by a quotation from Winters's essay "The Progress of Hart Crane," written in 1930, at the same time as some of the poems of *The Journey*: "The quality which we call 'restraint,' and which is here lacking, is a result of the feeling on the part of the poet that the motivation of his emotion is sound and needs no justification, that the emotion is inevitable; his problem, then, is only to give order to his emotion. In Mr. Crane we can see an attempt to emotionalize a theme" (*Uncollected Essays and Reviews*, p. 79). The truth or otherwise of Winters's description of Crane's poetic practice does not concern us here; what is interesting is that the passage accurately describes the movement from the predominant style of *The Proof* (1930) to that of *The Journey* (1931). Many of the poems of *The Proof* attempt to emotionalize their themes, to work them up by extreme means (I have already indicated the rather hys-

terical vocabulary and syntax of parts of this volume), and by Winters's
own criterion such attempts are made when the poet is unsure of the justice of what he is saying. The restraint which Winters remarks on as
being a sign of the poet's confidence in the soundness of his emotion is
fully evident in "The Slow Pacific Swell" and the other poems written in
heroic couplets at this time. Winters had passed through the uncertainties
of his change of poetic and philosophical direction and reached a state of
confidence in his new beliefs and practice. The poems of *The Journey* aim
at, and in the main achieve, a massive serenity (very different from the
crowded urgency of "The Invaders" or "The Realization"); we perceive
in them a mind alert to the world but intellectually anchored, not merely
drifting over the sea of its experience.

The title poem of *The Journey* repeats the transition (of *Fire Sequence*
and *The Brink of Darkness*) from brutality to a species of resurrection,
"in naked sunlight, on a naked world," and promise of a new life. In
its simultaneous presentation of Winters's own journey (both literal
and spiritual) from the environment of his early twenties to his new life
elsewhere it contains his finest tribute to the life of the American
wastelands—that anonymous persistence that had inspired so many of
the early poems:

> Small stations by the way,
> Sunk far past midnight! Nothing one can say
> Names the compassion they stir in the heart.
> Obscure men shift and cry, and we depart.

Like the title poem, and like other poems in *The Journey*, "The Slow
Pacific Swell" traces partly allegorically and partly directly Winters's own
emotional and intellectual development. One of the authors he named as
having influenced ("in a few poems each") his adoption of traditional
metrical forms was Robert Bridges. In a review of Bridges's *Shorter
Poems*, published in 1932, he praised the poem "The Summer-House on
the Mound" very highly. The poem is in heroic couplets; after a short
introduction it describes a boy, the young poet himself, lying on a hillside
watching ships passing in the distance. The poem's form, the setting, and
the activity of the protagonist are virtually identical in Winters's "The
Slow Pacific Swell," and a comparison of the two will show a remarkable
similarity of tone in the opening stanzas. (The poems close quite differently, but Bridges's poem was certainly, to some extent, the model for
Winters's).

In the first stanza the poet remembers himself as a child watching the sea "at thirty miles or more" from a hilltop. The writing is nostalgic, full of subdued passion, a sense of the pathos of lost innocence:

> The vision still
> Lies in the eye, soft blue and far away:
> The rain has washed the dust from April day;
> Paint-brush and lupine lie against the ground;
> The wind above the hill-top has the sound
> Of distant water in unbroken sky.

This revery, which inevitably reminds us of the tranced states of the early poems, is abruptly broken by the mention of passing ships which "seem not to stir. / That is illusion." The phrase "That is illusion" apppears to refer beyond its immediate context, denying the validity of the child's revery.

In the second stanza we see how deeply the child's entranced vision of "pale tranquillity" is mistaken. The poet describes how once, when on board ship, he had almost been drowned by a huge wave washing over the deck:

> the sea
> Hove its loose weight like sand to tangle me
> Upon the washing deck, to crush the hull;
> Subsiding, dragged flesh at the bone. The skull
> Felt the retreating wash of dreaming hair.
> Half drenched in dissolution, I lay bare.

Once free of the water's destructive power the poet crisply remarks, "That was the ocean," a phrase obviously meant to be set beside the "That is illusion," which denied the tranced distant vision of the sea. The ocean is not the calm vision of childhood but the destructive power he had faced as an adult. The stanza continues with a fine description of whales rising and sinking back into the ocean. The whales have an immense and majestic beauty, and they represent the equally immense and majestic beauty of the sea, which we now recognize as a potential destroyer.

Howard Kaye, in his essay "The Post-Symbolist Poetry of Yvor Winters," has remarked how in Winters's mature poetry, "sensory details are presented in language which also conveys philosophical ideas" (p. 180). The poem can be read on a purely sensory level, as "The Slow Pacific Swell" can be read purely as a poem about the sea, but this is not its whole meaning. One real difficulty with Winters's later poems is to unravel just what it is that the sensory details refer to beyond themselves. They are often the vehicle of a complex metaphor whose tenor is difficult to apprehend. Winters himself explained how his poem "A Spring Serpent" is about a particular kind of romantic symbolist poetry, though to the uninitiated it looks remarkably like a poem about a serpent in which the vocabulary has got rather out of hand. Howard Kaye comments on this poem: "The tenor is never explicit, nothing in the poem states that it is about symbolist poetry. One problem the poem presents is how we know what the tenor is" (p. 183). He continues, "The key to his intention, the bridge between vehicle and tenor, is frequently a word . . . slightly too abstract for its context. The word will prove on examination intelligible in terms of the vehicle, but its more immediate and fuller sense will be in terms of the philosophical ideas behind the poem" (p. 185). He instances, as an example, the word *dissolution* from the second stanza of "The Slow Pacific Swell." This word acts as a hint, if we have not realized already, that the poem is not merely about versions of what the sea is. Dissolution is the fear we are familiar with in Winters's work—the loss of definition, the dispersal of the mind into the undifferentiated chaos of experience, its destruction as a separate observing identity. The sea, we understand, is what Winters had described it as in the passage quoted from his essay on Stevens, "a universe, vast, chaotic and impersonal beyond his power of formulation or imagination and rendering him contemptible by contrast."

The sea in the poem represents the interminable flux of becoming that is the natural world as it exists over against the poet: this flux had seemed to him in youth to be something infinitely attractive, a state in which he would willingly sink himself in pantheistic communion—hence the trance of the poem's opening. But the attraction he felt sprang from his ignorance; a true invasion of the mind by chaotic reality is a drowning, an invasion of death. The first stanza is like a summation of Winters's early dream of "waking oblivion," the second a metaphor of the crisis which led him to reject pantheistic communion as a goal.

The last stanza opens "A landsman, I." The poet has rejected immersion in the flux of experience for the security of the intellect, represented by the land. However, he is still drawn to the sea,

> I would be near it on a sandy mound,
> And hear the steady rushing of the deep
> While I lay stinging in the sand with sleep.
> I have lived inland long.

The passage documents the tensions of Winters's later poetry—between the seductive and lulling promise of the natural world, and the equally strong desire for the security of "land." It is the tension between experience and the mind that in order to formulate experience both seeks and fears an intimacy with the world.

The poem ends with a passage of great power:

> the sea extends
> Its limber margin and precision ends.
> By night a chaos of commingling power,
> The whole Pacific hovers hour by hour.
> The slow Pacific swell stirs on the sand,
> Sleeping to sink away, withdrawing land,
> Heaving and wrinkled in the moon, and blind;
> Or gathers seaward, ebbing out of mind.

In this passage the immense, hypnotic power of the sea, its slow attrition of the land and its monstrous unformulable strangeness hinted at in the penultimate line, act as a magnificent metaphor for reality which is always beyond and infinitely greater than the poet, to which he is ineluctably drawn but whose dissolving strength he feels impelled to resist if he is to retain his identity and reason. The title of the poem is quoted in these lines, and we realize that it suggests a midway stage between the child "at thirty miles or more" from the sea and the adult who was almost drowned by its onslaught. The swell "stirs on the sand," the shore, the place where land and sea join, or in the scheme of the poem where experience and intellect meet in a wary intimacy; it is the province of the poet who is neither locked in the false dream of childhood nor borne down by the chaos of unformulable reality.

The later poem "Sir Gawaine and the Green Knight" deals with the same basic theme under the guise of telling, through a monologue by Sir Gawaine, the medieval legend. The poem is written in quatrains of iambic tetrameters, rhyming a b a b. The form is reminiscent of the ballad stanza and is therefore fitting for the narration of a traditional tale from folklore. (The ballad stanza as such is four lines in which the first and third are tetrameters and the second and fourth trimeters, only the second and fourth lines rhyming; however, variations of this scheme in certain of the ballads (for example, "Kinmont Willie") produced a form very close to Winters's Sir Gawaine stanza).

The poem opens with Sir Gawaine recounting how he had struck off the head of the green knight, and so involved himself in the future tryst in the knight's own country. The knight obviously (by his color, and by the description given him in the opening lines, "Reptilian green the wrinkled throat / Green as a bough of yew the beard") represents the natural world, which Sir Gawaine, who is the narrator and may be taken to represent the poet, thinks he can conquer. In the word *reptilian* we have an indication of this world's alien, inhuman qualities, and by the word *yew* it is associated with death.

However, Sir Gawaine's attempted conquest merely puts him in the knight's power. The central stanzas, which are the most significant in terms of the poem's allegorical meaning, describe the attempted seduction of Sir Gawaine by Morgan le Fay, the knight's wife, and, for the purposes of the allegory, his equivalent. But Sir Gawaine remains, though tempted, unseduced, and is freed "with what I knew":

> Although her body clung and swarmed,
> My own identity remained.
>
> Her beauty, lithe, unholy, pure,
> Took shapes that I had never known;
> And had I once been insecure,
> Had grafted laurel in my bone.
>
> And then, since I had kept the trust,
> Had loved the lady, yet was true,
> The knight withheld his giant thrust
> And let me go with what I knew.

That is, the poet remains unseduced by the beauty of the natural world, to which however he is strongly attracted; he does not sleep with the lady, he does not surrender himself to nature in the way that Wordsworth or Emerson advocated, but retains his separate identity. The mention of laurel in the second of the quoted stanzas reminds us of the laurel of the sonnet "Apollo and Daphne": it is laurel that Daphne becomes in order to flee Apollo's embrace. In both poems laurel indicates the natural world as it is alien to the mind. In the sonnet the emphasis is on the propriety of the mind's separation from reality; in the later poem it is on the seductive charm of that reality which seeks to induce the mind to leave its proper sphere. The poem ends with Sir Gawaine returning from his venture into the enchanted wood to the quotidian world of men:

> I left the green bark and the shade,
> Where growth was rapid, thick and still;

I found a road that men had made
And rested on a drying hill.

The stanza briefly echoes the symbolism of "The Slow Pacific Swell"—
the "drying hill," like the dry land of the latter poem, representing the
conscious intellect that provides a measure of security againt the mindless
energy and vivid chaos of sea or forest, unformulated experience. But, as
in "The Slow Pacific Swell," the implications of the poem are ambiguous. The final preference for land in the one and for the "drying hill" in
the other constitute the last word, but a great deal of the rhetorical force
of each poem has gone into making plain to us how strong the attraction
of sea and forest have been. The beauty of the inhabitants and representatives of the wilderness (the whales, Morgan le Fay) are potent symbols of
that invitation to surrender celebrated by romantic poets who saw nature
not as a threat to the intellect but as a resolving peace which would dis-
perse the problems of consciousness in beatitude. Winters's later criticism
is firm in its denunciation of such attitudes, but the evidence of his poetry, and not only his early poetry, is less overwhelmingly one-sided. The
very word *drying* in the phrase "drying hill" suggests that the journey has
been a kind of vivifying immersion or even rebirth. By remaining unseduced the poet is allowed to go "with what I knew," but had he never
embarked on the quest there would have been nothing to know. Howard
Kaye quotes J. V. Cunningham, "who called him [Winters] a 'congenital
Romantic' [and] recognized that Winters' concern with self-control arises
out of a specifically Romantic context. The temptations which the poet
of 'The Slow Pacific Swell' must resist are the temptations which Wordsworth and Crane invited" ("Post-Symbolist Poetry," p. 194).

Winters's insistence, in his prose, on the necessity for the intellect to
preserve its integrity, to resist all blandishments that invite it to lose itself
in revery or dream, must be read against the understanding of how very
real those blandishments were for him—particularly when they seemed
to offer a form of pantheistic communion with the natural world. Sur-
realism and the cultivation of the subconscious for its own sake had little
appeal for him; his interest was always external reality. Though he came
to condemn both Poe and Emerson, the nature-oriented vision of the latter was originally real and attractive to him, whereas the nightmarish
inward explorations of Poe held little charm for someone who had declared, "The subconscious, by any possible definition that justifies the
term, remains a mere fringe of one's spiritual existence" (*Uncollected Essays and Reviews*, p. 250).

Nature as a Benign Presence

The poems of my second suggested group clearly indicate this ambiguity in Winters's response to the external and natural world. These poems are mostly concerned with the past, and their tone is more or less constantly nostalgic. They are either concerned with the poet's own biography, or with episodes from California history. As Winters had spent part of his early childhood in California, the two subjects were probably associated for him. In these poems the natural world is less a threat than a symbol of lost beatitude, often indistinguishable from the traditional romantic beatitude of childhood. The implication of a lost Eden is reinforced in certain of the poems on California history by the descriptions of a fall—the sudden and violent transformation of California during the latter half of the nineteenth century. Of the autobiographical poems in *The Journey* the most important are "On a View of Pasadena from the Hills," "The Marriage," and the title poem, in which, however, the relation of the mind to external reality is more that of questing exploration than nostalgic revery. Of the autobiographical poems from the later volumes, which share the sense of nature as a benign presence, the most important seem to me to be "On Re-reading a Passage from John Muir" and "A Summer Commentary."

If we except the satire "The Critiad," which Winters did not reprint after its appearance in *The Journey*, "On a View of Pasadena from the Hills" is his longest and most ambitious poem in heroic couplets. In it he combined both personal and more public topographical history to make a poem that is a homage simultaneously to a particular landscape and its way of life, and to his own father. It is surely psychologically significant that the most substantial poem he retained from *The Journey* (1931, the year of his father's death; the volume is dedicated partly to his memory)—the volume in which his commitment to tradition becomes explicit and complete—should be in honor of his father.

The poem opens with a narrator watching, from a height, the gradual illumination of the valley below him as dawn approaches. His situation reminds us of that of the child at the opening of "The Slow Pacific Swell," who similarly watches the sea "from a hill / At thirty miles or more." In both cases there is a sense of the observer being at once above what he sees (literally and also in the hierarchical sense that he is a consciousness above the existence he perceives), but also excluded from any intimacy of knowledge. The first stanza describes the coming of dawn, and suggests in certain of its details the postsymbolist method, to use

Winters's terminology as defined by Howard Kaye. The details have their own fidelity to sensory experience but simultaneously indicate Winters's deeper concerns, as is evident in a couplet like

> Gray windows at my back, the massy frame
> Dull with a blackness that has not a name

where the darkness is given the unmistakable connotation of the un-defined in general. In a similar way the approach of dawn indicates the intellect's gradual comprehension of its subject—experience, or the world—and the moment chosen (the moment when darkness gives way to light) is like the shore of "The Slow Pacific Swell," the peculiar prov-ince of the poet.

The imagery of the first stanza is significant. The approach of dawn suggests images of flow and change ("the darkness spills / Down the re-moter gulleys"), and these images suggest and are associated with images of growth, the growth of the young gardens illuminated by the dawn. But contrasted with these images of flow and natural growth are images of definition; there is the "frame" in the above quotation, and the "con-crete walls" of the stanza's closing couplet:

> Drop by slow drop of seeping concrete walls.
> Such are the bastions of our pastorals!

This juxtaposition ("seeping," "bastions") is an encapsulation of one of Winters's chief preoccupations: the mind's attempts to define what is elu-sive, to be hypersensitively aware of flux, and at the same time to insist on the definitions and categories by which we necessarily live. It is the concern that underlies the title of his first book, *The Immobile Wind*, and which Thom Gunn summarized in his poem "To Yvor Winters, 1955," to "keep both Rule and Energy in view."

The second stanza contrasts the ordered gardens of the poem's opening with a memory of an older and more haphazard rural existence—an exis-tence which even in its heyday seemed removed from reality:

> Here are no palms! They once lined country ways,
> Where old white houses glared down dusty days,
> With small round towers, blunt-headed through small
>   trees.
> Those towers are now the hiving place of bees.
> The palms were coarse; their leaves hung thick with dust;
> The roads were muffled deep.

The dust that muffled leaves and roads was a literal sign of this land-scape's isolation from more urgent concerns, a sign of its Eden-like status. And the sense of observing a dreamworld is increased by our knowledge that the picture evoked belongs to an irrecoverable past:

> But now deep rust
> Has fastened on the wheels that labored then.
> Peace to all such, and to all sleeping men!
> I lived my childhood there, a passive dream
> In the expanse of that recessive scheme.

The expostulation "Peace to all such" is a sign of how Winters has come to terms with reality in these poems. The attitude evinced is not of a mind's hypnotized absorption in the minutiae of sensory experience (as in the earliest poems), nor of that hysterical horror of the undefined which we notice in many of the poems of *The Proof.* Rather we see that sense of propriety, of the mind's tact before experience and the world, which I have suggested is a persistent aim in Winters's later poetry. In saying "Peace to all such" the poet bids farewell to his own childhood's pastoral idyll (and its attendant pantheist musings), and to a traditional world now lost—a world he can respect and not hector. By this introduction of the past Winters prepares us for the appearance of his father in the poem, and he prepares us too for the tone of quiet respect with which he treats his father's values and life. What we witness is the poet's acknowledg-ment of the public and real world of humanity beyond himself. In the earlier, virtually solipsistic poems this world hardly exists—when other characters appeared they seemed mere paradigms for the poet's own emotions, or reminders of his mortality. But in this calm evocation of a vanished life, and in the poet's grave and tender reverence towards it and its representative (his father), we have the best evidence that Winters had been able to break out of the obsessive inwardness of his twenties into a more humane and civilized consciousness of the world beyond the poet, and the poet's role vis-à-vis that world.

The next two stanzas again contrast past and present. The past is evoked in images of a dusty, dreamlike landscape:

> The hills so dry, so dense the underbrush,
> That where I pushed my way the giant hush
> Was changed to soft explosion as the sage
> Broke down to powdered ash, the sift of age,
> And fell along my path, a shadowy rift.

The "powdered ash, the sift of age" in its dry crumbling is an image of the landscape's distance from present life, and this is confirmed by the ghostly unreality of the "soft explosion" as the friable, dead plants disintegrate. The present hillsides now visible to the poet are evoked in opposing images of damp and vivid growth, and the stanza ends with a fish pond, the schematic opposite of the past's "burning ashes."

So far in the poem we have had a description of dawn illuminating the gardens of the hills flanking the valley, and this present scene of ordered vigorous growth has been contrasted with memories of a more haphazard pastoral landscape, which, whatever its attractions, is associated with a dreamlike sense of death and disintegration. The last stanza of the poem continues the description of the scene now present to the poet's eyes— "the city, on the tremendous valley floor"—but before this stanza there interposes a passage about the poet's father. Up to this point the poem has contrasted past and present, but now we understand that the garden just described is that of the poet's father. That is, the past's representative is associated with, and is indeed responsible for, the present growth described in the poem. In the poem's weaving together of past and present we are shown that it is the past, or at least one aspect of it, that sustains the present. The past is presented as beguiling, then dreamlike and deathly, then as a sustaining force that informs and orders the present.

The poem ends with a description of the city, which is just emerging from night. It has passed from haphazard pastoral, to a garden, to the wholly man-made, each stage recognizably more ordered than the last. But this does not imply the poet's commitment to this subjugation of the natural world. The dead pastoral of the "powdered ash" and the more vivid order of his father's garden seem, each in their own way, to command more of his allegiance. The poem's close is reminiscent of the end of "The Invaders," another poem concerned with man's mastery of nature, in which Winters appeared as simultaneously fascinated and appalled by man's power. The final lines, in their suggestion of hubris and arrogance, and with their echo of the imagery at the end of "The Slow Pacific Swell," read as an admonishing reminder of the limits of man's capacities to transform the natural world:

> And man-made stone outgrows the living tree,
> And at its rising air is shaken, men
> Are shattered, and the tremor swells again,
> Extending to the naked salty shore,
> Rank with the sea, which crumbles evermore.

In a later poem, "An Elegy: For the USN Dirigible, Macon," which records a similar fascination with man's ability to manipulate natural resources (the ability is here symbolized by the airship) Winters wrote:

> Who will believe this thing in time to come?
> I was a witness. I beheld the age
> That seized upon a planet's heritage
> Of steel and oil, the mind's viaticum:
>
> Crowded the world with strong ingenious things,
> Used the provision it could not replace,
> To leave but Cretan myths, a sandy trace
> Through the last stone age, for the pastoral kings.

Here a future return to the dreamlike pastoral world is implied, and the beauty of the last stanza leaves us in no doubt that the poet approves of this; though man's power over nature fascinates him, he sees it finally as a hubris that invites punishment. His concern is, where possible, to work *with* the world, not against it, and the image of the garden is an indication of this (as is perhaps his breeding of Airedales and his interest in boxing—both activities where nature is, as it were, directed and trained rather than obliterated and denied). The haphazard pastoral of nostalgic romanticism is a kind of spiritual death (though a death whose attractions he was fully aware of); the brutal arrogance that destroys nature in the name of science or technological advance is a step too far in the opposite direction, a trespassing beyond Heraclitean limits. The mean is that intimate understanding of, and, as far as possible, cooperation with the natural world that neither surrenders to it nor seeks to destroy it. The ambivalence of Winters's feelings about nature is indicated by his two major symbols for it—the sea (as in "The Slow Pacific Swell"), which is quite unamenable to control or definition, and the garden (as in "On a View of Pasadena from the Hills"), where nature is ordered and tended.

A poem which beautifully celebrates the garden aspect of Winters's work, that tactful and sane intimacy with nature that guides and forms rather than destroying or seeking self-loss, is "The Marriage." Here the poet's marriage is paralleled by the marriage of flesh and spirit, whose ideal cooperation and almost indivisible intimacy are an image of a state desired and celebrated by the lovers. The poem suggests that man and wife ideally participate in that intimate interdependence that characterizes the relations of flesh and spirit. The point is made with great tact and tenderness—the first section celebrating the sensuous life of the couple, a sensuousness at once innocent and eager, evoked by images of pastoral felicity, and the second celebrating the spirit's fidelity and trust. The poem opens in the past tense and closes in the future, and the development in time parallels the development from flesh to spirit, from sensory to abstract. The final resolution of difference between both flesh and spirit and husband and wife must wait till death, and in this poem even death appears as beneficent. The annihilation of differences is seen as a symbolically apt finale to a life of interdependent intimacy, but the annihilation is invoked in no sense of pantheistic communion with a greater whole or good. Rather, the poem's close has a classical restraint which emphasizes privacy and unique individuality:

> And, in commemoration of our lust,
> May our heirs seal us in a single urn,
> A single spirit never to return.

The suggestion of the classical world in the word *urn*, and the emphatic particularity implied in the repeated *single* effectively prevent us from seeing the death here described in any romantic or Emersonian manner. The feeling is rather that of the poignance of particular lives passing, of the fragility and beauty of human youth and happiness: it is a sensibility similar to that of an inscription of the fifth century BC in Athens's Keramikos Cemetery, on a stele showing a mother holding her granddaughter: "I am holding here the child of my daughter, the beloved, whom I held on my lap when alive we beheld the light of the sun; and now I am holding it dead, being dead myself."

In two later poems, "On Re-reading a Passage from John Muir" and "A Summer Commentary," Winters reverts to the image of himself as he appeared in his earliest poems, a passive sensibility lost in trance before the natural world. This is from the "John Muir" poem:

> This was my childhood's revery: to be
> Not one who seeks in nature his release
> But one forever by the dripping tree
> Paradisaïc in his pristine peace.

And this from "A Summer Commentary":

> When I was young, with sharper sense,
> The farthest insect cry I heard

Could stay me; through the trees, intense,
I watched the hunter and the bird.

Where is the meaning that I found?
Or was it but a state of mind,
Some old penumbra of the ground,
In which to be but not to find?

In both poems the earlier stance is rejected: Winters has decided that poetry (and life) is for him a matter of finding rather than being, that mere empathy or innocence is not enough. But nature in these poems is not the destructive sea of "The Slow Pacific Swell," and far less is it the "subatomic roar" of "The Invaders" and "The Vigil"; it is a dream with which the poet has come to terms, one he recognizes but by which he does not feel threatened.

Three poems concerned with subjects from California history, "John Day, Frontiersman," "John Sutter," and "The California Oaks" suggest a vision of nature as a lost benign idyll. "John Sutter" opens with a vision of pastoral serenity and power:

I was the patriarch of the shining land,
Of the blond summer and metallic grain;
Men vanished at the motion of my hand,
And when I beckoned they would come again.

The earth grew dense with grain at my desire;
The shade was deepened at the springs and streams;
Moving in dust that clung like pillared fire,
The gathering herds grew heavy in my dreams.

The image of the "pillared fire" and the biblically authoritative language suggest a promised land, but the vision is wrecked by the discovery of gold, which leads to mayhem and murder; the life of the speaker, a life lived in harmony with a massive and idyllic nature, is contrasted with the violent destruction of those eager for gold. A line like "The shade was deepened at the springs and streams" epitomizes the narrator's relationship with the natural world, which is merely the intenser use of what is already there. This is contrasted with the frenetic rapacity of the gold seekers:

With knives they dug the metal out of stone;
Turned rivers back, for gold through ages piled,

Drove knives to hearts, and faced the gold alone;
Valley and river ruined and reviled.

In "The California Oaks" the historical movement is virtually the same, though covering a much greater span of time—from pastoral felicity to a destructive violation of the land and the archaic values it sustained. "John Day, Frontiersman" is a slightly more complex poem. It begins in a similar vein to the other two, with a celebration of pastoral solitude, but the protagonist of the poem is sent mad; here it is not man who threatens and destroys unregenerate nature, but unregenerate nature that threatens and destroys man, in a pattern reminiscent of that of "Sir Gawaine and the Green Knight" or "The Slow Pacific Swell." However, the poem ends in equivocal gentleness:

> The eminence is gone that met your eye;
> The winding savage, too, has sunk away.
> Now, like a summer myth, the meadows lie,
> Deep in the calm of sylvan slow decay.

The poem has shown that the vision of nature as wholly beneficient is illusory, but it closes on this vision, or something very close to it. The ambivalence is unresolved—nature in this poem is both dream and terror, and while the meaning emphasizes the terror the poem's shape ensures that it is the dream we remember.

I noted earlier that three of the sonnets from *The Proof* contained the word *hard* in their final line, and suggested that this was an indication that Winters saw poetry at this stage as an attempt to reach some kind of incontrovertible truth. The three poems discussed here (grouped together in *The Collected Poems*) similarly all contain one word in their final (in one case penultimate) lines. The word is *calm*:

> Deep in the calm of sylvan slow decay ["John Day"]

> What calm catastrophe will yet assuage
> The final drought of penitential tears? ["John Sutter"]

> And in the calm they guarded now abide. ["The California
> Oaks"]

In each case calm is the calm after tragedy, it is a stoic calm of acceptance. Both in the earlier sonnets and in these later poems on California history the movement of the poems is toward understanding, but in the sonnets understanding seems to imply an immense effort of will, and its result is either horror or a kind of grim determination not to flinch before whatever truth may be revealed—hence the recurring "hard"—reality is "hard" (difficult) and man must be "hard" (tough) to face it. But here understanding brings "calm," a resigned and sane acceptance purged of any suggestions of hysteria or even, by the time the end of the poem is reached, anger. One could say that the impulse is more towards wisdom than comprehension, that understanding has taken on an ethical appearance. The kind of grim delight that the Winters of *The Proof* seemed to take in demonstrating to himself that the world was as comfortless as he had guessed has given way to a steadier and deeper vision—the tone is one of acceptance rather than defiance.

I have suggested that Winters's poems imply two opposing views of nature, one seeing it as an idyll (usually locked in the past, as if this removal from immediacy is what confers grace on the landscape) and the other seeing it as a chaos that threatens to draw in and destroy the observer. A few poems suggest a third alternative, which is a kind of balance between these two extremes. In these poems the majesty and beauty of the landscape are presented in terms reminiscent of the idyllic poems, but the reader is warned that this majesty is wholly alien (not so much destructive as grossly incomprehensible). The note of terror that surfaces for a moment in "The Slow Pacific Swell," and dominates much of *The Proof*, is here subdued to a simple acknowledgment of the natural world's irreducible otherness. The headlong quest of Apollo for Daphne is replaced by the calm recognition that such a quest is an impossibility. In "The Manzanita" the tree symbolizes, as the laurel had done in the earlier poem, the natural world as it exists beyond our mental apprehension. The charm of the tree's appearance should not deceive us into believing that we in any way comprehend its existence:

> The skin is rose: yet infinitely thin,
> It is a color only. What one tells
> Of ancient wood and softly glinting skin
> Is less than are the tiny waxen bells.

In the last stanza the poet explicitly states that the life of man and that of the tree are wholly separate modes of being:

> This life is not our life; nor our wit
> The sweetness of these shades; these are alone.

There is no wisdom here! seek not for it!
This is the shadow of the vast madrone.

That third line—"There is no wisdom here! seek not for it!"—reads as self-admonition by one who was, or had been, only too prone to seek for wisdom in the natural world.

Time, Eternity, and the Mind

The simplest way to approach the poems dealing with time is to consider first those in which time is presented through the image of change in the natural world. This change is usually seen as a diminution of the human, and this implies a view of nature with which we are already familiar from Winters's poems, nature as destroyer. Such a poem for example is "The Last Visit, For Henry Ahnefeldt, 1862–1929":

The drift of leaves grows deep, the grass
Is longer everywhere I pass.
And listen! where the wind is heard,
The surface of the garden's blurred—
It is the passing wilderness.
The garden will be something less
When others win it back from change.
We shall not know it then; a strange
Presence will be musing there.
Ruin has touched familiar air,
And we depart. Where you should be,
I sought a final memory.

The familiar image of nature ordered by man (the garden) is used, and Winters contrasts it with the disorder of the encroaching wilderness, which here suggests what the sea suggests in "The Slow Pacific Swell," the chaotic natural world always poised to ruin man's attempts at definition and order. Time in this poem is the attrition of the products of the human will by "the wilderness," and it is significant that the poem commemorates a death—death had always been, even in the earliest poems, the most obvious sign of time for Winters. When time appears in his verse it is almost always as a destroyer; in the later poems it very rarely suggests growth or fruition, or if this aspect is presented the growth immediately shades off into ruin, as in "The California Oaks."

This concentration on the ruinous rather than the vivifying aspects of time gives Winters's poems on the subject an elegiac tone, stoic as in the above example rather than maudlin. The rhetorical indication of time's presence is made by slight nuances of diction and meter rather than by linguistic violence (it is noticeable how emotionally neutral his adjectives are, for example). A line like "Ruin has touched familiar air" with its momentary personification of ruin combined with the reticence of the verb and the slightly paradoxical "familiar air," reminding us of how what was local, particular, and known is becoming vague, generalized, and haphazard, is as powerful in its understatement as Wordsworth's "The unimaginable touch of Time." It may be that the juxtaposition of time, touch, and the idea of ruin in the Wordsworth sonnet are a source for Winters's line: in *Forms of Discovery* (p. 170) he singles out this moment as one of the best in Wordsworth.

In "For Howard Baker," placed next to "The Last Visit" in *The Collected Poems*, the end of a season means that two friends—the poet and the dedicatee—must separate, but the result of their conversation survives. Time in the poem is indicated by the seasons and the "wash of rain," the latter suggesting that attrition already referred to; what survives is "the firm mind," and the adjective points to the mind's freedom from time's attrition. Invariably, when Winters mentions the mind in his later poems it is associated (often explicitly, always at least by implication) with the nontemporal, a quasi-Platonic eternity of intellectual truth.

For someone as minutely conscious of time's presence in the natural world as we have seen Winters to be, this conception of the mind as participating in nontemporal reality poses a problem—that of the relations of the "eternal" mind with the temporal nature in which it is inextricably involved. Winters considers this problem in a number of poems and acknowledges that, from the standpoint of nature, eternity can only mean death. Life is change, but the mind is a product of life that seeks to emancipate itself from change, to move outside the processes of life in order to see clearly. To remain thoughtlessly immersed in change is to deny the mind, to attempt to transcend change altogether is to cut the mind off from that intimacy with the world that nourishes it.

"Inscription for a Graveyard," "The Grave," "Time and the Garden," "Prayer for My Son," and "To the Holy Spirit" are all concerned with such relations between physical, temporal existence and the eternal. If we consider the poems in the order I have just set out (the order in which they were published and probably written), a change of tone and emphasis is noticeable. In "Inscription for a Graveyard" the opposition between

the temporal and the eternal is seen purely as an opposition between life
and death:

> Death is Eternity
> And all who come there stay.
> For choice, now certainty.
> No moment breaks away.

The poem emphasizes that "absolute cleavage" between death and life
which Winters saw in Emily Dickinson's poetry and which is the subject
of his own sonnet "The Realization." Eternity is the incomprehensibility
of death. "The Grave" is similar in import, though the poet's concern
deepens to include a recognition of the pathos of life, which seeks to
comprehend eternity though it is caught in time. Eternity is seen as
peace; it takes on at least the shadow of a predicate:

> Here let me contemplate eternal peace,
> Eternal station, which annuls release.
> Here may I read its meaning, though the eye
> Sear with the effort, ere the body die.
> For what one is, one sees not; 'tis the lot
> Of him at peace to contemplate it not.

"Time and the Garden" compares the slow growth of a garden's plants
with the slow accumulation of understanding through an individual's
life. The desire, in early spring, to see the whole year's growth in an instant is like the desire to grasp at wisdom "not yet fairly earned." But as
man moves through time towards wisdom he also moves towards death;
the eternity of death is associated with an eternity of the intellect which
transcends change and particular lives. There is no suggestion in this
poem that this spiritual eternity is any other than a sum of the intellectual
labors of different generations, but "A Prayer for My Son" opens with an
invocation to the "Eternal Spirit":

> Eternal Spirit, you
> Whose will maintains the world,
> Who thought and made it true;

This suggests that theism to which Winters claimed he owed allegiance.
Eternity is here seen as a transcendent spirit, in which man is nevertheless able to participate. The eternal and temporal are seen as involved
with one another but separate; the relationship is alluded to in a brief
metaphor:

> The honey-suckle curled
> Through the arbutus limb,

and the poem is preceeded by an epigraph from Janet Lewis's poem "The Earth-Bound," "Tangled with earth all ways we move." (There is a fine propriety in Winters's use of an epigraph from his wife's poetry for a poem to their son; the poem involves the interdependence of body and mind, parents and child, and, by this epigraph, husband and wife). In this poem the "Eternal Spirit," while transcendent, seems accessible in some degree to humanity.

But in "To the Holy Spirit, from a Deserted Graveyard in the Salinas Valley" (probably the best of the few poems Winters completed after 1945) the meditation on eternity, aroused—as in "Inscription for a Graveyard" and "The Grave"—by the contemplation of the tombs of the dead, suggests that the "Holy Spirit" of the title exists wholly beyond man's apprehension:

> These are thy fallen sons,
> Thou whom I try to reach.
> Thou whom the quick eye shuns,
> Thou dost elude my speech.
> Yet when I go from sense
> And trace thee down in thought,
> I meet thee, then, intense,
> And know thee as I ought.
> But thou art mind alone,
> And I, alas, am bound
> Pure mind to flesh and bone,
> And flesh and bone to ground.

Man, caught in time, struggles toward the eternal, but because of his mortal nature must inevitably fail in his attempts to participate in the reality of the "Holy Spirit." The closing stanza leaves open the possibility, but not much more, of a religious creed which might ensure such participation after death. The poet asks, in a clear reference to Christianity's beliefs in the incarnation and resurrection, which would fuse the temporal and eternal—"Was there another birth?"—and answers himself,

> Only one certainty
> Beside thine unfleshed eye,
> Beside the spectral tree,
> Can I discern: these die.

(The "spectral tree," like the "dripping tree" of "On Re-reading a Passage from John Muir," would seem to refer to the natural world; "these" refers to the men buried in the graveyard that has occasioned the meditation). That is, the "Holy Spirit," to whom the poem is addressed, is certain, the existence of the natural world is certain, and death is certain. What is uncertain, or beyond man's comprehension, is the relationships among these entities. The "Holy Spirit" of the poem is not that of traditional Christianity, as the poem's suspension of judgment on that religion shows; yet it is clearly suprahuman and therefore something more than the corporate mind adumbrated in "Time and the Garden." The poem approaches the ineffable, as it admits—"Thou dost elude my speech"—and there is a strange circularity in Winters's concern with ineffable numinous truth; this had been the goal of his early "waking oblivion." But there the truth hinted at had been wholly immanent, here it is transcendent. Winters had begun be believing in an immanent divinity, or at least numinousness, moved to a belief in the human mind as a repository of the only values accessible to man, and towards the end of his life approached a notion of transcendent divinity close to that of traditional religion. His definition of himself as a theist, though it confirms such a development, does not greatly help us in the interpretation of what Winters meant by the "Holy Spirit"; his theism was largely a matter of finding a source for ethical beliefs, and it is not ethics which is primarily at issue here. The "Holy Spirit" invoked is closer to the transcendent God of Christian theology than to a mere ethical equivalent of Aristotle's Prime Mover.

    The poem opens with the phrase "Immeasurable haze," and at the beginning of the second stanza the time is given as "high noon." The triggering of quasi-metaphysical meditation by observation of the haze of noon or summer is common in Winters's poems (for example, "Inscription for a Graveyard," "The Empty Hills," "An Elegy: For the USN Dirigible, Macon" among others). The experience was clearly real to Winters, but it was perhaps confirmed by his reading of Valéry, in whose poems, especially "Cimètiere Marin," we perceive a similar transition. (Valéry's work, especially "Ebauche d'un serpent," which Winters considered to be possibly the greatest poem in existence, certainly influenced Winters's "To the Holy Spirit," in which the relationship of consciousness to eternity echoes the scheme of Valéry's poem.) A sense of being dazed by the brilliance of the sunlit landscape is a common concomitant of such scenes, as if the intellect is somehow dissolved in light. This dazed state in Winters's poems on the subject suggests a direct apprehension of the world's being, unmediated by the intellect, an intuitive insight that re-

minds us of the earlier poems. But dark or more especially moonlit landscapes are also common in his work, and these two extremes—the
intense clarity of noon and the vague, elusive brilliance of moonlight—
take on symbolic connotations, suggesting polarities between which the
conscious mind exists, a kind of Scylla and Charybdis of the intellect.
The intense clarity of noon in which meanings and distinctions seem to
dissolve suggests the mind's abasement before external reality: nature or
the world is suddenly revealed in inapprehensible brilliance, and there is a
hint in the immobility and silence of these sunlit landscapes of a partly
divined meaning beyond time and change—a hint very close in feeling to
some forms of Christian mysticism. If there are slight suggestions of divinity at these sunlit moments it is a wholly transcendent divinity; by
contrast, the poems of night or moonlight suggest an almost unwilling
inwardness and subjectivity—the poet's equilibrium is upset not so much
by external grandeur as by intimations of internal chaos, and the suggestions of the supernatural imply chthonic and subhuman forces rather than
transcendent divinity. R. P. Blackmur wrote of Wallace Stevens's use of
moonlight, "Moonlight, for Mr. Stevens, is mental, fictive, related to the
imaginations and meaning of things" (*Language as Gesture*, p. 225). Winters uses moonlight in roughly the same way, except that his moonlit
scenes contain an edge of fear wholly his own.

In a late critical essay, "The Poetry of T. Sturge Moore," Winters
quotes and partially explicates a passage by Moore dealing with a moon
goddess. His comments are extremely revealing when applied to his own
poetry, as much to as to Moore's:

> Medea sacrifices her humanity in order to achieve the peculiar kind
> of perfection demanded by Artemis; but Artemis is complex
> within what seems her simplicity, and her complexity is inhu-
> man—she is "manifold Delia," goddess of several names and
> natures,
>
> > Orthia, she drinks blood . . . Hecate . . . there
> > You blench! those names are hers as much
> > As Cynthia is . . .
>
> As one commits oneself more and more wholly to this goddess
> alone (or her to her principal adversary, Aphrodite) one commits
> oneself more and more to despair, and perhaps to self-destruction.
> [p. 3]

As Winters comments, the attributes of this goddess are complex and
ambiguous: as the virgin sister of Apollo, Artemis shares something of

his perfect disdain for mortality; as Orthia, who presided over the bloody rites of young people who fought in front of her altar, and Hecate she is mistress of a moonlit world of phantasmagoric violence. Artemis for Winters, like the moon for Stevens, represents the imagination; her blank infertile light is an icy, unearthly vision associated with poetic creation—Winters's poem "To the Moon" opens "Goddess of poetry / Maiden of icy stone"—but it also represents hallucination and terror:

> Moonlight from sky to earth, untaught, unclaimed,
> An icy nightmare of the brute unnamed.
> This was hallucination. ["Moonlight Alert"]

The imagination, the source of poetic vision, is acknowledged as demonic and beyond reason. The terror evoked by the goddess reminds us of Winters's abiding fear of the undefined, and was probably associated by him with intimations of demonic evil. Reading through *The Collected Poems* we see the poet poised between the opposing extremes of sunlit revery (associated with external reality and particular landscapes) and subjective moonlit hallucination. Both threaten to obliterate the mind's distinctions and categories, but the poet is unable to renounce either. The hallucinatory world of Artemis is the source of poetry; the blaze of noon seems to indicate a truth the poet can neither ignore (committed as he was to seeing poetry as the "quest for reality") nor define. The definitions of his poetry represent something of a balancing act between these two areas of the undefined, one demonic and tending (literally) to the lunatic, the other a sunlit intimation of some ineffable transcendent reality. (It is remarkable—for a poet who prided himself on definition—how often the words *haze* and *dazed* appear at crucial moments in these "sunlit" poems, as if the lack of definition of the landscape is a suggestion of a truth in which rational distinctions are submerged or nonexistent). Winters's distrust of the undefined arose from his fear of the "moon-lit" world, but he extended it to any lack of definition, and this appears to have dissuaded him from any attempt to explain or develop that suggestion of the numinous that ghosts the "sunlit" poems. It is left as just that, a suggestion, beyond reason and language, while the poems concern themselves with the definable.

Not all the "moon-lit" poems deal with the irrational aspects of the imagination, but all are concerned with vision beyond the apprehension of immediate existence, and in all this vision implies a sudden access of meaning which the mind cannot order and therefore fears. In "Moonrise," for example, the first two stanzas describe the moon rising through

leaves, and two lovers awake watching the process and each other. Then
follows the third stanza:

> We turn from sleep
> And hold our breath a while,
>   As mile on mile
> The terror drifts more deep.

Almost nothing so far in the poem has prepared us for "the terror"
(though the second stanza does end with the slightly minatory line "We
know the hour grows late"), and at first reading the reader wonders what
it is doing there. What prompts "the terror" is the icy sub specie aeter-
nitatis vision of human mortality, of the inevitable separation of the
lovers, by death if nothing else:

> So we must part
> In ruin utterly—
>   Reality
> Invades the crumbling heart.

The vision of reality is not that of a sunlit plenitude of Being, but of individual mortality and the impotence of love against time. The mind's
vision, abstracted from the quotidian and immediate, aware of death and
time beyond present love, is equated with the cold light of the moon.
The success of the poem depends on the fact that the metaphorical meaning is discreetly suggested *through* the fact of the moonlight. The moonlight is still moonlight throughout the poem (whereas the spring-serpent
in the poem of that name almost ceases to be a serpent), so that the metaphor works simultaneously on both levels.

Winters's most complete exploration of his "moon-lit" apprehension
of the world is in "Moonlight Alert: Los Altos, California, June 1943":

> The sirens, rising, woke me; and the night
> Lay cold and windless; and the moon was bright,
> Moonlight from sky to earth, untaught, unclaimed,
> An icy nightmare of the brute unnamed.
> This was hallucination. Scarlet flower
> And yellow fruit hung colorless. That hour
> No scent lay on the air. The siren scream
> Took on the fixity of shallow dream.
> In the dread sweetness I could see the fall,
> Like petals sifting from a quiet wall,

Of yellow soldiers through indifferent air,
Falling to die in solitude. With care
I held this vision, thinking of young men
Whom I had known and should not see again,
Fixed in reality, as I in thought.
And I stood waiting, and encountered naught.

The calm of the opening lines, a calm menaced by incipient fear as the night is disturbed by the siren's wail, reminds us of the opening of "Moonrise," but in this poem the sense of dread communicated by the description of the moonlight is justified by the war that is the poem's background. In the previous poem the dread had been personal; here it derives from a public, identifiable concern, war. In both poems the moonlight brings a vision of death, but the vision in this later poem is generalized beyond the poet himself, and it is the death of the generation now fighting which he perceives.

What is significant about the poem is the way that the poet's vision is both true and untrue. The moonlight's spectral patina is a deceit, a "hallucination," which drains reality of sensory immediacy. The siren's wail and the lack of scent add to the unreality of the landscape, and this unreality reaches an extreme in the poet's vision of falling petals as soldiers falling to death. But this "hallucination," this "icy nightmare," is an image of the truth—this is what was happening in Europe at that time. That is, the phantasmagoric vision that contradicts immediate visible reality reveals another, more comprehensive reality. If it leads away from one kind of truth it points to another, more urgent and poignant than the immediate present. In this poem, as in "Moonrise," the mind is able to detach itself from local reality about it to perceive a wider (and far more desolate) vision. The moonlight represents the imagination, and the imagination's lie is truer than the immediate and tangible world.

The penultimate line of the poem, "Fixed in reality, as I in thought," refers to this interweaving of visionary truth and external reality. The poet is fixed in thought, the mental world implied by the moonlight which removes him from immediate reality. The soldiers are fixed in the reality he perceives, the imminence of death. The poet's physical distance from the war is a paradigm of the distance between the mental, imaginative world and the present, external world. Despite—or even because of—this distance, it is the imagination that is able to perceive truly. In the last line the vision dissolves and the poet is left facing "naught"; this is not only the nothingness that was his vision—its illusory nature—but also that nothingness his vision implies, the "naught" of death and the moral "naught" of the war.

In these poems, then, Winters characterizes the moonlight as producing that dissociation from the immediate world which enables the imagination to perceive a profounder and more comprehensive truth. But such a dissociation is hazardous and the "moon-lit" poems are pervaded by that sense of terror Winters always associated with the undefined. The dissociation has its own pathos too, as of a mind cut off from reality and given over to Goyaesque dreams which threaten to become nightmares. This sense of the mind's separation from reality, particularly the creative mind's, would seem to be the subject of the poem "Midas." Here Winters uses the myth of the king whose every touch transformed the world to gold as a haunting metaphor for the self-enclosed creative sensibility:

> Where he wandered, dream-enwound,
> Brightness took the place of sound.
> Shining plane and mass before:
> Everywhere the sealèd door.
> Children's unplacated grace
> Met him with an empty face.
> Mineral his limbs were grown:
> Weight of being, not his own.
> Ere he knew that he must die,
> Ore had veinèd lip and eye:
> Caught him scarcely looking back,
> Startled at his golden track,
> Immortalized the quickened shade
> Of meaning by a moment made.

The curiously hypnotic meter, a perfect vehicle for a poem on this subject, is defined by Winters as an "iambic tetrameter with the initial unaccented syllable omitted" (*In Defense of Reason*, p. 110); though the meter is not uncommon in English poetry, Winters appears to have originally found it in the works of Robert Greene, whose use of it he draws attention to in his 1939 essay "The Sixteenth Century Lyric in England."

The poem is reminiscent of the sonnet "Apollo and Daphne," in which Apollo-mind seeks Daphne-reality and touches laurel. Here the king seeks reality and touches gold, both gold and laurel implying the imagination's transformation of reality, reality's paradigm even, but not that tangible truth the mind despairs of reaching. The transformation is not celebrated as it would be in, for example, Wallace Stevens's work; Apollo and Midas would prefer Daphne and the world to laurel and gold. What is gained is not reality but the result of the mind's contact with reality—a still, hard beauty that is a denial of that evanescence the mind seeks.

Howard Kaye writes of this poem: "The tenor involves the consequences of the Symbolist aesthetic, and the vehicle is the story of Midas. (Winters viewed the romantic mystique as self-destructive, and therefore made Midas turn himself to gold, destroyed by the power he coveted)"("Post-Symbolist Poetry," p. 191). Though it is probable that he meant the poem to refer specifically to the dangers of romantic symbolism (he himself stated that this was the subject of "A Spring Serpent"), we cannot read the poem wholly as a condemnation of methods of which Winters disapproved. The poem does not read as exhortation but as revery, and though the reader may be meant to assume condemnation—as Midas's self-destruction suggests—that condemnation is not implicit in the poem's tone. It has to be imported into the poem, which reads as plaint rather than polemic. Winters has clearly experienced the state he describes; he was, or one part of him was, Midas.

The Poems on Greek Myths

Apart from the sonnet "Apollo and Daphne" most of the poems that involve Greek myths are fairly late (in terms of Winters's poetic oeuvre, that is, not in terms of his life; he produced little poetry during his fifties and sixties). They all proceed by the same method as "Apollo and Daphne": the myth is presented as the vehicle of an implicit metaphorical argument. I shall discuss the two longest of these poems, "Theseus, a Trilogy" and "Heracles." These mythological poems have been impressively analyzed by Grosvenor Powell in his book *Language as Being in the Poetry of Yvor Winters*, and my discussion is indebted to his work, though I disagree with his interpretations of particular moments of the poems.

"Theseus, a Trilogy" is divided into three sections: the first is concerned with Theseus's rape of Hippolyta, the second with the story of Theseus and Ariadne, and the third with Theseus's relations with the bride of his old age, Phaedra. As Powell points out, all these women are "avatars of the moon," and the poem is concerned with man's relationship with the "moon-lit" world as hypostatized in the poems discussed above. The first thing that must strike us about these three relationships—Theseus-Hippolyta, Theseus-Ariadne, Theseus-Phaedra—is that they all involve deceit and violence of one form or another and that they are all failures. Hippolyta is raped; Ariadne is killed (in Winters's version by Theseus himself); Phaedra tricks Theseus into demanding the death of his own son. In dealing with the last relationship Winters glides quickly over Phaedra's treachery but emphasizes treachery from another source, Lycomedes, which results in Theseus's death. This death appears as retribution for the protagonist's violent career. Winters implies that man's relationships with the "moon-lit" world, the world of the imagination and visionary truth, but also the world of the chthonic and undefined, are a venturing into a prerational and ahuman landscape that exacts its own revenge for such trespass. We are given to understand that the moonlight of man's life is so constituted that there can be no peace between it and man's conscious mind, and no satisfactory equilibrium is possible.

The language of the first section, "The Wrath of Artemis," is full of references which, when the reader is familiar with Winters's vocabulary, signify danger or fear. There is not only the moonlight itself,

> the night
> Blue with insistence of the staring eye,

and its representatives, Hippolyta and her Amazons, but also Artemis, who is described as the "evasive demon," and in Hippolyta's defeat,

> her women
> Fell as they came, like water to dry earth,
> An inundation of the living moon.

This language closely recalls the dry-wet symbolism of "The Slow Pacific Swell" and the close of "Sir Gawaine and the Green Knight" (and, incidentally, other poems such as "Elegy on a Young Airedale Bitch"), where wetness stands for the seething mass of experience which threatens to engulf the mind, and dry for the discrete integrity of the intellect and its individual survival. In Winters's terms the lines suggest not only the inundation of the earth, but also the inundation of the mind by the imagination, of consciousness by the arational. This suggestion of wetness as an almost evil fecundity is increased by the following passage describing Hippolyta:

> In Attica, the naked land, she strode,
> Brooding upon the secrets of the goddess,
> Upon the wet bark of the Scythian forest,
> The wet turf under bare foot.

(Powell points out that the goddess here is probably the Ephesian Artemis, the many-breasted goddess of fertility, rather than the chaster Artemis of the Greek mainland.) The writing here certainly suggests hallucination, that derangement of rational mental processes which Winters meant by the moon, and here by its avatar, Hippolyta.

But the important fact around which this first section of the poem revolves is the rape. I have already suggested that Winters's poems imply a tact before experience as the most desirable stance, a sense of things in their just places, and that to attempt to go beyond these limits—as does Apollo in "Apollo and Daphne" or as do the despoilers of rural America in "John Sutter" or "The California Oaks"—is to defy a natural order. Theseus's rape of Hippolyta is such a defiance, and if we take Theseus as representative of the conscious mind (as we are encouraged to do by the large number of Winters's poems in which this is the obvious function of the protagonist), and moonlight-Hippolyta as representative of the imagination and the subconscious, then the rape is symbolic of that descent into the unconscious mind which Winters has deplored in so much romantic and postromantic poetry, but which was, for him too, at least a necessary prelude to poetic creation.

The result of the rape is Theseus's and Hippolyta's son, Hippolytus, who therefore represents the union of the conscious and the subconscious, the intellect and the imagination. Winters used the shore in "The Slow Pacific Swell" and dawn in "On a View of Pasadena from the Hills" as representatives of that meeting of the defined and the undefined which is peculiarly the province of poetry, and Hippolytus too, by the symbolic nature of his parentage, represents such a meeting point. He is the most highly characterized personage of the poem, but his characterization is extremely ambiguous:

> Insolent, slender, effeminate, and chill,
> His muscles made for running down the stag,
> Dodging the boar, which Theseus would have broken,
> Keeping step with the moon's shadows, changing
> From thought to thought with an unchanging face.
> He, judging Theseus from his narrow wisdom,
> Yet judged him, and exiled him from his quiet,
> The wrath of Artemis grown part of Theseus,
> A man of moonlight and intensive calm.

The potent charm of this is undeniable, and we cannot believe that its creator was immune to it, but disapproval is clearly implied: "Insolent, slender, effeminate and chill," "his narrow wisdom." The "quiet" from

which he exiles Theseus and the last line, "A man of moonlight and in-
tensive calm," imply that Hippolytus is a representative of that trancelike imaginative state that so fascinated and repelled Winters throughout
his life. It is probable that here, as in "Midas," Winters is concerned with
a specific imaginative stance, attractive but destructive—however, the
implications of the passage are wider than polemic against a particular
poetic practice. As in the case of "Midas" the reader has to import any
condemnation into the poem, which reads as rapt, fascinated revery.

The second section, "Theseus and Ariadne," is certainly the most obscure of the poem. It opens with a retrospective glimpse of the slaying of
the minotaur, and again the language is thick with implications of horror, especially when we recall the personal associations of Winters's
vocabulary:

> After the mossy night and the wet stone,
> The grappling with the wet hair of the beast,
> After the slow and careful fingering
> Of the pale linen on the cold return,
> Theseus emerged. Ariadne awaited him,
> Her face half hidden with black hair and shame.

Theseus, having killed the minotaur (and Winters is careful to emphasize
its moon-lineage), takes Ariadne as his mate, and she too, like Hippolyta
before her, represents the moon. (Her mother's name—Pasiphaë, meaning "all-shining"—is often taken as referring to a moon-goddess, and
Winters has adopted the implication as it fits the poem's scheme.) Theseus has killed one representative of the dark chthonic world ruled over
by the moon (the minotaur, characterized by Winters's typical fear word,
wet), only to have another before him: "Theseus emerged. Ariadne
awaited him."

In Winters's version of the story Theseus, instead of abandoning Ariadne on Naxos, kills her, as he had previously killed the minotaur. She is
not an alternative to the minotaur, but an emblem of those same forces
Theseus had been attempting to overcome when he slew the minotaur.
The murder of Ariadne represents an attempt at purgation, the mind's
rejection of that moonlit world with which it has become inextricably
involved. The failure of the attempt to kill the minotaur—a failure in the
poem's symbolic scheme because Theseus is immediately confronted by
Ariadne, who represents what the minotaur represented—should warn
us that this attempt too will probably fail, and indeed in the third section
we find Theseus partnered by Phaedra, yet another representative of the

moon. As Grosvenor Powell puts it, "He kills Ariadne as an effort to escape the entanglements of the dark side of experience. Such escape is not possible: the very motive force of his action is the dark side that he tries to purge."

But Phaedra is far younger than Theseus, and he is beyond her comprehension or influence. (Winters glides over the betrayal of Hippolytus, which would have established in the reader's mind Phaedra's ascendency over Theseus's decisions.) Winters seems to be implying a gradual emancipation of the mind from the imaginative and subjective realm of moonlight—Phaedra exists in this section as a kind of solace, a reminder of life and danger now past, rather than as the potent adversary that Hippolyta had been.

And as the mind emancipates itself from subjectivity it moves into the more public responsibilities of statecraft. In section 1 Theseus is presented as a mere pirate; in section 2 he is shown as conscious of his dilemma and struggling to free himself; by section 3 he has virtually emancipated himself from the subjective turmoil of the earlier stages and is presented as a man desiring the more external struggles of the public world. His life of subjective passion is alluded to as a parenthetic (though very beautiful) revery. This move from the inward world to the outer is seen in the development of Winters's verse as a whole and becomes particularly pronounced from his mid thirties on. If we compare successive stages of his poetry we notice a gradual movement from solipsism—where only the subjective mood is considered valid—to a sense of tension between the claims of external and internal reality—this characterizes the verse of his late twenties and early thirties—to the attempt to write wholly public verse, in which the individual sensibility is subordinated to the creation of that representative and normative vision implied by satire or panegyric. Theseus's development thus echoes Winters's own.

But the state too rejects Theseus and he dies betrayed. Neither the inner world of the imagination nor the outer world of public action can accept him: both threaten to destroy him, and one finally does so.

One aspect of this poem that has not received attention hitherto is its pervasive but obscure eroticism. Grosvenor Powell remarks that the characters whom Theseus confronts "significantly . . . are all women," but he does not explicate this significance. I have indicated that the poem is primarily concerned with man's relationship with those arational and imaginative aspects of life which fascinate and threaten to dominate him. Sexuality is an obvious example of such unwilled fascination, of an at-

traction that defies reason, and Winters exploits its metaphorical possibilities. But Winters's association of the indefinable (and uncontrollable)
with evil and horror produces a peculiarly nervous and fraught atmosphere of distaste, a distaste which issues in violence, reminding one of
the atmosphere of, say, *Measure for Measure*. The rape of the first section,
which is like an exasperated surrender to impulse, corresponds to the
killings (of the minotaur and Ariadne) of the second section, where the
protagonist attempts in self-disgust to rid himself of the taint of the irrational. It is worth remarking that this obscure, violent, and fearful eroticism is found in one other poem of Winters's, "A Vision," and it is
perhaps worth glancing at this poem before passing on to a discussion of
the second of Winters's chief mythological poems, "Heracles."

In "A Vision" the protagonist is at first alone in a familiar room,
"Changing and growing dark with what I knew." Then a couple enter, a
Widow (capitalized by Winters) and her lover, and the speaker realizes
that he has been transported to another time. The Widow has an unexplained power over her lover, who is presented as weak, dependent and
desperate, and his dependence is specified as sexual. Despite his mute plea
for her to desist, the widow displays to him a severed head. At this point
the lover fades from the room and the speaker takes his place. He takes
up the head and immediately,

> My blood drew from me, from the neck flowed red,
> A dark pulse on the darkness. The head stirred
> Weakly beneath my fingers, and I heard
> A whispered laughter, and the burden grew
> In life and fury as my strength withdrew.

Sapped by the loss of blood, the protagonist attempts to flee, pursued by
manic laughter (of the lover?), but he is everywhere confronted by "The
Widow like a corpse." The poem breaks off with a final scream that
"Shattered my being like an empty dream." The poem is Winters's most
obscure and I do not pretend fully to understand it; the structure is like
that of a nightmare (particularly the close), the head that gains strength as
the speaker forfeits his is like the demon mentioned at the end of *The
Brink of Darkness*, the Widow is perhaps partly, it has been suggested, a
figure embodying his fear of his mother's occult interests. It is curiously
similar to Robert Lowell's poem "The Severed Head" and may be a
source for that poem; in the Lowell poem the blood flow is connected
with the writing of a manuscript, and it is possible to read this meaning

back into "A Vision." Read in these terms the poem becomes an allegory for literary creation with the Widow as a monstrous and pitiless muse. This may be part of her meaning, but it does not exhaust her significance. She and the lover are identified as "demons," which immediately recalls to us Winters's sense of the malevolence of whatever lay beyond the illuminated circle of human reason. The Widow's fierce scorn is akin to that of Hippolyta in "Theseus, a Trilogy"—and, though Hippolyta is the victim and the Widow the predator, both exist as an alien disdainful presence whose destructive fascination is a concomitant of their sexuality. "Theseus, a Trilogy" and "A Vision" are the two darkest poems by Winters, not only in the sense that they are pervaded by an undefined aura of malevolence and fear, or in that they are largely about darkness and take place in darkness, but also in that they are the two poems in which the individual sensory details seem most charged with obscure emotion. In both poems the narrative that supports the allegory is (partly) concerned with sexual attraction, in both cases an attraction associated with disgust and violence. I have indicated in discussing other poems by Winters that it is sometimes difficult to tell which aspect of the metaphor is vehicle and which tenor, and it seems to me to be true that these poems are to some degree *about* sexuality, rather than merely using it as a device to present an allegorical meaning. This would go some way toward explaining their relative obscurity, as if Winters's sense of tact were preventing him from dealing with the subject more openly. If we accept this view, it must be admitted that the poems show a rather bleak view of sexual attraction, seeing it as a violent and destructive force subversive of reason, which Winters valued as the central defining quality of humanity. Given his views on reason and instinct this conclusion is consistent with his general intellectual position, though whether it was merely an aspect of that position or a more radical perception partly responsible for generating that position is a question that must remain open.

"Heracles" is a much clearer, more sharply etched poem than "Theseus, a Trilogy," and its allegorical structure consists of more easily identifiable one-to-one equivalents. It is also, perhaps for this very reason, for me at least, less powerful in its final impact than the Theseus poem. It has the clarity and beauty of a demonstrated equation, but it lacks the sense of problematic struggle, of an overpowering and enveloping reality, that is the mark of "Theseus, a Trilogy." The difficulties of the Theseus poem inhere in the matrix of the poem itself and are probably irresolvable as the poem stands; the difficulties of the Heracles poem are much more exter-

nal to its central meaning—they are chiefly reducible to the one difficulty
of decoding the numerous mythological references with which the poem
is encrusted.

Winters added a note to the poem: "Heracles is treated as a Sun-God,
the particular statement used being that of Athon's *Classical Dictionary*.
Allegorically he is the artist in hand-to-hand or semi-intuitive combat
with experience" (*Collected Poems*, p. 189). As we have seen, many of
Winters's later poems are basically allegorical, and the fact that he singled
this one out for an explanatory note (rather than, say, "Midas" or "Theseus") indicates that he felt it to be, to an extreme degree, a poem à clef,
almost substanceless without its key (whereas both "Theseus" and "Midas" can be read with some pleasure and understanding even if the reader
remains all but unaware of the allegory).

Heracles in his role as sun-god is reminiscent of Apollo in the sonnet
"Apollo and Daphne," another deity associated with the sun and used by
Winters as an allegorical expression of the artist's relations with reality.
The poem opens with Heracles being called to Eurystheus's throne and
entrusted with his labors, which are identified with the signs of the
zodiac. The completion of the labors is the movement of the sun through
the zodiac's signs, the establishment and demonstration of harmony and
law, the reduction of experience to order.

Heracles is not entirely successful, however, in his subjugation of experience, or rather the subjugation is not effected without sacrifice:

> And yet the Centaur stung me from afar,
> His blood envenomed with the Hydra's blood:
> Thence was I outcast from the earthy war.
>
> Nessus the Centaur, with his wineskin full,
> His branch and thyrsus, and his fleshy grip—
> Her whom he could not force he yet could gull.
> And she drank poison from his bearded lip.
>
> Older than man, evil with age, is life:
> Injustice, direst perfidy, my bane
> Drove me to win my lover and my wife;
> By love and justice I at last was slain.

The Centaur is equated with life (it is he who is "older than man, evil
with age") and in particular with the sensual aspects of life. Heracles,
much as Gawaine thinks at the opening of his duel that he can deal with
the Green Knight, thinks that he can deal with the Centaur, but it exacts

its own revenge by guile. The Centaur had attempted to seduce Heracles' wife, Deianira, but had failed, killed by Heracles' poisoned arrow. As he died he offered Deianira a cup of his blood, promising her it would act as a love potion; she, when Heracles later wished to abandon her and re-marry, sent her husband a garment impregnated with the blood, hoping thus to win him back. The poison burnt into Heracle's flesh, and in re-morse Deianira hanged herself. The poem thus explicitly states that life exacts its own revenge on those who would order and control it; that the artist is defeated by the life he appears to subdue. A similar judgment is implicit in the first two sections of "Theseus, a Trilogy"; the avatars of the moon, though raped and killed by Theseus, retain their ghostly hold on him—he is as much their victim as they are his.

Heracles is driven by the will of Hera and cannot resist his fate:

> my life was not my own,
> But I my life's; a god I was, not man.
> Grown absolute I slew my flesh and bone;

In that last line we have the notion, familiar in Winters's work, that the mind should transcend the particulars of immediate sensuous life in order to partake of and add to an atemporal life of the intellect. The tragedy of such a course is that though the mind is impelled to strive for such an absolute, it can reach it only by renouncing the very life in which it is grounded. Heracles' translation to godhead implies this renunciation.

In the last stanzas of the poem a change of mood is discernible. The sense of pain and stress which has so far informed the narrative gives way to a saddened intimation of loss, a sense of muted nostalgia. Indeed, the stanzas are curiously reminiscent of the sestet of "Apollo and Daphne":

> This was my grief, that out of grief I grew—
> Translated as I was from earth at last,
> From the sad pain that Deianira knew.
> Transmuted slowly in a fiery blast,
>
> Perfect, and moving perfectly, I raid
> Eternal silence to eternal ends:
> And Deianira, an imperfect shade,
> Retreats in silence as my arc descends.

In the same way that Apollo and Daphne separated into different realms so do Heracles and Deianira, and in the same way that Daphne's remo-tion was effected by a metamorphosis, so is Heracles'. The silence and the retreating shade of the last lines echo the sonnet even in imagery and cadence:

> And like a cloud of silence or a name,
> The god withdrew into eternity.

The similarity is because the basic subject is the same—the distance of the mind from the reality it seeks and from which it is finally estranged. Heracles' very perfection separates him from Deianira; his solace is the "eternal ends" of art. The poem becomes complex in its implications in these closing lines. So far the metaphor for the mind's experience of reality has been one of combat, here it is one of love. But this mingling of love and combat as paradigms for the mind's relations with the world is common in Winters's work. If we take love in the sense of sexual union there is the evidence of "Theseus, a Trilogy," in which the protagonist's relations with Hippolyta and Ariadne both involve violence and love; "Apollo and Daphne" with its attendant rape; and "Sir Gawaine and the Green Knight," in which Sir Gawaine fights with the knight and is made love to by his lady, both knight and lady representing the world as it exists over against the mind. If we take love in the sense of overwhelming affection, there are the poems on California history in which the affectionate tact of the early settlers is contrasted with the violation of the land by the later arrivals.

In "Heracles" we see again that ambivalence toward external reality already noted in Winters's work—it is both to be fought against and loved. It is both omnipresent chaos threatening to destroy the mind's integrity and independence, and lost idyll calling to the mind over a distance of time or space. But there is a difference between the love of Heracles and Deianira and that of Apollo and Daphne. Apollo never possesses Daphne and renounces her, as he must, before knowing her. Heracles and Deianira have been husband and wife, and Heracles' renunciation of her as he moves into eternity is a renunciation after intimacy and knowledge. There is not the frustrated searching of Apollo, but the calmer renunciation of completed experience. This is perhaps simply because the latter poem is the work of an older man; the sonnets of *The Proof* are the poems in which Winters bade farewell to his youth, and they carry with them a sense of youthful impatience and anger, a sense of the *search* for reality. "Heracles" implies an acceptance of experience, and a willingness to forgo it or in some sense rise beyond it. (I should add that Winters is careful to suppress reference to Heracles' later love and his wish to remarry; though we are abstractly aware of this feature of the story—as the motive

THE LATER POETRY   131

for the blood-soaked garment's being sent—it is not allowed to intrude into the given detail, and we are left with the impression that Deianira is Heracles' true beloved.)

There remains the problem of Eurystheus. Grosvenor Powell says of him, "He is one of the 'dead living' and fears the truly living" (*Language as Being*, p. 132; the phrase "dead living" is from Winters's poem "The Bitter Moon," and it also occurs in his essay on Louise Bogan's poetry). Eurystheus is presented first as "trembling" when he calls on Heracles to perform his labors and then as ungrateful when they are performed. Further, he is the king at the center of the "corrupted state," and here in his "den of brass" he is shielded from that reality with which Heracles struggles. If he represents the "dead living" he also represents the public world, as the later Theseus does in the last section of "Theseus, a Trilogy." On this reading, Heracles—the "artist in hand-to-hand or semi-intuitive combat with experience"—appears as a spiritual guardian of the race, one whose orderings of reality are necessary for the maintenance of that world governed by Eurystheus, though Eurystheus only intermittently realizes this, and he is for the most part content to despise Heracles. This notion of the artist as the despised guardian of the race's intellectual heritage is one that is prominent in Winters's public poems.

Public and Occasional Poems

In tracing Winters's poetic development I have drawn attention to the way in which this was, in part, a development away from privacy toward a recognition of reality as it exists separate from the poet, and an engagement with its problems. The poems which follow on from *The Proof* (in general, the poems of Winters's thirties) are chiefly concerned with this tension between the observing, organizing mind and the external reality which is its raw material. Reality is here basically conceived of as the natural universe, in which the poet appears as an isolated consciousness attempting to comprehend the data presented to it. But in the two poems utilizing Greek myths which have been discussed it was noticeable how particular figures, Theseus himself in the third section of "Theseus, a Trilogy" and Eurystheus in "Heracles," exist as representatives of the public world of the state and political action. Poems concerned with such themes became more prominent in Winters's oeuvre as he grew older. In these poems reality is not so much the natural world as the human world of government, laws, and the state, and Winters's conception of the poet has, accordingly, implicitly shifted in emphasis. In such poems the poet appears less as a sensibility entering into a relationship with something alien to its nature—a relationship of combat, love, fear, trust, distrust, or whatever—than as a representative and guardian of an ethical norm to which the public world is admonished to adhere.

Such public poetry presupposes an ethical norm, and the fact that it has rarely been written, in English at least, with much success since the eighteenth century is perhaps an indication that universally accepted norms of behavior are no longer thought to exist. As a self-confessed absolutist Winters could not accept the ethical relativism implied by the absence of such public poetry, and he appears to have given himself the task of singlehandedly recreating a rhetoric adequate to the writing of poetry that invoked a civic ethical standard.

Broadly, public poetry concerned with ethics can work in one of two ways. It can either positively indicate the desired behavior and offer an illustration of how it is fulfilled (in which case it is some kind of eulogy or panegyric) or it can proceed by pointing out how the people, customs or laws which it describes fail to embody the standard desired. In this case it is satire. English poetry has normally preferred the latter form, but in general Winters proceeded by the former method, and his public poems therefore read as eulogy rather than satire.

However there is one major exception to this last statement, Winters's poem "The Critiad." It was excluded from the *Collected Poems*, and did not even find its way into the more complete volume *The Collected Poems of Yvor Winters*, published in 1978, which managed to gather together most of the poems missing from Winters's own selection; but as it is his only substantial attempt at satire it is worth brief consideration. The poem was published in 1931 as the introductory poem to *The Journey* and is therefore contemporary with "The Slow Pacific Swell," "The Marriage," and "On a View of Pasadena from the Hills"; like them it is written in heroic couplets. It is thus earlier than most of Winters's public and occasional poems and its subject is narrower—not the world of politics or war but that of literary criticism. The poem opens with Winters considering recent criticism of his own poetry and proceeds to an examination of the work of various critics then active. Most are lampooned; some are praised. It is noticeable that the lampooned critics are generally dismissed with a line or two, but those in whose work Winters finds something valuable are discussed more fully. Two of these stand out— Allen Tate and Irving Babbitt. The poem ends with a list of those poets Winters admired but whom he felt were unduly neglected; the list includes Thomas Hardy, Allen Tate, William Carlos Williams, and Wallace Stevens.

Two points are noticeable from this quick survey of the poem. First, the concluding section of the work, and preceding portions of it, are concerned with praise (albeit qualified) rather than satire. Winters is as much interested in spelling out what he admires as what he condemns; indeed we are given to understand that it is the neglect of what he admires that provokes his anger. Second, he assumes, with an almost formulary world-weariness, that what is to him admirable will be, by most people, despised or neglected. These two factors (that the core of the poem is a positive commitment, rather than mere disdain, and that this commitment is slighted by the world in general) inform most of Winters's public poems. We are never in much doubt as to what Winters believes is right, but equally he does not seem to expect to win many converts. He does seem to have believed, from his late twenties onwards, that the world was made up largely of the "dead living," from whom not much in the way of comprehension could be expected. Many personal experiences probably contributed to this opinion—his stormy relations with certain of the Stanford English faculty, the anger aroused by some of his critical essays and (perhaps decisively) the Lamson trial. For whatever reason this opinion seems to have gained in strength as he grew older, and the bitterness evident in some of his later work is, for many readers, a serious blemish—though one that it is possible to ignore when one has become familiar with his work as a whole.

Besides the poems that deal with political power, the law, and the nature of the state, there are two other kinds of poems included in this public and occasional category. These are poems addressed to members of the poet's family (in which the individual is often placed in a wider social and ethical context) and poems on the public aspects of scholarship and learning. This latter group leads on from the concerns of "The Critiad." Three poems are connected with William Dinsmore Briggs: one has already been discussed as one of the sonnets from *The Proof*; the other two are "Dedication for a Book of Criticism" and "For the Opening of the William Dinsmore Briggs Room." The "Dedication" is written in what Winters referred to as the "plain style" and consists of simple declarative statements. There is no imagery, as is consistent with the most extreme examples of the plain style. The main theme of the poem is stated in the couplet that opens the second stanza,

> Strong the scholar is to scan
> What is permanent in man.

The word *permanent* alerts us to Winters's concerns—with absolute truths which persist despite the vagaries of particular generations, with the nature of tradition, and with ensuring the tradition survives. Briggs is honored as what Winters saw as the best kind of scholar, not a man who merely disinters the past but one who makes available to the present the best that has been thought in the past; as the poem makes plain, to make this available one must be able to understand and participate in it. The scholar's task is evaluative as well as purely expository. The poem's stony simplicity (at variance with the sophistication that is its subject) gives the impression of an honest and humble tribute, but the trouble with universal truths is that everyone has heard them many times; though this does not make them less true, it does mean that the author must work particularly hard if he is to convince the reader that he has arrived at these truths for himself. The simple exposition of the poem's premises in the first stanza barely escapes banality, though the remaining stanzas, in their dignity and balance, go some way toward demonstrating those qualities of mind with which the poem is concerned.

In "For the Opening of the William Dinsmore Briggs Room" Winters's preoccupation with beleaguered truth is given a particular validity by the fact that the poem was written in wartime and specifically refers to the war, which carries an allegorical implication beyond its immediate meaning:

> Because our Being grows in mind,
> And evil in imperfect thought,
> And passion running undefined
> May ruin what the masters taught;
>
> Within the edge of war we meet
> To dedicate this room to one
> Who made his wisdom more complete
> Than any save the great have done.
>
> That in this room, men yet may reach,
> By labor and wit's sullen shock,
> The final certitude of speech
> Which Hell itself cannot unlock.

The first two stanzas contrast definition and the undefined. This is done abstractly and by implication in the first stanza, and by means of the imagery of the room (the subject of the poem) and the war (the context within which the poem is written) in the second stanza. The room, the defined space, symbolizes the virtues of definition (the room exists for the pursuit of scholarship) and the war indicates the evils of "imperfect thought" and "passion running undefined." The second stanza ends with an example of just such definition as the room exists to encourage. In the last stanza the theme is summarized—definition, laboriously achieved, brings certainty which no extremity of evil can undo. The poem is summed up by the opposition between the capitalized word in the first line (Being) and that in the last line (Hell). Being refers to humanity's Being, which for Winters was its intellectual heritage, Hell to "passion running undefined," the war, the forces that would annihilate Being. If we remember Winters's dependence on Aquinas for his definition of evil (as privation, a lack of being), the contrast between his Being and his Hell becomes even clearer.

The threat of the real war which hovers behind this poem reinforces a symbolic scheme which was by this time (1942) becoming habitual with Winters. We can accept the reality of this poem's abstractions because we are able to perceive the immediate context out of which they grew. The circumstances of the poem's concern are given to us, and we can therefore sympathize with that concern, whereas the context of the "Dedication" is as general as life itself, and sympathy presupposes in the reader an evaluation of life similar to Winters's. Many of his later poems, like those of a writer he especially admired, Fulke Greville, appear to have been written, in Greville's words, "to those only that are weather-beaten in the sea of this world, such as . . . study to sail on a right course among rocks and quicksands."

Two other poems on literature and the intellect confirm the theme of the hard, defined core of worth which it is the poet's and scholar's care to create and preserve against the attrition of the world. "A Dedication in Postscript, Written to Agnes Lee Shortly before Her Death" utilizes the symbol of "the statue, pure amid the rotting leaves," to convey the meaning (the symbol is borrowed from Agnes Lee's own poem "A Statue in a Garden"). In "On Teaching the Young" a similar opposition between the defined work of art and the vague imprecisions of transient life is indicated:

> A poem is what stands,
> When imperceptive hands,
> Feeling, have gone astray.

The hands are those of students attempting to understand the poem. The word *feeling* is a quiet pun. We have the visual image of hands attempting to know something by touching it, and failing; and there is also the meaning of feeling as experiencing emotion—the students go astray because they feel rather than understand, they work with emotion rather than with intellect. The poem ends with a summary statement of Winters's own Parnassianism (the term he had applied to Agnes Lee's poem):

Few minds will come to this.
The poet's only bliss
Is in cold certitude—
Laurel, archaic, rude.

Besides "For the Opening of the William Dinsmore Briggs Room" Winters wrote other poems against the background of the Second World War—one has already been discussed ("Moonlight Alert") in connection with his use of moonlight as a symbol for the imagination. "Night of Battle" and "To a Military Rifle" are both chiefly concerned with war as a time when

The private life is small
And individual men
Are counted not at all.

The poems contain a vision of "giant movements" in which "Only the common will" has meaning. Winters's instincts—committed to discrimination and the individual intelligence—were to withdraw from such activity, even though he may have assented to some of its manifestations. His description of himself as "I / Who alter nothing" implies a pessimism about the value of individual action which extends beyond the specific context of the war. As in the poem on the reading room at Stanford, the war suggests not only itself but the more permanent chaos of life in general, in which the individual consciousness, while being the only source of moral discrimination available, is all but powerless.

In this phrase, "moral discrimination," we have the central concept of Winters's public poems, which are almost entirely concerned with moral vision and the will which must implement the choices discerned. If Winters saw this will as being all but powerless, this did not prevent him from deploying it when necessary, as is clear from the episode of the Lamson trial.

The circumstances of this trial, and the three poems that arose out of it, throw a great deal of light on Winters's attitudes and preoccupations. They are perhaps his most important public poems, written within the context of the particular trial but transcending that context by their implications, so that the trial and its personages become paradigms of the hazards of the ethical life. As is the case with the poems on the Second World War, the particular circumstances of this trial must have confirmed in Winters views that he had already developed (on the solitary nature of moral integrity, on the evils of mass emotion, on the necessity for absolutes as the only force that can withstand this emotion, and, not least, on the reality and power of evil). The trial, with its absolutes (the law), its exemplars of integrity and venality, its exposure of the mistaken and evil nature of much mass opinion, and its demonstration of the superiority of reason over emotion as a guide to truth, must have seemed to Winters an almost miraculous demonstration of his own beliefs. He was too urgently involved in the business of saving an innocent man's life to have approached it in this spirit, but the appositeness of the trial's details to his beliefs cannot have escaped him.

The poems become more accessible if we understand the background to the trial. David Lamson was sales manager for the Stanford University Press. On 30 May 1933 he discovered his wife dead in the bathtub of their home. She had a deep wound in the back of her head, and the police officer whom Lamson called quickly decided that she had been murdered by her husband. The collection of evidence was cursory, and the trial, accompanied by a good deal of gossip, was something of a travesty of justice. Lamson was found guilty and condemned to death. One of the prosecution experts (who testified, incorrectly as it later appeared, as to the nature of the wound Allene Lamson had received) was a Dr. Meyer of Stanford University. Winters (in common with many other people) was convinced that Lamson was innocent, and he worked hard to procure a retrial. While Lamson was waiting in the condemned cell Winters and another member of the Stanford English faculty, Frances Theresa Russell, wrote a pamphlet, *The Case of David Lamson*, which set out the lackadaisical and even vicious methods of the prosecution. (Among many examples of carelessness perhaps the most flagrant is that marks in the Lamson house which a prosecution expert asserted to be human blood turned out to have been made by a child's crayons). The pamphlet establishes that Allene Lamson had slipped, probably as a result of a faint, in the bathtub, violently cracked the back of her head against the washstand, and died as a result of bleeding from the wound. After the first trial two more trials followed—both with a hung jury—and a mistrial caused by someone interfering with the box from which names of jurors were drawn. The state then dismissed the case. Lamson later became a neighbor and close friend of Winters; he died in 1975.

Although many people agreed with Winters that Lamson was innocent, many more did not, and it required some courage to stand out
against what appears to have been virtual mob hysteria stirred up by the
prosecution's innuendoes about Lamson's sexual life. Apart from the
sheer justice of the case I believe two important factors contributed to
Winters's deep sense of involvement with Lamson's predicament. First,
the behavior of Lamson was eminently dignified and stoical throughout
the proceedings, and dignity and quiet stoicism were two qualities Winters greatly prized. When condemned to hang, Lamson addressed the
judge as follows: "I understand that under the law and verdict you have
no alternative save to pronounce the death penalty. I should like you and
the people of this state to know that my conscience is clear before your
judgement and the judgement of God. I know in my heart that I have
been a good husband to Allene. I have done her no harm. I am as innocent of her death as you yourself. That is all" (Russell and Winters, *The
Case of David Lamson*, p. 26). This was in sharp distinction to the behavior of the prosecuting lawyers, one of whom descended to reading out
the murder of Nancy by Sykes from *Oliver Twist* in order to impress the
jury.

Second, the hysterical emotions aroused by the trial, which only
served to obscure the truth of Lamson's innocence, seem to have swept
away supposedly sane and reasonable men until the proceedings degener-
ated into a species of witch hunt. Winters was especially bitter that some
members of Stanford University were caught up in this hysteria and did
not appear concerned that an innocent man would die as a result of it.
This confirmed two of Winters's beliefs—that the source of evil is emotion (and that the complacent academic mind is as susceptible to this evil
as any other) and that the common fate of undemonstrative virtue was to
be vilified by fools. The concluding paragraphs of the pamphlet written
in Lamson's defense bear all the marks of Winters's prose:

> We have seen men eminent as scholars, fully aware that no man is
> universal master of any field of knowledge or even of a limited part
> of any, testifying hastily on subjects which they were ill-prepared
> to discuss and so giving casual opinion the force of authoritative
> statement to the minds of an ignorant jury, and, when their testi-
> mony was questioned or met with reasonable argument, becoming
> testy and violent as if it were their honor, rather than the natural
> limits of their knowledge, that was being explored, behaving as if
> they themselves were on trial for their reputations as scholars, as if

they were not thus impugning their own common-sense and common humanity, and, lest we forget it, as if David Lamson were not on trial for his life. [Pp. 94–95]

This querulous insistence on truth, and the bemused contempt for those who would put their own reputations before it, are typical of Winters's critical writings. Of course, everyone will agree with Winters here—the truth was more important than a scholar's reputation because a man's life depended on it. But Winters clearly felt that truth was always more important than individual reputations, and he wrote accordingly, thereby managing to alienate a large number of disagreeing critics.

The first poem of the three is "To Edwin V. McKenzie, on his Defense of David Lamson." McKenzie was Lamson's defending counsel. The poem is concerned with the nature of heroism, and—fittingly—is written in heroic couplets (though we now associate the heroic couplet chiefly with the mock heroic, we should remember that Pope's *Iliad* preceded his *Dunciad*). The poem is in two sections. The first begins with the line "The concept lives, but few men fill the frame," and the second ends with the line "Yourself the concept in the final hour." The poem sets out a universal concept as a standard difficult to attain and claims that a particular individual, the defense lawyer, has succeeded in becoming a living embodiment of the concept.

As it is defined in the first section, this concept is not only that of justice but of a completeness of humanity, a kind of vigilant, civilized care that seems almost mythical rather than merely human. And in the last lines of the section the mythical implications are focused:

> This is the great man of tradition, one
> To point out justice when the wrong is done;
> To outwit rogue and craven; represent
> Mankind in the eternal sacrament—
> Odysseus with the giant weapon bent.

The metaphor is not developed but its implications are plain: Odysseus, as he is here portrayed, uses his strength and skill to outwit the rabble of suitors, obviously equated with those working for Lamson's condemnation and death. The physical strength of Odysseus, his mastery that puts the suitors to shame, is an analogy for the lawyer's moral and intellectual superiority to his opponents. The "eternal sacrament" refers to what Winters saw as man's chief concerns—the establishment of truth and the identification of his own Being, as far as possible, with the absolutes of traditional wisdom. As Odysseus's bow shot establishes the legitimacy of his claims and scatters the parasitic suitors, so the great lawyer, by his forensic skill, establishes a truth that silences the sophistry of men more concerned with reputation than justice.

The second section opens with lines eloquent of Winters's disgust at those members of the Stanford faculty who had abetted the prosecution:

> When those who guard tradition in the schools
> Proved to be weaklings and half-learnèd fools,

and the poet describes the solitary battle of the lawyer which finally establishes him as the embodiment of the "concept." The last three lines of each section are a triplet after four heroic couplets, and the added rhyme in each case works as a rhetorical emphasis, an expression not only of the poet's depth of concern but also of the fixed integrity and will of the lawyer. The lines aim at both indignation and grandeur:

> I saw you, mantled in tradition, tower;
> You filled the courtroom with historic power;
> Yourself the concept in the final hour.

The second poem is addressed to the defendant's sister, "To a Woman on Her Defense of Her Brother Unjustly Convicted of Murder." This poem, like the previous one, is concerned with the difficult defense of truth and the innocent in hostile circumstances, but as it is addressed to someone intimate with Lamson the rhetoric itself is, especially in the closing stanzas, more intimate; the emphasis is on the innocence rather than the truth. The poem aims less at the grandeur of formal statement than at a sympathetic admiration of its subject's passion. The poem opens with two stanzas that list the forces against which the sister had to battle, summed up by the line, "Outrage and anarchy in formal mien." The "formal mien" is not only the formal guise of the functionaries of the law court, but also the quasi-professional evidence given by experts who were in fact no experts and who were more interested in hiding this fact than in arriving at the truth of the case. The line is of course a paradox—the law and its experts exist to combat "Outrage and anarchy"; here they embody them. The third stanza, a statement of how complete and vicious seemed the opposition to the possibility that Lamson may have been innocent, recalls Winters's theory of demonism—the active malevolence of evil directing its forces against the human mind:

> These for an evil year now you have fought,
> Which for three weeks, through nervous nights awake,

> I learned could break me, for the Devil wrought.
> May God support you, for your brother's sake!

Stanzas 4 and 5 are probably the best of the poem:

> There is a special Hell for each of these:
> The brute, succumbing where his judgements err,
> Compels the cringing fool to perjuries;
> The friend begs comfort of the perjurer;

> The scholar, now discovering his allies,
> And turning to himself to stay his doom,
> Finds but his pride amid a nest of lies,
> A dire obsession in an empty room.

Winters picks up the theological implications of "Devil" and "God" from the previous stanza, and these lead to the Danteesque notion of a "special Hell" for "brute," "cringing fool," "friend," "perjurer," and "scholar." The first of the two stanzas gives a picture of the blind leading the blind—one form of insufficiency turning for help to another. The "brute," discovered in his errors, forces the "cringing fool" to perjury to support him, and perjurer and "friend" (presumably those of Lamson's friends who deserted him in his trial—that there were such is apparent from *The Case of David Lamson*) cling together in an attempt to convince themselves and each other that they are right. Significantly, the "scholar" is given a stanza to himself. With sufficient intellect to understand the nature of his "allies" but not with sufficient character to renounce them, he is left with himself. He cannot turn to others for support but must turn inward; here he finds only "pride amid a nest of lies"; his only substantial attribute is his pride, which is a "dire obsession" in the midst of emptiness. *Dire* means "having dreadful or terrible consequences"; the terrible consequences are twofold, the condemnation of Lamson and the spiritual damnation of the scholar himself. It is the traditional damnation of a deprivation of grace, of having allied oneself with evil—the punishment is the understanding of this. The last line of these stanzas, "A dire obsession in an empty room" both characterizes the scholar's spiritual state and is an image of the man alone with the fact of his damnation—the knowledge that he has abetted evil and is insufficiently strong to break free. The closing stanzas, like the closing lines of the poem to McKenzie, postulate an absolute which the subject of the poem and her brother embody. But here the absolute is more entangled with the specific lives which demonstrate it; it is less potent in its grandeur but more moving in its humanity.

The last of the three poems is addressed to Lamson himself, "awaiting retrial, in the jail at San José." The poem is in the comparatively rare meter in which Winters wrote his "Midas" and "Before Disaster." The formality of diction of the opening lines may disturb readers who equate colloquial language with authenticity of emotion: it functions not only as an indication of Winters's seriousness in this poem, but as the linguistic equivalent of those traditional and timeless concepts that these three poems evoke. The poem rehearses, as have the other two, the forces arrayed against Lamson. Again the best lines are reserved for the scholar, an indication of how strongly Winters felt about this *trahaison des clercs*:

> How great scholars failed to see
> Virtue in extremity;
> How the special intellect
> Fortified them in neglect,
> Left their feelings brutal, wild,
> By inconsequence beguiled.

The lines are a tissue of abstractions, but because of their metrical control and their close focus on their subject (no one could be in doubt about what the poet is discussing) they have a cogent eloquence.

The poem then turns to Lamson himself, "Hidden in the county jail." It is his quiet stoicism, "Unchanged amid disease," that wins Winters's admiration:

> Who, unchanged amid disease,
> Wrote with power and spoke with ease,
> Who, though human thought decayed,
> Yet the dissolution stayed,
> Gracious in that evil shade.

Winters here repeats the device he had used in the poem to McKenzie— he introduces a triplet of rhymes after a series of couplets, and this gives the end a rhetorical emphasis and power. The word *stayed*, a momentary stumbling block to some readers, is being used in the same way it was in the poem to Lamson's sister, "And turning to himself to stay his doom"—that is, it is used transitively to mean "hold back" or "prevent." In both cases there is a sense that the staying may prove only temporary—deservedly so in the scholar's case, tragically in Lamson's. The last line of the poem, "Gracious in that evil shade," is typical of Winters's habits of thought in its juxtaposition of two opposing abstractions. "Gracious" is a pun: it refers on the immediate level to Lamson's superficial ease and charm in such an appalling situation, but more deeply it refers to

the spiritual grace opposed to evil, that is, the grace of truth and innocence. Largely because of these closing lines, in which Winters's habit of
seeing human experience in terms of the absolutes it implies is here mag-
nificently justified by the subject matter, this poem seems to me the best
of the three connected with the Lamson trial.

A poem that follows on from the Lamson group in its themes is "Socrates." It is a monologue spoken by the philosopher just before drinking
the hemlock to which he has been sentenced by the Athenian state. The
poem emphasizes the solitary nature of Socrates' career, the individual of
integrity and reason brought down by mob emotion. But it goes beyond
the fact of tragedy in its suggestion that Socrates has "raised the Timeless
up against the times." Though he is condemned to die by "the times" it is
"the Timeless" that "bids me drink the judgement up." He assents to the
rule of the city-state and its laws, though he knows they are mistaken in
their present judgment, because they embody, however imperfectly,
those principles of universal law his reasoning has discerned. (The situation is distantly analogous to the condemnation of Billy Budd by Captain
Vere, an episode that Winters greatly admired in its presentation of the
problems of individual tragedy and the absolute nature of law.) By his
teaching and death Socrates participates in "the Timeless," which exists
as a constant admonition to "the times" and whose values can be passed
on by individuals of sufficient integrity and will. In his remarks on the
drama Winters wrote, "There might well be tragic possibilities in the
predicament of the German and other European professors who refused
to betray the principles of scholarship at the insistence of the Nazi government" (*The Function of Criticism*, p. 31). Such notions of personal
integrity heroically maintained against the pressure of a brutal environment, which we see in the Lamson poems, in "Socrates," and in the comment on the German scholars under the Nazis, were clearly profoundly
moving to Winters; the heroism called forth his admiration, and the venality of the environment confirmed his worst suspicions of the "dead
living."

I wish to mention one more poem by Winters that is concerned with
public action and the nature of the state, his sonnet "The Prince." If Winters conceived of the scholar or philosopher as one whose stance was primarily defensive, a jealous guardian of truths slighted by the community
at large, he conceived of the statesman far differently. The statesman
must act in the world in a way that the scholar need not, and he must
necessarily accommodate himself to the world's strategies and needs. The
prince of Winters's poem reminds us of his Theseus and Heracles rather
than of the more stoic stance implied by many of the poems considered

in this section, where the individual's role is to observe, suffer, and understand, rather than to actively engage with what he understands. Here is the poem:

> The prince or statesman who would rise to power
> Must rise through shallow trickery, and speak
> The tongue of knavery, deceive the hour,
> Use the corrupt, and still corrupt the weak.
>
> And he who having power would serve the State,
> Must now deceive corruption unto good,
> By indirection strengthen love with hate,
> Must love mankind with craft and hardihood:
>
> Betray the witless into wisdom, trick
> Disaster to good luck, escape the gaze
> Of all the pure at heart, each lunatic
> Of innocence, who draws you to his daze:
>
> And this frail balance to immortalize,
> Stare publicly from death through marble eyes.

The relish for the struggle, which never loses sight of what the struggle is about, is typical of the best of Winters's poems of his thirties, in that the tone is defined by the tension between the mind's perceptions and values (here, what the prince's struggle is actually for) and the nature of the world in which the protagonist must live and act. This tension between mind and world simultaneously establishes a sense of intimacy with the world, and a confidence in the mind's standards. Such a tension is the hallmark of Winters's finest poems—in the earliest work the mind often seems swamped by the data of the world, and certain of the last poems have withdrawn so far from intimacy with quotidian reality that their abstractions must be taken on trust. But the best poems keep both world and mind in balance; "Wisdom and wilderness are here at poise," as Winters wrote of Melville. That poise is visible in "The Prince," and indeed invoked in the "frail balance" of the penultimate line.

The last poems to be discussed are those addressed to or concerned with members of the poet's own family. Three such poems have already been mentioned: "On a View of Pasadena from the Hills," which is partly concerned with Winters's father; "The Marriage," which we may take as referring to his own marriage; and "A Prayer for My Son." The qualities of tact and tenderness which inform these poems are also present in "To My Infant Daughter," "A Testament, To One Now a Child," and one of

his last poems, "At the San Francisco Airport," addressed to his daughter.
What distinguishes these poems as a group separate from Winters's other
occasional poetry is their poignant sense of the uniqueness and fragility of
individual lives. This quality is fleetingly present in many poems of *The
Bare Hills*, but its first extended appearance is in "The Marriage." In these
later poems (to children) the sense of the vulnerability of the lives entrusted to our care is omnipresent. The vision implied by these poems is
one of constant attrition: the oppressive sense of time ineluctably passing
and destroying (the chief perception of his early poetry) has combined
with an understanding of the human world's potential for evil (the theme
of much of his later poetry) to produce an all but overwhelming conception of the world as "this appalling place" ("A Testament"). The child of
these poems is beleaguered both by natural process and by human evil.
The sustaining power into whose care the child is committed is a notion
of surviving spiritual truth, handed on despite such "appalling" odds:

> God is revealed in this:
> That some go not amiss,
>   But through hard labor teach
>   What we may reach.
>
> These gave us life through death:
> Jesus of Nazareth,
>   Archaic Socrates,
>   And such as these. ["A Testament"]

"To My Infant Daughter" is in two sections. The first is a lament for
the distance between child and father, and the father's impotence to help
the child in the vicissitudes to which life will expose her. This estrange-
ment is finely expressed in the last stanza by the evocation of the child's
death at some unnamed distance in time among people now unknown,
when the poet himself will presumably be dead:

> Whose hands will lay those hands to rest,
> Those hands themselves, no more the same,
> Will weeping lay them on the breast,
> A token only and a name?

The second section is more subdued in its rhetoric and attempts to
warn the child by precept of the dangers ahead of her. That warily defensive stance already referred to as typical of Winters's attitude to the world
is recommended:

> Take few men to your heart!
> Unstable, fierce, unkind,
> The ways that men impart.
> True love is slow to find.

The precepts remind us of Winters's descriptions of the Elizabethan "plain style," and this section of the poem is clearly modeled on the practice of Googe or Raleigh. Of the two dangers that threaten the child—those of natural process and human evil—the first section generally is concerned with the former, and the second with the latter.

"At the San Francisco Airport" is concerned, on the immediate level, with the poet's seeing his daughter off on a flight. The farewell is given the deeper implication of the father's watching his daughter move out of his immediate care and influence into the world of her own life. The poem emphasizes how the two figures are necessarily separate, though the separation is shadowed by the poet's unavailing care:

> And you are here beside me, small,
> Contained and fragile, and intent
> On things that I but half recall—
> Yet going whither you are bent.
> I am the past, and that is all.

But they are interdependent in their concern for the child's future, in

> The passion to acquire the skill
> To face that which you dare not shun.

"That which you dare not shun" suggests the child's future journey through life, on which the poet cannot accompany her. The understated stoicism of the end is very moving, particularly if we recall that this was virtually Winters's last serious poem (it was followed in the *Collected Poems* only by "Two Old-Fashioned Songs"):

> This is the terminal, the break.
> Beyond this point, on lines of air,
> You take the way that you must take;
> And I remain in light and stare—
> In light, and nothing else, awake.

The closing image is not only a fine evocation of the father left alone, momentarily fixed in private thought, withdrawn from the airport's public glare, but it suggests too that light of the intellect which had become

Winters's chief concern, the intellect which sees and understands but knows that it is cut off from the life it loves and watches.

Winters's mature poems rarely startle the reader with brilliant discrete images; neither do they suggest unformulable meanings (they do not deny that such meanings may exist, but they refuse the sleight of hand of pretending to say what, by definition, cannot be said). The momentary brilliance of a startling image and the evocation of irresolvable ambiguities are two of the most prized strategies of modern poetry, and Winters's avoidance of both is one explanation of why his poems have received such scant attention.

In the first essay he ever published, he praised Edwin Arlington Robinson for focusing his mind "upon the object"; in the same way his own poems belong to what they are about. Though an individual personality is clearly discernible from the *Collected Poems*, it is there as an inevitable residuum of the poet's "quest for reality"—it is never presented as an end in itself. The coruscating image that draws attention to the cleverness (or mental stress) of its creator rather than to that which it is meant to illumine, the indefinable suggestions of imprecise language that blur rather than clarify, and the exhibition of personal eccentricities were all, for Winters, hindrances in the path of good poetry. The metaphors of his poetry work subtly through the whole substance of the poem, and both halves of the metaphor are given equal weight. The sea and the forest of "The Slow Pacific Swell" and "Sir Gawaine and the Green Knight" *are* sea and forest as well as being instruments of an allegorical argument. The metaphor is not there as a mere statement of the coincidental visual resemblances between its constituents, but as a presentation of reality charged with meaning. This reality and meaning pervade the whole poem of which they are an aspect; the metaphor is not a detachable moment.

But Winters's poems achieve their effects as much by their metrical and formal structure as by allegory and the postsymbolist method. It is clear that their traditional form, their regularity and metrical precision, are meant as a paradigm of the intellectual position Winters worked out in his late twenties and early thirties. The poems are meant as artifacts, defined against the flux of life. As they are meant to oppose definition to flux, they move towards clarity and certainty, though their author is more aware than most of the difficulties of arriving at such certainty. The diction frequently enacts such apprehensions of truth—the common device in Winters's poems of repeating words or phrases across stanza and line breaks gives us the motions of a mind claiming a concept for its own, moving in on its reality and apprehending it part by part.

If the author of the earlier poems had appeared drawn to the minutest specifics of the natural world, the mature work shows a quite different concern for fixed, immoveable grandeur, whether of the natural world (the ocean at the close of "The Slow Pacific Swell," the California oaks and the Manzanita in the poems so named) or of moral heroism ("Socrates," the Lamson poems, the opening of "On Re-reading a Passage from John Muir"). This concern with the constant and abiding is one aspect of what appears as an almost temperamental need in Winters's later work; in the natural world and in human life he searches for and is clearly moved by what is solitary, heroic, permanent. His poems therefore rarely proceed by the lavish delineation of incidental details. Rather, their extended allegories and the finality of their meters indicate a concern with general truths clearly perceived, with a rocklike weight and irrefutability. In the same way his vocabulary is removed from the quotidian and fashionable; it aims at an atemporal and even archaic dignity, and its registers are rarely those of colloquial speech. In the best work, and it is extensive, such dignity of language, the firm metrical control and an unobtrusive use of the postsymbolist method (what I refer to above as reality charged with meaning) together produce poems of a grandeur and finality comparable to that of their subjects.

5 The Later Prose

The passion to condense from book to book
Unbroken wisdom in a single look . . .

Winters's early criticism, as discussed in Chapter 2, was largely concerned with matters that had a direct bearing on his own development as a poet. He reviewed new poetry and he attempted to define the problems facing contemporary poets. In common with others of his generation he saw the problems as being partly technical (the subtitle of *The Testament of a Stone, Notes on the Mechanics of the Poetic Image*, shows this), but, with his gradually emerging view of poetry as a means of evaluating reality and conveying meaning, he soon became convinced that the chief problems facing the modern poet were more or less metaphysical. The technical problems were then seen as deriving from an underlying metaphysical confusion. His attempts to define and come to terms with this metaphysical problem received their most cogent expression in his essay "The Extension and Reintegration of the Human Spirit" (1929).

His later writings on literature appear, at first sight, to be the work of a far more disinterested critic, a professional student of literature whose essays on say the Elizabethan lyric or the American novel in the nineteenth century attempt to reach a just and, in so far as such a thing is possible, objective evaluation of these works' significance and worth. And in one sense this is true: after he had joined the staff of Stanford University Winters obviously decided to make his living as an academic, and the prodigious amount of criticism which he published in the 1930s was in part his claim to academic status and his contribution to academic debate. And in this he was greatly encouraged by his new mentor, W. D. Briggs, who especially recommended him to concentrate his attention on the evaluation of American literature.

But if we examine Winters's later criticism we see that it falls largely into three groups. There is the work on twentieth-century poetry, and this we can consider as a continuation, albeit on a deeper level, of the preoccupations of his earlier essays, which were, as we have seen, also concerned with modern poetry. Second, there is a large body of writings on what is usually called the lyric, and what Winters himself preferred to call the short poem. The writing on various aspects of the short poem, whether the particular essay is concerned with the Elizabethans, with

149

Tuckerman, or with Valéry, resolves itself into a discussion of a single group of copiously illustrated problems: What is the short poem? How does it work? When is it successful? These questions are usually discussed in as absolute a fashion as possible; that is, Winters makes as little concession as he can to the time in which the poem was written. The *Weltanschauung* of the poet may be interesting as a source of his ideas, but his job as a poet remains, for Winters, constant, and the practice of Shakespeare is comparable to, say, that of Wallace Stevens. Winters's discussion of the short poem, in its various historical contexts, is therefore not merely for him an act of scholarship. It can be seen rather as a kind of poet's education. It is the work of a poet examining his models and peers, who are, for the purposes of his examination, his spiritual contemporaries. Winters does not traduce the past or attempt to reinterpret it from a twentieth-century point of view, rather he sees that certain problems—of form, content, emotion, meaning—are perennial, and he is, as a poet, naturally inquisitive to know how these problems have been approached by his predecessors. There is the further implication that he is making available to modern poets possibilities from the past which their own temporal provincialism—their sense that whatever is new is therefore better—has led them to overlook.

Third, there is a group of writings, largely contained in *Maule's Curse* (1938), on nineteenth-century American literature, both prose and verse. Here Winters is, almost obsessively, concerned with the history of ideas. His essays on Hawthorne, James, and Henry Adams all contain lengthy descriptions of the intellectual climate of nineteenth-century American civilization, particularly in its most self-conscious manifestation, that of New England. Many of the essays contain attacks on Emersonian romanticism; if we recall the nature of Winters's early poems, and his own diagnosis of their solipsism as being an unconscious expression of such romanticism (a solipsism which led him to the crisis through which he passed before turning to what we may call, for brevity's sake, reason and traditional form) we can understand that here again his criticism is serving, obliquely, the needs of the twentieth-century American poet. He considered that the metaphysical confusion in which poets of the early twentieth century, including himself, found themselves was a direct result of the similar confusions of their predecessors. His writings on nineteenth-century American literature are his attempt to explain this antecedent confusion and to understand how the major authors who experienced it either succumbed to it or were able to build up some strategy of survival. The vitiation of the Western intellectual tradition by romanticism is a major theme of Winters's criticism, whether he is considering eighteenth- and nineteenth-century English literature or nineteenth-century American literature, but it receives its most eloquent indictment in his diagnosis of the spiritual ills of New England. This is because, I believe, Winters saw himself and his contemporaries as the heirs of this confusion. It is no exaggeration to say that he held the writings of Emerson, Poe, and Adams to be responsible for the intellectual uncertainties (including his own) that he perceived in the writings of his contemporaries, and for the suicide of Hart Crane. In Winters's version of intellectual history he was able to save himself because he saw the romantic confusion for what it was—an invitation to abdicate the central integrity of the mind and plummet, like Melville's lookout drugged with his sense of the infinite, to death—whereas Crane was its dupe. His discussion of romanticism, particularly in its American manifestations, was therefore more than a matter of merely academic concern.

Winters and Babbitt

Winters's appraisal of romanticism, which varies from the irritated to the contemptuous to the horrified, was the result of deep personal conviction and, as has been indicated, can be traced to the experiences of his twenties. However there is also an external source for it, Irving Babbitt's *Rousseau and Romanticism*.

Apart from the passage in "The Critiad" devoted to him, Winters makes three fairly extensive references to Babbitt. The first and briefest is in his essay "Poetry, Morality, and Criticism," a contribution to *The Critique of Humanism: A Symposium* (1930). This essay is, for the greater part, a restatement of the ideas of "The Extension and Reintegration of the Human Spirit." Winters's main interest in the morality of poetry is here concentrated on "the spiritual control in a poem," which is "simply a manifestation of the spiritual control within the poet." Morality is seen as the result of an engagement with experience rather than as an abstract scheme imposed on it. As in "The Extension and Reintegration of the Human Spirit," one of Winters's chief exemplars of the attitude he is praising is Baudelaire, whose poetry Babbitt disliked. Though Winters praises Babbitt highly, he sees the latter's moral concern as "wisdom in a vacuum" ("Poetry, Morality, and Criticism," p. 331), an abstract scheme incapable of responding to the forms of spiritual control in which Winters was then interested. The second reference is in the essay on Henry Adams from *The Anatomy of Nonsense* (1943). Here *Rousseau and Romanticism* is called Babbitt's "most valuable book" (*In Defense of Reason*, p. 385); Winters then uses the quasi-Aristotelean Babbitt of this book as a stick with which to beat the later, more religious, and, to Winters, quasi-Emersonian Babbitt. The third reference is in the opening essay of *The Function of Criticism* (1957), "Problems for the Modern Critic of Literature." The passage is generally hostile in tone and is chiefly an account of how Winters's generation turned for literary guidance from Babbitt to Pound.

Despite the predominantly unsympathetic tone of these references, if we read *Rousseau and Romanticism* with Winters's later criticism in view we cannot fail to notice how deeply Babbitt's "most valuable book" impressed itself on Winters's mind. It is not merely a question of the ideas in the book but of the very tone and vocabulary used. In so far as external influences were operative rather than Winters's own experiences, it was this book which codified Winters's feelings about romanticism and which gave him the vocabulary and intellectual framework within which he could deal with the development of literature after the appearance of Lord Shaftesbury.

There are first Babbitt's descriptions of the genealogy, practice, and results of romanticism. Like Winters after him Babbitt saw Shaftesbury as the originator of many of the basic tenets of the romantic movement, and this led him to push its origins back to the beginning of the eighteenth century, so that he considered many of the authors of what is usually called the Age of Reason as essentially romantic, allied on the side of emotion and instinct against the primacy of reason. He refers to "the shallowness that I have noticed in the 'reason' of the eighteenth century" (*Rousseau and Romanticism*, p. 32) and says that "Pope . . . from the truly Classical point of view . . . is about as inadequate as Voltaire" (p. 33). In this judgment, as to the essential unreasonableness of much of the poetry of the Age of Reason (and the poetry not only of the protoromantics like Collins and Gray, but also of its chief representatives like Pope) Winters joins with Babbitt.

Babbitt was also impatient with a great deal of what is more generally accepted as romantic poetry, finding it imprecise in reference and prone to cultivate sensation for its own sake, and in this judgment too he is followed by Winters. Though it is true that the first decades of the twentieth century saw a critical turning away from romantics like Shelley and Byron, and that in their distaste for these poets' vague enthusiasms Babbitt and Winters were not isolated figures, nevertheless Babbitt's whole-hearted contempt for Blake and his suspicion of Wordsworth were more radically original judgments. Here he is on Blake: "Blake was a Romantic aesthete who was moving in his imaginative activity towards madness and seems at the end actually to have reached his goal" (*Rousseau and Romanticism*, p. 152), and on Wordsworth: "His assertion that the light of setting suns and the mind of man are identical in essence is at best highly speculative" (p. 286). The double condemnation in the sentence on Blake, of aestheticism and of madness as a desirable goal, is typical of both Babbitt and Winters after him—and Winters's later view of Blake was essentially identical to this. What is striking in the judgment on Wordsworth is the wry literalism with which Babbitt has read the more purple passages of romantic rhetoric. He demanded that their meaning be identifiable and, once identified, verifiable against man's reasonable experience of the world. Wordsworth's rhetoric blatantly appeals to another bar than that of rational definition, but Babbitt ignores the appeal and implies that it is illicit. In this literal reading of romantic rhetoric Babbitt is often echoed by Winters, and Winters's judgments frequently have the same mixture of stubborn literalism and slightly arch irony. A good example is his comment on the "Sandburgian mysticism" of Crane's poem "The River": "I believe that nothing save confusion can result from our mistaking the Mississippi Valley for God" (*In Defense of Reason*, p. 592). In the quotations from both Babbitt and Winters the literalness and irony are aimed at disentangling a romantic confusion between landscape and feelings of moral exaltation.

Babbitt's distaste for madness, and for extreme states of mind in general, is apparent from his remarks on Blake. One of the most direct statements of this attitude occurs in the introduction to *Rousseau and Romanticism*: "'All those who took the Romantic promises at their face-value,' says Bourget, 'rolled in abysses of despair and ennui.' If anyone still holds . . . that it is a distinguished thing to roll in abysses of despair and ennui, he should read me no further" (p. xvi). Here too we can note a tone echoed by Winters: it is more than a slight raising of scholarly eyebrows at the stupidity of the unregenerate (though it is at least that)—it is an implicit appeal from whatever is extreme, eccentric, and uncontrolled to the central, abiding, and ordered in human life, coupled with a washing of one's hands of those who cannot see that this is, per se, desirable. The same attitude appears in Winters's work as early as the "Notes on Contemporary Criticism" (1929): "If it be objected that there should be an end to a controlled and harmonious life, I answer that, if life is all we are given, a controlled and harmonious life is the only available end and its value should be self-evident" (*Uncollected Essays and Reviews*, p. 223).

Babbitt's basic objection to romanticism is stated on the first page of the main text of his book: "This inability or unwillingness to define may itself turn out to be only one aspect of a movement that from Rousseau to Bergson has sought to discredit the analytical intellect" (*Rousseau and Romanticism*, p. 1). And he goes on to stress "the importance of definition, especially in a chaotic era like the present." It is easy to overlook the importance of Babbitt's association of definition with the "analytical intellect" and therefore with abstract thought. For precision and definition were also rallying cries of the imagists, who saw themselves as turning away from the undefined enthusiasms of romanticism, but whose interest in the "analytical intellect" was minimal. Though in their search for clarity and a fidelity to the sense's—especially sight's—experience of the external world they were, in their own eyes, an alternative to romanticism, Babbitt saw them as but another version of romanticism, and in this he is again echoed by Winters in *Primitivism and Decadence*. The romanticism of delirium and the cooler romanticism of primitivism were, to Babbitt and Winters, but aspects of the same abandonment of rational definition as the guiding principle of man's relations with experience.

It is instructive to compare Babbitt's and Winters's uses of the words *primitivist* and *primitivism*. Here is Babbitt: "The primitivist means by 'nature' the spontaneous play of impulse and temperament . . . he inclines to look on reason . . . as the opposite of nature" (*Rousseau and Romanticism*, p. 38). With this definition in mind he refers to the "primitivistic trend of the eighteenth century" (p. 80). Winters's extensive use of the word *primitivism* in his major work on twentieth-century poetry, *Primitivism and Decadence*, at first sight differs from Babbitt's. He defines the primitive poets as "those who utilize all the means necessary to the most vigorous form, but whose range of material is limited" (*In Defense of Reason*, p. 90).

But in his example of William Carlos Williams, who, he writes, "is wholly incapable of coherent thought and . . . had not the good fortune to receive a coherent system as his birthright" we notice a similarity with Babbitt's definition, in that both are concerned with a shying away from reason and abstract thought. Babbitt's primitivist rejects abstract thought because it is "unnatural," and when Winters talks of a limited "range of material" he means limited by exactly this rejection of what is dependent on abstraction. That there is a fundamental unity of conception underlying Babbitt's and Winters's uses of the word *primitivism* should be clear from the following passage from *Rousseau and Romanticism*, a passage of which the later Winters would clearly have approved and which equates the primitivist and imagist: "If the Rousseauistic primitivist recognizes the futility of his symbolizing, and consents to become a register of outer perception, if for example he proclaims himself an imagist, he at least has the merit of frankness, but in that case he advertises by the very name he has assumed the bankruptcy of all that is most worthwhile in poetry" (p. 298).

Winters had begun his career as a poet as what I have termed a cool romantic—an imagist—but this primitivism, with its invitation to revery and trance, slipped imperceptibly towards the delirious romanticism of his contemporary and correspondent Hart Crane (such a descent is apparent in the poems of *The Proof*). Babbitt's refusal to see primitivism as anything but a version of romanticism, though it saw itself as an alternative to romanticism, must have corroborated Winters's own early experiences.

For Babbitt, and for Winters after him, the intellectual climate of modern (that is, early twentieth-century) American society was still predominantly romantic, and the state of contemporary poetry was evidence of this. They are clearly alarmed by their own diagnosis, and in both writers the alarm is chiefly for the deleterious effects they believe such notions to have on society. They search for some countervailing certainty, some rational bastion which would stem what Babbitt called "the pursuit of delirium, vertigo and intoxication for their own sake" (*Rousseau and Romanticism*, p. 180). Their alternatives to such a pursuit are very similar, being reducible to two basic ideas: the central importance of ethics (and therefore of the world as it exists separate from the individual's consciousness of it), and of an Aristotelean-based classicism.

Both authors show a simultaneous awareness of and irritation with the epistemological doubts of post-Cartesian philosophy; for both the existence of the outside world is indubitable (see Babbitt, *Rousseau and Romanticism*, pp. xiv–xvi, and Winters, *In Defense of Reason*, p. 407). Their concern is with the individual's relations with the external world whose existence he must accept and respect, what Babbitt calls "the problem of conduct." That is, their central concern is ethical, and both extend this concern to their understanding of the nature of poetry. As Babbitt wrote, "One needs, in short, to deal with both art and life from some ethical center" (p. 173), a claim frequently echoed by Winters (see, for example, *In Defense of Reason*, pp. 29, 505).

Man's experience of the world, for both Babbitt and Winters, involves him in ethical considerations, and this inevitably leads to the problem of a standard by which to evaluate experience. For both, the solution of the problem is unequivocal. Standards imply an absolute against which they can be measured. Babbitt declares himself an absolutist with apparent serenity; Winters does so with some discomfort, but unambiguously. Babbitt roundly declared that "all the ethical values of civilization have been associated with fixed beliefs" (p. xii). In "Notes on Contemporary Criticism" (1929) Winters seems to hope that he can minimize the need for divine authority: "That such an ethic is not parasitic upon religion is sufficiently demonstrated by the dependence of the Christian ethic upon the Greek systems, or at least by the unanimity of the Church, Aristotle, and in a measure the Stoics, upon most essential points" (*Uncollected Essays and Reviews*, p. 220). But in the opening essay of *In Defense of Reason* (1947), Winters admits that "my absolutism implies a theistic position, unfortunate as this admission may be" (p. 14).

Usually when philosophical or ethical questions are involved the name invoked by Winters is that of Aristotle (or his medieval follower, Aquinas)—and here too he is in agreement with Babbitt. Babbitt's use of Aristotle is involved with his concept of experience as the ultimate test of a theory's validity. His appeal is to what he calls "a general nature, a core of normal experience," which "according to Aristotle one is to get . . . not on authority . . . but is to disengage it directly for himself from the jumble of particulars he has before his eyes" (*Rousseau and Romanticism*, p. 17).

Two factors are important here: the appeal to experience and the concept of the significance of a central, shared humanity—a "classical" humanity—as the worthy object of the artist's concern (as against the extraordinary and eccentric experiences sought and celebrated by the romantic artist). An appeal to experience and a belief in absolutes that transcend the particulars of experience would seem to suggest a possible contradiction. The reconciliation, if it is one, is brought about by Babbitt's claim that experience reveals such a core of constant truth, what he calls "the universal." The perception of the universal is the achievement of "true classicism," which rests on "an immediate insight into the universal." Winters tends to avoid the word *classicism*, but his conclusions are the same. In a famous passage in the introduction to his last book, *Forms of Discovery*, he uses the analogy of breeding dogs to explain his position: "The breeders who devised the standard and created the breed, however, started with neither a perfect standard nor perfect specimens; they started with a general idea of what they wanted and a multiplicity of variously crude specimens with which to begin their breeding. One improves one's understanding of the general by examining the particular; one improves the particular by referring it to the general" (p. xiv). The universal is seen as a type towards which or away from which particular specimens tend. In this analogy, Winters, like Babbitt before him, is making a plea for an inherent absolute—the standard by which experience must be judged must itself be extrapolated from experience. This problem, whether standards necessarily imply a measure which is absolute and transcendent, or whether such a measure can somehow emerge from the judged material itself, is one that I do not think Winters ever managed to completely resolve for himself. For ethical purposes his analogy is clearly insufficient: the standards of a breed are arbitrary, fixed by human whim, which is exactly what absolute ethical standards (or absolute standards of any kind, such as, for example, those Winters wished to apply to poetry) by definition cannot be.

Babbitt's notion of a universal ("classical") humanity leads directly to his notion of decorum. A few quotations should clarify this:

> Decorum is in a way the peculiar doctrine of the classicist. [*Rousseau and Romanticism*, p. 22]

> To follow nature in the classical sense is to imitate what is normal and representative in man and so to become decorous. [p. 38]

> The hônnete homme . . . [was concerned] not with expressing himself . . . the first virtue in his eyes was a sense of proportion. [p. 54]

I have noted the preference apparent in Winters's poetry for just such a sense of proportion, of things in their just places, and of how frequently disaster in his poems is the result of the upsetting of such an equilibrium. Babbitt's contempt for artists who are primarily concerned with "expressing themselves" is shared by Winters, as in his gleeful retailing of the anecdote about a young girl who told her drawing master that if she drew as he wished she could not express her personality, to which the master replied that no one but mama was interested in her personality (*Function of Criticism*, p. 144).

Babbitt's classicism, and his rejection of the eccentric and willful, led him to a belief in "sound models" (*Rousseau and Romanticism*, p. 64), a belief constantly echoed by Winters. And such a belief was not merely a matter of poetry: "Mr. Babbitt stresses the moral effect of example at all social levels. This I believe to be sound" (*Uncollected Essays and Reviews*, p. 267).

A further result of Babbitt's belief in proportion, which had profound and far-reaching echoes throughout Winters's criticism, is his interest in "motivation." What he means by this should become clear in the following quotations: "The pursuit of the unrelated thrill without reference to its motivation"; "The disproportion between the outer incident and the emotion that the Rousseauist expends on it is often ludicrous" (*Rousseau and Romanticism*, pp. 58, 215). In the context of Babbitt's arguments these remarks indicate little more than a scholarly irritation that so much un-defined emotion should be presented to him as serious literature worthy of his critical attention, but in Winters's theories of what constitutes a good poem the ideas implicit in them—that there should be a justice and proportion between the motivating experiences and the emotion to which it gives rise—assume a central place. One of Winters's constant criticisms of romantic poetry is in essence Babbitt's: its sense of emo-tional proportion is untenable; the emotion implied, and in which we are asked to share, has been cultivated for its own sake, as what Babbitt calls "an unrelated thrill," rather than as a just response to a particular experi-ence. The culmination of such a reversal of the classical order (the emo-tion produced by an incident becomes much more important than an understanding of the incident) received, for Winters, its most ludicrous formulation in Eliot's, or Santayana's, idea of the "objective correlative," where the artist *begins* with an emotion and then casts about for a situa-tion to justify it.

The last aspect of Winters's debt to Babbitt to which I wish to draw attention is his adoption of elements of Babbitt's vocabulary and even, to some degree, his tone. This must in part be due to a similarity of basic outlook (a firm belief in the ethical nature of literature, a concern with civilized values as expressed in literature, and a related concern that a great deal of romantic literature seemed to betray those values). I have already remarked on their common use of the word *primitivism*, and there are other minor details which can be paralleled, such as their insistence on "sound models," but the similarity in many cases goes beyond this. There is in both Babbitt and Winters a distinctive sense of the moral re-sponsibilities of a writer, expressed by both in typically hortatory lan-guage. Babbitt speaks of "genuine spiritual effort," "spiritual or moral indolence" (*Rousseau and Romanticism*, pp. 150) and refers to some lines of Browning as "perhaps the most flaccid spiritually in the English lan-guage" (p. 287). This implied moral calisthenics cannot but be familiar to any reader of Winters's later criticism, in which Frost is referred to as "a spiritual drifter" and Sidney as "spiritually indolent." There is also Babbitt's anger, again an anger echoed by Winters, at those who confuse revery with meditation. Babbitt repeatedly distinguishes between the two, and Winters adopts the distinction (see *Rousseau and Romanticism*, pp. 289, 342, 349, and Winters's *In Defense of Reason*, p. 491). As one would expect, both authors prefer the discipline of meditation to the laxity of revery. Their distrust of revery has a common source, a suspicion of any activity that threatens the conscious will, a fear of underlying anarchy. In a passage extraordinarily similar to many moments of Winters's criticism, Babbitt can only deplore "any . . . surrender to the sub-rational . . . any such encroachment of the powers of the unconscious upon conscious control" (p. 270).

Winters's debt to Babbitt is on any showing extensive: he echoed Babbitt's genealogy of romanticism, and his view of the Age of Reason as essentially romantic; he read romantic texts with a literalism that wittily deflated their vatic claims; he appealed to a central and abiding humanity rather than the extremes and eccentricities of romanticism; he rejected primitivism—and therefore imagism—as a romantic stance; he diagnosed most modern poetry as being essentially romantic despite its contrary claims; he gave a central importance to ethical questions, and he worried about the location of the absolutes that his ethical concerns implied; he echoed Babbitt's critical vocabulary and tone. A few such resemblances could be considered coincidental but their accumulation indicates a direct influence. However, this influence did not preclude substantial differences between their views. Babbitt professed a distaste for romantic subject matter per se and implicitly demanded that the writer turn his back on it. Winters with more profound insight understood the all but overwhelming attractions of romanticism and was most impressed by those modern writers whom he considered able to face and evaluate these attractions. The difference is clearest in their evaluation of Baudelaire: for Winters he was one of the greatest poets of the last two hundred years; for Babbitt he was little more than a degenerate.

A further divergence between the two is Winters's disdain for the notion—central to Babbitt's thought—of an "inner check" as a guide to conduct. This was an intuitive mechanism that, if attended to, would guide its possessor toward right action, somewhat like Socrates' daimon. Winters saw the guide to right action as conscience and pointed out that "when Aquinas comes to define conscience, he identifies it with reason" (*In Defense of Reason*, p. 386). He considered Babbitt's intuitive substitute for reason as a form of sentimentality, and commented that "Babbitt's final position seems to be little better than a starting point for a short-cut back to Emersonian mysticism" (p. 386). And he had little respect for Babbitt's response to poetry. Though he continued to admire him as a historian of ideas, his attitude to Babbitt's abilities as a guide to poetic worth is summed up in his essay "Problems for the Modern Critic of Literature": "But for the young men of my generation Babbitt was the professor in person: the other professors were an indistinguishable crowd. And Babbitt had a way of saying stupid things about great poems: so we looked elsewhere for enlightenment" (*Function of Criticism*, p. 12). Babbitt's criticism seeks an overall view and moves towards historical generalizations. This is its strength, and it is these generalizations which were useful to Winters, but Winters was also looking for an informed and intelligent response to the texts of individual poems, which he did not find in Babbitt. He had to look elsewhere for sensitivity to poetic texture. The sentence that follows the above quotation reads, "We found our enlightenment in Ezra Pound."

Winters and Pound

Winters's chief critical debts to Pound are more a matter of manner and approach than of substance, and though stylistic traits traceable to Pound's influence persist throughout his prose they are most noticeable in the earliest work. The taxonomic slant of essays like "The Testament of a Stone" (1924) and "Notes on Contemporary Criticism" (1929) was probably learned from Pound, as was the allied habit of writing in extremely succinct and dogmatic paragraphs. Less definable but no less obvious is a similarity of tone—a general aura of pugnacity and ex cathedra omniscience, combined with an impatience with those who disagree. Pound's vocabulary, his (at the time) idiosyncratic mixing of linguistic registers (since imitated ad nauseam) was not of course adopted by Winters. But there is one aspect of his verbal usage that does find echoes in Winters's prose; this is the use of extremely (for critics committed, as these two were, to "clarity and precision") vague epithets of approbation and condemnation used liberally and without definition: words like *good* and *beautiful* abound in the criticism of both authors, and what exactly is meant by them is left to the reader to divine as best he can from the general thrust of the criticism. The trait is persistent in Pound's prose; in Winters it is chiefly confined to the earlier criticism. They appear to have given approximately the same value to *beautiful*, both of them assigning it to works of a certain kind of beauty—delicate, fin de siècle, slightly precious, what Pound called Chinese. As an indication of Rémy de Gourmont's "sense of beauty" Pound uses the sentence, "The mist clings to the lacquer," and it is this kind of evocation that both he and the early Winters characterize as beautiful (*Literary Essays of Ezra Pound*, p. 343).

The preoccupation with the clear and precise so characteristic of the literary theorists of the earlier part of this century seems to have been started, in English-speaking countries at least, by Pound; he himself traces it to a comment of Stendhal on the virtues of prose (virtues which Pound was attempting to reintroduce into poetry): good prose, Stendhal claimed, can give "*une idée claire et précise des mouvements du coeur*" (*Literary Essays of Ezra Pound*, p. 54). But we should distinguish between different kinds of clarity and precision. Despite the subjective implications of the Stendhal quotation, for Pound these qualities were chiefly the means of representing the visible world clearly, for the vivid reproduction of surface and appearance (from such a representation internal responses may result, but this is a subsequent event). His distrust of abstract language ("Go in fear of abstractions" [p. 5]) seems to have been based on the notion that such language cannot be as precise as language that refers directly to the physical world.

Though Winters echoed this distrust in the reviews of his early twenties, his later position on the place of abstract language in poetry was fundamentally opposed to Pound's. Indeed, the more abstract the language of a poem was, other things being equal, the more likely the later Winters was to approve of it. For Winters clarity meant above all clarity of *thought*, and only secondarily clarity of representation, which was Pound's concern. Nevertheless there is a common root to their attitudes, if only in what they were opposed to, that is, the undefined and excessively emotional, the pervasive *Weltschmerz* of so much late Victorian poetry. The gist of the following passage from Pound's *A Retrospect* (1918) is something one can imagine Winters wholeheartedly agreeing to: "As to twentieth century poetry . . . it will, I think, move against poppy-cock, it will be harder and saner. . . . It will be as much like granite as it can be, its force will lie in its truth. . . . At least for myself, I want it so, austere, direct, free from emotional slither" (p. 12). Hardness and sanity are qualities we associate with Winters's own crusades, as is the insistence on truth as a criterion for poetic force. Both writers believed that poetry was good only in so far as it concerned itself with the presentation of some

form of objective truth and was bad in so far as it drifted away from or
veiled in heady language that presentation. When Pound writes, "One
moves the reader only by clarity" (*A Retrospect*, p. 22), we can again presume Winters's agreement, but we should remember that their definitions of clarity did not quite overlap.

But Winters's chief debt to Pound is in his use of the past, his approach
to the literatures of previous centuries (and of other cultures). Pound's
attitude to the past was perhaps unique at the time, and Winters certainly
learned a great deal from it.

First, neither critic was any great respecter of reputations, and both
harbored a strong suspicion of the epic narrative, as a form lending itself
to ungainly pomposities and sleights of hand, and of the drama as being a
radically impure form. Both saw themselves as something of a new
broom (and this involved an appeal to their own experience as the test of
a poem's truth), an overhauler of the literary canon and an establisher of a
new canon based on new criteria. This suggests the creation of an idiosyncratic tradition, and both writers provided one. (The traditions overlap in some areas—a rejection of much nineteenth-century poetry, for
example—but diverge in others; Pound preferred the Petrarchans to the
plain stylists among the Elizabethans, and Winters did not share Pound's
enthusiasm for a great deal of medieval verse).

Pound's wholly ahistorical attitude to literature was connected with his
establishment of a new and personal tradition: he deliberately juxtaposed
poems from quite different times and cultures (for example, Arnaut
Daniel and the Greek Anthology) and claimed to perceive not only similar qualities in the poems' textures but, by implication, a similarity of intention and attitude on the part of the poets concerned. All poetry is seen
as theoretically contemporary. Winters's juxtapositions are less flam-
boyant (he will, for example, compare a poem by a sixteenth-century author with one by a modern author) but he does make use of the same
technique. Most important, he explicitly rejects the idea that a writer
must be so conditioned by his historical milieu and culture as to render
any such comparison meaningless. Like Pound he sees the strategies and
concerns of past poets as being available and significant to the modern
writer, and arguments as to the difference of environment fail to impress
him; he rejects all notion of historical determinism. This ahistoricism is
of course in sharp contrast with Babbitt's historicist approach to literature, which, as I have indicated, also influenced Winters. He extracts
himself from the dilemma by insisting that if a poet becomes conscious of

the forces that are molding him he can understand those forces and, by reason and will, emancipate himself from them. He considered his own relation to the romanticism which he believed destroyed Hart Crane to be an example of such emancipation.

Pound, and Winters after him, saw criticism as a process of selection according to defined criteria (Pound justifies the procedure etymologically [*A Retrospect*, p. 30]) which were held to be operative irrespective of historical pressures. These criteria also operated as a means of selecting within the oeuvre of a given author. Both critics can adopt a remarkably superior tone to the authors whom they praise; neither, having approved of one work by a writer, will trust that writer when their own taste rebels. Pound selects fairly drastically within the work of Henry James, for example, (like Winters after him he is suspicious of the later novels) and justifies his action thus: "The laziness of an uncritical period can be nowhere more blatant than in the inherited habit of talking about authors as a whole" (p. 304). His comments on Shelley could be echoed, with suitable substitutions, by many judgments of Winters on other poets: "Shelley's 'Sensitive Plant' is one of the rottenest poems ever written . . . yet Shelley recovered and wrote the fifth act of *The Cenci*" (p. 51). And he even carried the method into the texts of particular poems: "Surely among poems containing a considerable amount of beauty, this is one of the worst ever written" (p. 51). In this too he was followed by Winters.

Selection within an author's work, high praise for some parts and fairly comprehensive damnation for others, led Pound to make lists of what he thought were the most important poems, that is, the ones that fitted his criteria of excellence. Winters also made such lists (the criteria differ but the lists occasionally overlap; for example, they both praise Mark Alexander Boyd's single surviving sonnet very highly), and this is his most noticeable tactical debt to Pound. Both writers place their emphasis on the quality of specific works rather than on the personality of the author or on the interest of the individual vision presented by his works as a whole; neither uses psychological interest to justify what he considers as minor aspects of a writer's oeuvre (though Winters does use details of personal life to explain an author's preoccupations—for example, in his book on Robinson). Poetry rather than poets is their interest, and this arises in part from a shared distaste for the romantic cult of the artistic personality.

A concentration on the works of art themselves, rather than on the psyche of the artist, led Pound to emphasize questions of technique rather than psychological imponderables, and this in turn led to the suggestion that the modern poet bear in mind certain "models"—and here he was in agreement with Winters's other mentor, Babbitt. Both Winters and Pound frequently appear to be writing their criticism largely for the benefit of would-be poets, directing the neophyte's attention to what they take to be excellent. The careers of both were largely propaganda for the type of poetry they admired, even down to the writing of their own verse, which occasionally seems to exist less as verse pure and simple than as a series of examples of its writer's principles. The critical gift they shared, one that cannot be learned from another, is the ability to direct us to previously ignored (or relegated to minor status) poems of great power and freshness; and it is interesting that though both were finally men concerned with modern poetry, their most spectacular rediscoveries of English verse were in the Elizabethan period—Pound's championing of the Elizabethan classical translators, and Winters's of the plain stylists.

Apart from the less easily definable (because he left no book) influence of Briggs, Babbitt and Pound were the two authors who were most useful to Winters in the elaboration of his intellectual position—Babbitt largely by his diagnosis of the nature of romanticism, Pound by the example of his critical method. He also adopted one or two hints from elsewhere. He took over, for example, I. A. Richard's terminology in discussing metaphor (tenor and vehicle), a terminology since used by many critics. And his analysis of nineteenth-century American literature owed a considerable amount to the work of the historian H. B. Parkes; this will be discussed in the appropriate section.

Winters's later criticism, by which I mean that written during and after the 1930s, is fairly constant in its concerns and judgments. Two related interests dominate his critical writings: the nature of poetic technique and the definition of a particular kind of subject matter and of different writers' attitudes toward this subject matter.

His concern with poetic technique is clearly connected with his own technical experiments during his twenties and his subsequent conversion to traditional poetic form. Behind all his writings on poetry there is the sense of Winters himself, as a poet, testing the poetry he reads, of whatever age, against his own needs and understanding of the nature of poetry. As he wrote in *The Function of Criticism*, "The poet, as poet, tries to write as well as possible . . . he reads other poets as he reads himself, to discover what is really sound, to discover what might be improved, and in this way to improve his own intelligence and composition" (p. 22).

His mature view of the nature of poetry is implicit in all his later writing; it is given explicit definition in his essay "Problems for the Modern Critic of Literature" (1956; reprinted in *The Function of Criticism*, 1957): "Let me repeat first of all the assumption on which I invariably proceed as a critic. I believe that a poem . . . is a statement in words about a human experience. . . . In each work there is a content which is rationally apprehensible, and each work endeavors to communicate the emotion which is appropriate to the rational apprehension of the subject. The work is thus a judgement, rational and emotional, of the experience" (p. 26).

A poem, then, is concerned with the understanding and judgment of experience. The primary act of poetry is one of rational understanding (in the above brief quotation the word *rational* and its derivative *rationally* appear three times); the emotion involved in a poem is a subsequent result of such an apprehension—it is the emotion "appropriate" to our understanding of the truth with which the poem deals. Discussing, in 1939, the plain style of certain Elizabethan poets, he wrote, "The wisdom of poetry of this kind lies not in the acceptance of a truism, for anyone can accept a truism, at least formally, but in the realization of the truth of the truism; the realization resides in the feeling, the style" ("Sixteenth Century Lyric," pp. 95–96).

The mention of wisdom implicitly suggests that wisdom is something which should be intimately connected with poetry—an assumption that involves us in just those areas of understanding, and the personal acceptance of understanding, which Winters considered to be the particular goal of poetry. To apprehend the direction of his concern one has only to contrast this assumption of the centrality of wisdom with the two other main contending theories of the first half of this century's American criticism—that poetry should seek chiefly to render the appearance of the world cleanly and clearly (as with the imagists) or that it should be "dramatic" (as with Eliot's reading of metaphysical poetry). The aims of the imagists Winters saw as legitimate but circumscribed: their lack of interest in, indeed their hostility toward, universals, their reduction of reality to a succession of discrete particulars, appeared an abdication of that "rage for order" that is man's distinctive intellectual need. He therefore saw the movement, with Babbitt, as a species of primitivism. The desire for the dramatic he considered as an invitation to confusion; for Winters poetry, implying wisdom, involved judgment: dramatic verse, with its cultivation of the eccentric and distinctive voice and its illusion of immediacy, deliberately narrows the gap between the observer and the observed—it has as its *aim* the presentation of reality through an obsessive distorting emotion, so that the reader's attention is focused more on the quirks of the speaker's rhetoric than on his supposed subject. The blurring of speaker and subject in this way precludes any notion of evaluation or understanding intervening between the apprehension of reality and its emotional expression. (This was to be the main reason for Winters's distrust of the drama as a form, as will appear later).

In what way does Winters's idea of a poem differ from its truth, from its paraphrasable content? The answer is contained in the word *realization* in the above quotation. Winters uses the word in its literal sense of "making real"; the truism is made real for the writer (he understands it, in the usual sense of realize), and he then has to make it real for the reader. It is the ability to make it real for the reader, so that he intellectually and emotionally understands and accepts the precise truth of what is stated, that is the mark of the great poet. And this making it real does not lie in the author's drawing attention to his own emotions about the subject (as in so much romantic poetry, in which the poet's emotional response to his subject tends to outweigh in significance the subject itself, or in which emotion is presented pure and simple, unmotivated by any subject), but in simply directing the reader's intellectual and emotional attention toward the reality that is to be conveyed. The emotion is attendant on understanding; it is not a substitute for understanding. For Winters great poetry points to some important truth of the human condition, and its language brings this truth home to the reader, so that the reader internalizes it, so that his being is modified by its apprehension. The emotions attendant on the acceptance of this truth will be there of themselves, and the poet need only suggest, by the subtlest of rhetorical means, the direction or appearance of such emotion. Emotional overemphasis ("dramatic" speech) or decoration that obliterates what is being decorated can only blur the essential apprehension by distracting the reader with irrelevance.

Winters admitted that such rhetorical effects, indicative of the "appropriate" emotion attendant on the understanding of the truth which is the poem's subject, were extremely difficult to describe or discuss ("Rhythm, for reasons which I do not wholly understand, has the power of communicating emotion" [*In Defense of Reason*, p. 12]). Nevertheless he claimed they were real, and that they constituted a large part of the unique efficacy of poetry. Much of *Forms of Discovery*, his last critical work, is given over to discussions of meter; this was because he believed that meter was the principal way in which such a "making it real" could be effected by the poet. (Though he did allow a place for imagery, it was a far smaller place than that accorded it by most other modern critics; he delighted in pointing out that certain universally admired poems—such as Wyatt's "Blame Not My Lute"—contain virtually no images at all and that their rhetorical power must therefore depend on something other than imagery). We should also recall that in the mid 1960s (when *Forms of Discovery* was written) few American poets were interested in the possibilities of traditional meter, and his analyses were probably meant as—in part—an admonition to consider a strategy then largely ignored.

The particular area of subject matter which engaged Winters's attention is more difficult to define, but it is clearly recognizable to anyone familiar with his mature poetry. He was especially moved by works of literature that recognized man's unique position as an isolated rational consciousness in a universe "vast, chaotic and impersonal beyond his power of formulation or imagination." This universe is seen as indifferent, or demonically menacing, threatening to engulf man in its impersonal processes—it is a view remarkably close to that of Manicheism, which saw the physical universe as wholly inimical to the life of the spirit. (One should remember, though, the ambivalent nature of the evidence in Winters's own poetry of his attitude towards the natural world). The destructive process that Winters identifies most readily in the writings of those authors with whose work he expresses a critical sympathy is time, and the end toward which time carries individual lives—death. Further, he demands of those writers whose work he finds most intellectually coherent and satisfying that they acknowledge the "absolute cleavage" between the life of man—or at any rate his spiritual and mental life—and that of the physical world. Any attempt to overcome this cleavage he views with profound suspicion, seeing it as an attempt to subvert the intellect, which lives only by the maintenance of its independence from the flux of time and physical life. Nevertheless, the intellect and spirit are embodied in individuals who are subject to time and death—and this is their tragedy. The spirit in man cannot emancipate itself from time and can therefore never participate in or apprehend the purposes of God, who is pure spirit; the Jansenist notion of a *dieu caché* who imposes moral obligation but is inconceivable, distant, and never immanent in human affairs appears, at least in his later life, to have greatly attracted Winters, and he shows a deep sympathy with authors (for example, Valéry) in whose work he perceives such notions. Man's ignorance of his true state and of the nature of metaphysical truth, coupled with a strong ethical sense and a deep psychological need for moral certainty in a cha-

otic world are concerns evident in the works of literature Winters particularly admired, whether they be by Elizabethan authors like Jonson and
Greville, nineteenth-century authors like Dickinson and Melville, or
modern authors like Stevens and Valéry. He had little time for writers
who seem never to have wished to address themselves to such problems,
who seem free of all metaphysical anxiety and who therefore cannot see
the need for that wary stoicism which Winters's writings, whether in
verse or prose, implicitly recommend.

The area of subject matter which interested him perhaps more than any
other is man's apprehension of that "absolute cleavage" between his own
intellectual being and that of the physical universe. As the evidence of his
own poetry (and of his short story *The Brink of Darkness*) indicates, he
was himself acutely conscious of this cleavage and the, to him, absolute
necessity of maintaining it. He believed that a great deal of nineteenth-
century literature, particularly American literature, had as its avowed aim
the destruction by one means or another of the chasm between man and
the world as it exists over against his mind—a destruction he could only
view as an invitation to insanity or suicide (or both). His critical writings
on the works of this period were therefore far more than the academic
definition of the nature of a particular area of literary activity. They were
the diagnosis of a spiritual malaise from which, he believed, American
literary culture still suffered. I shall therefore begin my discussion of
Winters's attitudes toward specific writers and their works with an examination of his criticism of nineteenth-century literature.

Winters's Critical Writings on Nineteenth-Century Literature

If we look through *Quest for Reality*, the anthology of poetry Winters edited shortly before his death, we find that there is not a
single poet represented between Charles Churchill (1731–64) and Jones
Very (1813–80), and there is not a single British poet between Churchill
and Thomas Hardy (1840–1928). Blake, Keats, Shelley, Byron, Wordsworth, and Coleridge are all absent. *Quest for Reality* represents Winters's last public thoughts on the subject, but his criticism conveys the
same general impression of impatience with the authors of the early nineteenth century (with the possible exception of Landor). Indeed, the British representatives of romanticism are hardly mentioned in his critical

writings; out of sympathy with the intellectual (or, as Winters would have said, antiintellectual) preconceptions of their work, he remained largely unmoved by their rhetoric—though occasionally (less frequently as he grew older) he was willing to admit that the work of, for example, Blake or Keats indicated a high natural talent for poetry. Typical is his treatment of Wordsworth in *Forms of Discovery*; parts of the "Ode to Duty" are praised, as are the concluding lines of the sonnet "Mutability," though the rest of the poem is treated with derision. These two poems appear to have been singled out for partial praise as much for their Wintersian subject matter as for their language, the "Ode to Duty" for its implicit stoicism and the sonnet because it treats of the destructive effects of time in exactly the manner Winters found sympathetic. By the time he wrote *Forms of Discovery* the insights of the criticism of the 1930s had tended to become somewhat ossified. It is a far less open and generous book than its predecessors and many poets are demoted from the positions Winters had previously accorded them; nevertheless its treatment of Wordsworth and his fellow British romantics is basically that which could be deduced from any of Winters's critical writings.

But the romanticism of American literature he took far more seriously, largely because he felt himself to be living in a milieu still corrupted by its writings and beliefs. His own flirtation with romantic pantheism, which he took to be the peculiarly American form of romanticism, had been conducted when he still lived under the threat of tuberculosis, and it is possible that the physical disintegration of the disease was, on some level of his mind, associated with what he took to be the spiritual disintegration of the doctrine. What terrifies Winters in his later poetry is a sense of the self's dissolution, and he saw romantic pantheism as an invitation to just such a dissolution. When we consider that he suffered from both "diseases" at the same time—his teens and early twenties—the parallel with the physical process of the disease is compelling.

His view of Emerson is fundamental to his writings on nineteenth-century American literature. He wrote of Emerson, "In Emerson the terms of New England mysticism and of Romantic amoralism were fused and confused so inextricably that we have not yet worked ourselves free of them" (*In Defense of Reason*, p. 173). The reference to a modern dependence on Emerson's ideas is in itself significant—his attack on Emerson was meant as an attack on something still vital. He located the two sources of Emerson's thought in "Romantic amoralism" and "New England mysticism." His views on the origins of romanticism and its attendant "amoralism" were largely those of Babbitt; his views on "New

England mysticism" are repeated throughout his study of nineteenth-century American literature, *Maule's Curse*, and elsewhere (in *Maule's Curse* they occur in the essays on Hawthorne, Melville, and Henry James; they also appear in the essay on Henry Adams from *The Anatomy of Nonsense*, and in his book on Robinson). This extensive repetition is some indication of how seriously Winters took the matter.

Winters's critical forte was the close examination of individual texts. He also had a considerable flair for explicating the preconceptions that lie behind a particular text, but when discussing the origins of such ideas he tended to trust other authorities; we have seen his dependance on Babbitt for his analysis of the intellectual origins of romanticism. For his analysis of the history of New England thought he was indebted to the scholar H. B. Parkes, as he made abundantly clear (he called him "a writer to whom I am more deeply indebted than I can indicate in any series of footnotes" [*In Defense of Reason*, p. 268]).

Winters's debt to Parkes

H. B. Parkes was an Englishman who emigrated to America in 1927, when he was twenty-three. He made a study of American history, concentrating particularly on the religious background. Winters mentioned Parkes's book *The Pragmatic Test* (1941) as a major source for his own characterization of nineteenth-century American thought, and in particular cited the first two essays of this volume, "The Puritan Heresy" and "Emerson." Both essays had appeared in *Hound and Horn* while Winters was the western regional editor of the magazine; the issue that contained the essay on Emerson also contained Winters's story *The Brink of Darkness*, his most emphatic rejection of the Emersonian invitation to relax the limits of the conscious self.

That Winters was deeply impressed by Parkes's analysis of American Puritanism is apparent from the number of times he returned to it: it is explicitly cited in the essays on Emerson and Hawthorne and is the obvious source for the discussions of Puritanism in the essays on Henry James and Henry Adams. He cited other works as sources for some of his facts, but his interpretation of those facts followed Parkes's work closely. Parkes's analysis bears much the same relation to Winters's writings on the American nineteenth century as Babbitt's analysis of romanticism bears to Winters's criticism of that movement. It was the framework by which he ordered his material.

Describing his approach, in the introduction to *The Pragmatic Test*, Parkes wrote: "I endeavored to use the philosophy of the Catholic Church as a standard by which to judge the other varieties of Christianity. . . . I still believe that the best way of understanding Puritanism is to examine how it deviated from Catholicism" (p. 3). This was Winters's approach, too, and it may well have been what led him to find Parkes's version of this phase of the history of ideas sympathetic, as it was only a short time before the appearance of Parkes's essays in *Hound and Horn* that Winters had, at Briggs's suggestion, undertaken his study of Aquinas. The introduction contains other ideas and attitudes that are typical of Winters, for example, an insistence that "philosophical beliefs exercise a pervasive (and often harmful) influence upon conduct . . . this influence is apt to be especially important when its effects are not consciously recognized." Like Winters, Parkes argued that man's goal is "the extension of consciousness and the exercise of control . . . the development of reason and will." Most important, both men shared the supposition that the Puritan experiment had been a massive intellectual mistake whose deleterious results were still apparent, not least of which was the discounting of the importance of reason and will.

Parkes was chiefly concerned with the development of the Puritan doctrine as such, and Winters with its legacy to American nineteenth-century thought. Winters was therefore interested less in Parkes's reconstructions of the historical movements of Puritanism (though he did allude to them) than in those strands of Puritan doctrine which became, imperceptibly, the received opinions, the folk wisdom, of the nineteenth century. Like Parkes he was of the opinion that beliefs which were hardly consciously held at all, that were a habitual reflex of mind, had a "pervasive (and often harmful) influence." The beliefs that he considered the Puritans had bequeathed to American intellectual life were so pervasive as to be considered axiomatic, and in Winters's terms definitely harmful.

If we omit Parkes's (extremely interesting) analysis of the historical development of religious thought in America and concentrate on those habits of mind which he believed Puritanism and its offshoots fostered, we arrive at the following list: "a refusal to accept authority; a tendency to obey impulse as the voice of God; a worship of enthusiasm; a willingness to fancy that perfection was not impossible in this world; a belief that the will was bound and that the soul was a mere bundle of reactions" ("Puritan Heresy," p. 190). The refusal to accept authority was not merely the refusal to accept an external authority (the sole law was "the Spirit's secret witness" in the heart of the believer) but also a refusal to accept the authority of human reason, called by Luther "the whore of the devil." As neither reason nor any other kind of external standard could be appealed to, "each inhabitant of New England believed that he knew God's will; and the annals of its parishes are an unending series of quarrels. . . . every man was his own pope" (p. 177). The identification of "the Spirit's secret witness" with impulse was a slow process completed by the transcendentalists. It resulted in the deification of emotion and a further denigration of reason. Emphasis on emotion naturally led to a "worship of enthusiasm" and again a suspicion of reason's distinctions.

Parkes further showed how those who believed that they belonged to the elect took the view that being saved they could not sin; from being a religion emphasizing man's degeneration the later versions of Puritanism gave the elect ethical carte blanche; all their impulses were from God and therefore good. Finally, Calvin's absolute insistence on predestination meant that the human will was powerless. If the will is powerless and intuition is the voice of God, it is foolish and sinful for man to attempt to follow either reason or will. Parkes was careful to indicate that all these beliefs were not held at once—and that some of them were apparently contradicted by the believers' actions (Winters pointed out that a great deal of Puritan energy went into exhorting men to repent while Puritan theology, believing all events to be predestined and the will to be impotent, held that repentance was impossible); but the list represents what he considered was the legacy of "unconscious" Puritanism to nineteenth-century American thought.

Winters followed Parkes closely in his characterization of the background of American intellectual life during this period; if we examine this characterization it is not difficult to see why, with his already-recorded regard for reason and the conscious will, he found American authors' work of this period either vitiated by these ideas or able to achieve distinction only by a determined rejection of them.

I wrote above that the subject which almost more than any other engaged Winters's interest was the "absolute cleavage" between man's intellectual being and the physical universe. The problem presents itself in different guises—as a split between man and nature, between the mind and the world, between meaning and experience. In his criticism Winters frequently implies that the problem is perennial (he locates it in Shakespeare's work, for example) but he certainly considered it to be peculiarly acute in nineteenth-century American literature. He believed that the habit of mind encouraged by the Puritanism Parkes described encour-

aged men to hope that this "cleavage" could be overcome by a surrender
to impulse which would dissolve the hitherto-isolated self in some undefined pantheist All. This was the attitude of Emerson and his disciples
(like Whitman); it was naturally, given his beliefs, anathema to Winters.
He saw writers like Hawthorne and Henry James as struggling with a
different aspect of the same problem—the relation of meaning to experience. Two writers, Herman Melville and Emily Dickinson, he considered, in their best work, to have approached the problem in a spirit he
found both sympathetic and laudable.

Emerson

Winters's interest in Emerson went back to his adolescence. Emerson
was the author who confirmed in him, if confirmation were necessary,
those solipsistic and quasi-pantheist feelings by which he felt assailed in
his youth. For both Parkes and Winters Emerson displayed in a singularly unadulterated form most of the traits listed by Parkes as being typical of the Puritan legacy.

Both writers, in describing Emerson as a transcendentalist, agreed on
the origins of his ideas. Parkes described transcendentalism as "Edwar-
dean [that is, deriving from Jonathan Edwards] Calvinism modified by
European Romanticism" ("Puritan Heresy," p. 186), and Winters echoed
this doctrine with specific reference to Emerson: "Emerson took the essential doctrines of European Romanticism and restated them in terms of
Edwardian Calvinism" (*Uncollected Essays and Reviews*, p. 291).

There was agreement too in the conviction that Emerson's trust in impulse as a sure guide to conduct was a result of the fact that his own acts
"were qualified by tradition for he was the descendant of a line of clergy-
men, and his character had been formed by the society which they and
their kind had formed, so that his impulses were no doubt virtuous" (*In
Defense of Reason*, p. 267). Both men saw him as destroying the tradition
which had formed him; Parkes concluded that "the whole tendency of his
philosophy was to destroy the tradition in which virtues such as his own
could be cultivated" ("Emerson," p. 581). Winters was typically tren-
chant, writing that Emerson and his like were "moral parasites upon a
Christian doctrine they were endeavoring to destroy" (*In Defense of Reason*, p. 587).

Winters was hardly interested in Emerson's work itself; his discussion
of the texture of his writings, as against the ideas contained in them, is

virtually nil. Rather his concern was with Emerson's influence on other writers. It is noteworthy that his most contemptuous and lengthy attack on Emerson appeared in his last essay on Hart Crane (in which he makes him virtually responsible for Crane's suicide) and that this is closely followed in strength of feeling by the references in the essay on T. S. Eliot where Emerson's work is taken as the archetypal expression of the "mystical determinism" he found so distasteful in Eliot's criticism.

He apparently found the whole tissue of Emerson's work an unpleasant mess, but attention is drawn to three particular Emersonian doctrines: the surrender to impulse, the denial of the efficacy and worth of reason and will (the "mystical determinism" of the essay on Eliot) and the doctrine of pantheistic mysticism. The first two are the obverse and reverse of the same doctrine, and for Winters were merely the logical result of the romanticism that had been slowly gaining ground in Europe and elsewhere since the time of Shaftesbury; "exactly the same conclusions are deducible from the 'Essay on Man'" (*In Defense of Reason*, p. 55). The surrender to impulse led to moral relativism, or what Parkes memorably referred to as the state in which "every man was his own pope." But the notion that aroused Winters's intensest opposition was the last mentioned—"pantheistic mysticism."

The reason is not far to seek. The doctrine had been his own during his adolescence and early twenties, encouraged, as he tells us, by his own temperament (and presumably by the tenor of his youthful reading). That destruction of the barriers between the observing subject and observed object which is the recognizable goal of his earliest imagist verse, and which is recommended in his early prose, was an attempt to participate in the pantheistic trance that is Emerson's constant theme. He came, for whatever personal reasons, to view such experiments with profound distrust: he saw them as a spiritual suicide, and Crane's literal suicide was mere confirmation for him of where such beliefs led. For Winters the invitation to revery, an invitation repeatedly extended by Emerson, was a flirtation with an undefined destructive power he did not hesitate to call demonic. The peculiarly American version of romanticism, the Emersonian version, was, according to Winters, one that saw the dissolution of individual existence as desirable. Winters had taken these ideas seriously in his youth, and had seen his contemporary and fellow poet succumb to them. He himself had drawn back, but he had felt the attractive power of the romantic invitation to annihilation. It is because he had experienced the attraction that he was so vehement in his denunciation of it. If the criticism of his thirties (almost everything he wrote on Emerson was written during this period) is to be read, as I believe it is, largely as a self-created bastion against those forces he characterized as demonic, the intensity of his dislike for Emerson's doctrines and their influence is not surprising. For Emerson had characterized as benevolent and desirable precisely those areas of experience Winters feared and shunned.

An interesting footnote to Winters's view of Emerson is his championing of the work of the neglected poet Jones Very. He finds in Very's poetry the corrective to Emerson. Very *appears* to experience nature in much the same way as Emerson, but Winters is at pains to distinguish their attitudes: Very's God is ultimately distinguishable from Very himself, he is transcendent, whereas Emerson's God is nebulously immanent, indistinguishable from Emerson's impulses: "The gulf between Emerson and Very if not wide was yet immeasurably profound. . . . Emerson tried to explain to Very that truth is relative, and Very tried to point out to Emerson that truth is absolute" (*In Defense of Reason*, p. 270). Emerson's invitations to pantheistic revery are not mysticism in Very's sense: "He had no mystical life to give . . . he never experienced that which he recommended" (p. 279). This was also Parkes's view—he called Emerson "a pseudo-mystic" ("Emerson," p. 588). Very did not proselytize and Emerson did. Winters called him "the most influential preacher to appear in America after Edwards" (*In Defense of Reason*, p. 268); Very was "at core . . . a saint" whereas Emerson was "at the core . . . a fraud and a sentimentalist" (p. 279). If we recall Winters's essay on Hart Crane and "Professor X" we find a similar relationship echoed: Crane believed and acted on ideas that Winters considered mistaken; he is honored for his sincerity and commitment. Similarly, Very believed and acted on ideas Winters considered mistaken, and he too is honored for this. Emerson and "Professor X" are popularizers, parasites who do not realize the true implications of notions they peddle at small risk to themselves. It was the sincerity of the commitment to what he believed to be an absolute truth that moved Winters in Very's work, and it was the "fraudulence" that he discerned in Emerson that aroused his contempt.

However, this does not, I believe, wholly account for Winters's interest in Very and his poetry. If we examine Winters's own mature verse the natural world is presented ambivalently; it is both destructive and a lost idyll seen through a haze of beatitude; the tone of rapt contemplation that pervades the idyllic poems is like a calmer, more reflective version of the hypersensitive absorption of his earliest imagist verse. This tone of

charged seriousness, of an intellectual immobility or trance before the
natural world, did not lose its imaginative hold on Winters, for all his
rejection of the demonic in nature; it is a constant tone in many poets he
intensely admired (for example, Sturge Moore, Valéry, Edgar Bowers)
and it is, I believe, one of the chief reasons for his championing of the
neglected Very's work. He recognized the authenticity of the experiences
recorded in Very's poetry, their truth to psychological reality, from his
own experiences. He claimed that he found Very's beliefs alien, and so
they were to his conscious later beliefs, but they corresponded to a part of
himself that, as certain of his own later poems testify, was still powerful,
and he was clearly moved by the truth of their record.

Hawthorne and Henry James

Winters considered Hawthorne as "essentially an allegorist" (*In Defense of
Reason*, p. 157) and believed that this predisposition was derived from the
Puritan background of New England. He quoted H. W. Schneider on the
Puritan outlook: "Nature was instructive to them only in so far as it suggested the hidden mysterious operations of designing agents . . . natural
events were . . . to be understood only in so far as they showed evidence
of some divine or diabolical plot" (p. 161). This is the view of experience
we find in *The Scarlet Letter*—or rather it is the view held by the novel's
characters, though there seems some doubt when we ask ourselves how
far it is the author's view. He appears to both endorse and reject such direct links between the natural world and moral or divine meaning. For
Winters, Hawthorne was a man who, constitutionally and by the influence of his New England background, was an allegorist who was able to
complete one perfect and wholly allegorical work (*The Scarlet Letter*) by
setting it within a framework (that is, the early settlements of Puritan
New England) in which "allegory was realism, the idea was life itself"
(p. 165): he was then ruined by his attempts to produce the effects of allegory while dealing with intractably unallegorical material—the universe
as it was to the nineteenth-century mind, an uneasy mixture of scientific
nominalism and Emersonian transcendentalism. Hawthorne searches for
allegorical meaning where, he suspects, there is none. There is the uninterpreted world or there are the mind's schematizations of reality that
seem on examination to have little connection with the world of experience. As with Emerson, Winters draws attention to the representa-

tive nature of Hawthorne's plight, and, by implication, to its continuing relevance:

> His dilemma, the choice between abstractions inadequate or irrelevant to experience on the one hand, and experience on the other as far as practicable unilluminated by the understanding is tragically characteristic of the history of this country and of its literature; only a few scattered individuals, at the cost of inordinate labor, and often impermanently, have achieved the permeation of human experience by a consistent moral understanding which results in wisdom and great art. [p. 174]

Winters's own poetry moves between the two extremes here suggested. The extremes again indicate that separation between experience and the mind which was one of Winters's major preoccupations. The permeation referred to in these remarks was the aim of his own postsymbolist method, an aim which he can be considered to have achieved in the best of his later poetry.

Winters was dissatisfied with allegory as a method (he attacks its arbitrary nature in *The Function of Criticism*, pp. 44-45), but his best poems are modified allegories. He tried to eliminate the arbitrariness by making the poem function with equal precision on both levels, the purely sensuous as well as the abstract, and by making one level exist as a manifestation or extension of the other (the essence of the postsymbolist method). His early imagist poems give us a mind that waits in rapt trance for meaning to be disclosed by the particulars of the natural world. His later belief was that meaning is wholly of the mind; the world does not disclose meaning, the mind constructs it by reference to the universals it discerns (a belief he probably derived from Aquinas; see *Summa contra gentiles* 1.26.5 and 1.53.3). In a sense Hawthorne's progress was Winters's in reverse—after he had abandoned allegory (the attempt to unite meaning and experience) he was left with the rapt contemplation of the apparently meaningless particulars of the natural world. Winters quotes a passage from Hawthorne's *Septimus Felton* and, following Percy Boynton, suggests it is a self-portrait of the later Hawthorne:

> As for Septimus, let him alone for a moment or two, and then they would see him, with his head bent down, brooding, brooding, his eyes fixed on some chip, some stone, some common plant, any commonest thing, as if it were the clue and index to some mys-

tery; and when, by chance startled out of these meditations, he
lifted his eyes, there would be a kind of perplexity, a dissatisfied,
foiled look in them, as if of his speculations he found no end. [*In
Defense of Reason*, pp. 172–73]

The picture is of a man hypnotized by minute specifics (very like the
Winters of the early imagist poems) but who can find no meaning in
them; he is transfixed by the uninterpretableness of things, unable to accept them merely as they are and equally unable to suggest what they
might mean.

Winters's view of James is very similar to his view of Hawthorne. He
begins by claiming him as a typically New England novelist, and this enables him to substantially repeat his diagnosis of Hawthorne's metaphysical ills and fictional problems as being the result of New England's
cultural history. In the same way that Hawthorne was seen by Winters as
deriving the method and substance of his fiction from a metaphysic (that
of the Puritans) in which he could no longer believe, so James and his
characters are seen as operating in a milieu that has severed "its connection with the one and only source of its nourishment, the Aristotelean
ethical tradition as embodied in the Catholic Church" (*In Defense of Reason*, p. 305). According to Winters, the moral sense in James "was a fine,
but very delicate perception, unsupported by any clear set of ideas, and
functioning, not only in minds of very subtle construction, but at the
very crisis in history at which it was doomed not only to be almost infinitely rarified but finally to dissolve in air" (p. 306).

Hawthorne's obsession with meaning is seen as the result of the Puritan
habit of the allegorization of experience; James's moral hypersensitivity
as the result of centuries of minute ethical enquiry and introspection, encouraged by the Catholic and Anglo-Catholic churches. Neither author
can accept the metaphysical presuppositions that would provide a context
for their concerns. Thus Hawthorne allegorizes where he does not believe in allegory, and James's moral complexities, for want of a plain and
absolute standard beyond which there is no appeal, become more and
more subtle and indecipherable. In Winters's terms both writers are parasitic upon an older tradition without being truly conscious of this—they
operate without a metaphysical context, and this is the source of their
difficulties and even of their particular tone.

There is a parallel, implied by Winters, between this metaphysical
homelessness and the extreme degree to which James's characters exist in
a cultural and moral vacuum. Winters points out that his characters are

usually isolated from "the influence of ethical habit and of social pressure
as they appear in the guise of manners or of economic necessity." His aim
is to "isolate the ethical consciousness . . . more perfectly than it is to be
found isolated in life. In this respect his art approaches that of the allegorist or symbolic poet" (*In Defense of Reason*, p. 312).

The mention of the allegorist again reminds us of Hawthorne, and
Winters draws a parallel between Hawthorne's hypnotic perusal of discrete particulars and James's equally obsessive quizzing of his characters'
motives and perceptions. On *The Awkward Age* he writes of "the excessive subtlety with which the characters scrutinize each other and the
whole situation. . . . They remind one . . . of Hawthorne scrutinizing Dr.
Grimshaw's spiders with insane intensity but with no illumination" (*In
Defense of Reason*, p. 321), and in the same essay he remarks that "the en-
tire drama of the typical Jamesian novel is the effort of some character or
group of characters . . . to understand what is going on" (p. 317).

Both Hawthorne and James attempt to decipher reality, as if the world
and the people in it are part of some larger meaning that will not quite
disclose itself. In both cases, if we accept Winters's analysis, the author's
simultaneous desire for significance and his implicit rejection of a wider
metaphysical context which would provide such significance encourages
a desire to read into experience a meaning far in excess of what is war-
ranted. The creators of the fictional world find it as much a puzzle as do
their readers. Of *The Spoils of Poynton* Winters wrote, "We . . . have an
intense situation, developed with the utmost care, so far as the succeed-
ing facts and states of mind are concerned, but remaining at nearly all
times and certainly at the end uncertain as to significance" (*In Defense of
Reason*, p. 320), and he made very similar remarks on *The Sacred Fount*
and *The Turn of The Screw*. He does not quite accuse James of bad faith—
of kidding the reader that more is going on than actually is—but this is
only because he sees James to be as much in the dark as are his characters.
Of *The Sense of the Past* he wrote: "James is nearly as hallucinated as Pen-
drel. . . . James, like the characters of *The Awkward Age*, becomes so
watchful for symptoms that he appears to be self-hypnotized; in this
again he resembles the later Hawthorne" (p. 324).

This leads to a consideration of James's later style, in which the writer
appears to be dependent on the consciousness of his characters for his information. Winters objects, quite violently, to this procedure, and considers it a deterioration in James's technique as a novelist. His objection
turns on his view of the functions of art and the duties of an author. It is
not so much the obscurity of the later works to which he objects as to the

author's implicit abdication of judgment over his characters. On *The Ambassadors* he wrote, "Our final attitude to Chad is unresolved, and thus resembles our final attitude to Owen Gereth in *The Spoils of Poynton*; this may not be untrue to life but it is untrue to art, for a work of art is an evaluation, a judgement, of experience, and only in so far as it is that is it anything; and James in this one respect does not even judge the state of uncertainty, but, as in *The Spoils of Poynton* he merely leaves us uncertain" (*In Defense of Reason*, p. 334). Winters is insisting that an author keep his moral bearings. His belief that art is an evaluation of life (rather than merely, say, a reflection or distillation of it) involves him in a belief in moral absolutes by which a situation or character can always be judged. In James's later novels the moral sense is fragmented, interiorized, and individualized to such an extent that a final judgment is often impossible (we may consider, for example, the quite opposing valuations, by different critics, of the conduct of the characters of *The Golden Bowl*). The data for making a judgment are always suspect, and no one, not even the author, has sufficient independence of the novel's action to offer an evaluation of it. It is this moral relativism of James's later novels that arouses Winters's distaste—his strictures on these novels are in essence identical to his strictures on the drama as an inherently flawed form.

Though it should be emphasized that Winters thought the above problems to be of only minor significance when set against the splendor of James's achievement, which he considered to be unsurpassed in the history of the novel, nevertheless his critical interest was fairly narrowly focused on two aspects of James's art: the lack of a coherent metaphysical context, which led James to interiorize the search for meaning, and the moral relativism of the later style. The latter issue was, for Winters, an aspect of the former, and both were related to the underlying problem of the relation of significance to experience, which Winters perceived as common to the American writers of the nineteenth century and as still pressing for their successors.

Melville and Emily Dickinson

The two writers of the nineteenth century with whom Winters clearly felt the most kinship—with the possible exception of F. G. Tuckerman—were Herman Melville and Emily Dickinson.

That Winters had a particularly high regard for Melville's work is evi-

dent not only from the personal testimony of his students but also from
the tone of his essay on Melville in *Maule's Curse*, and by his two poems
on the subject. In "To a Portrait of Melville in My Library" Winters describes the face portrayed as one in which "Wisdom and wilderness are
here at poise"—the line I have used as the title of this book. The phrase
not only characterizes Melville's work, it summarizes the major effort of
Winters's own mature poetry, indeed of all his later writings, whose chief
preoccupation was the relation between the conscious mind and "wilderness," both internal and external—the strategies by which the mind attempts to know and evaluate the disorder of experience. The "poise" in
particular suggests that tact which was of such importance in Winters's
sense of the world—neither mind nor experience obliterating the other
but each held in precarious balance. Melville's work, for Winters, epito-
mized a concern and achievement with which he felt an exceptionally
close kinship.

His discussion of *Moby Dick* is extraordinarily illuminating when considered in relation to his own poetry:

> The symbolism of *Moby Dick* is based on the antithesis of the sea
> and land; the land represents the known, the mastered, in human
> experience; the sea the half-known, the obscure region of instinct,
> uncritical feeling, danger and terror. [*In Defense of Reason*, p. 200]

Further in the same essay we read,

> The ocean is the home of demons and symbols of evil too numer-
> ous to mention. It is the home specifically of Moby Dick, the
> white whale, the chief symbol and spirit of evil. . . .
>   . . . His approach to water is represented as an approach to
> chaos, death and hell. [Pp. 201, 204]

And most thoroughly and explicitly:

> The symbolism of the whale is part of the symbolism of the sea.
> The sea is the realm of the half-known, at once of perception and
> of peril; it is infested by subtle and malignant creatures bent on
> destruction; it is governed by tremendous destructive forces, the
> storms, the calms, currents, tides, depths and distances, amid
> which one can preserve oneself by virtue only of the greatest skill,
> and then but precariously and from moment to moment. Of all the
> creatures in the sea, the whale is the greatest, the most intelligent

and the most dangerous. . . . It is . . . in a general way, the symbol
of evil and death, and this symbol is developed from beginning to
end of the book carefully and elaborately. [Pp. 212–13]

The progression of things which the sea represents, cited in the first of
these extracts, is particularly significant: from the "half-known" to—as if
this were the natural consequence of the "half-known"—"danger, and
terror"; that is, reality not under human control or comprehension is au-
tomatically seen as terrifying and destructive. That the symbolism here
set out is plainly that of Winters's poem "The Slow Pacific Swell" is made
particularly clear when we recall the whales of that poem's second stanza.
My concern here is not to suggest a direct influence in the choice of symbolism (this is of course possible, but if there is a literary source for Winters's land-sea symbolism it is as likely to be Wallace Stevens as Melville)
but to suggest that Winters's profound respect for Melville's achievement
derives from what he considered to be a shared apprehension of the nature of reality; Winters's own version of things was more substantially
confirmed and deepened by Melville than by almost any other author.
The sense in Melville's works of a malevolent and demonic evil which is
associated with instinct, chaos, and the unknown—and of man as necessarily embattled against such evil—is exactly the sense that informs *The
Brink of Darkness* as well as a great many of Winters's most characteristic
and important poems.
    Of Ahab he writes:

His sin, in the minor sense, is monomaniac vengeance; in the major the will to destroy the spirit of evil itself, an intention blas-
phemous because beyond human powers and infringing upon the
purposes of God.
    . . . He is convinced of the true existence of the "demonism of
the world." He thus endeavors to step outside the limitations of
man . . . he is Promethean. [*In Defense of Reason*, pp. 211, 213]

He calls Ahab's act "a defiance of natural order." These passages are concerned with a violation of natural limits, a rejection of that tact mentioned
above as being an important constituent of Winters's beliefs. They are evidence of his suspicion of the Promethean or Faustian view of humanity,
and of his allegiance to a more classical sense of balance and restraint. The
killing of the whale, when considered in this way, reminds us of the recurrent rape and violence of "Theseus, a Trilogy": here too the symbolic
scheme illustrates man's relations with the undefined and perilous—and

here too the relationship is one of violence, the willed destruction of evil, a violence explicitly condemned by the author but seeming to retain a monstrous fascination over his mind.

Again we are reminded of Winters's own preoccupations and poems when he writes, "As the whale represents death and evil, Ahab's ivory leg represents the death that has become part of the living man as a result of his struggle with evil, it is the numb wisdom which is the fruit of experience"(*In Defense of Reason*, p. 209). This intuition, that to do battle with experience and gain wisdom is to slowly sacrifice one's life, so that the complete wisdom is death beyond change, is a recurrent theme of Winters's poetry, particularly of those few poems he wrote after his thirties were over; it receives its most explicit expression at the end of "Time and the Garden."

It would be possible to illustrate further the peculiarly intimate relations between Winters's reading of Melville and the themes of his own poetry (his interpretation of Starbuck as the rational intellect, his comments on the look-out's pantheistic reveries, for example) but one more quotation should suffice: "The relationship of man to the known and the half-known, however, is not a simple one, he cannot merely stay on land or he will perish of imperception, but must venture on the sea, without losing his relationship to the land; we have, in brief, the relationship of principle to perception, or, in other words, the problem of judgement" (*In Defense of Reason*, p. 202). This is as succinct an exposition of the principles of his own poetry as one could wish for, the poet as "Adventurer in / living fact," but an adventurer whose ultimate task is understanding rather than immersion. We can add too that it is possible to trace Winters's own development as a gradual shift of emphasis from one side of this equation to the other; if the sea of indefinite experience is the element of his early poetry, he wrote of himself in "The Slow Pacific Swell" as "A landsman I," and his later work came more and more to reveal the judgments of the land rather than the experiences of the sea. But he was aware of the danger this involved: "he cannot stay merely on land, or he will perish of imperception."

Like Melville, Emily Dickinson occupied a special place in Winters's view of the nineteenth century, and at the end of his essay on her in *Maule's Curse* he brackets them together: "Except by Melville, she is surpassed by no writer that this country has produced"(*In Defense of Reason*, p. 299). Indeed he considered that her subject matter in her best poems was broadly similar to Melville's, which, as we have seen, means broadly similar to the concerns of his own poetry. Discussing her poem "I started early," he writes, "The sea is here the traditional symbol of death; that is, of all the forces and qualities in nature and in human nature which tend toward the dissolution of character and consciousness" (p. 285), a familiar enough formulation in Winters's criticism. Familiar too is his praise for her rejection of pantheism and her recognition of "the essential cleavage between man . . . and nature . . . the plight of man, the willing and freely moving entity, in a universe in which he is by virtue of his essential qualities, a foreigner . . . the nostalgia of man for the mode of being which he perceives imperfectly and in which he cannot share" (p. 292). The nostalgia referred to is that which permeates Winters's own earliest verse (and some of his later poems) and which he felt impelled to consciously reject. The natural world in most of Winters's later verse and, he claimed, in Emily Dickinson's, "remains immitigably the symbol of all the elements which corrupt, dissolve, and destroy human character and consciousness; to approach nature is to depart from the fullness of human life, and to join nature is to leave life. Nature may thus be a symbol of death" (p. 292).

But what particularly attracted Winters to Emily Dickinson's work is indicated in the subtitle of his essay on her, "The Limits of Judgement." This is apparent in his comments on her poems connected with death: "The observer watches the death of a friend, that is follows the friend to the brink of the comprehensible, sees her pass the brink, and faces the loss" (p. 291). The description could almost apply to Winters's own sonnet "The Realization." More important, we have here an explicit reference to "the brink," that limit beyond which comprehension cannot pass, the "brink of darkness" that divides not only consciousness from the unknowable but also life from death.

Winters draws attention to "the awareness on the part of Emily Dickinson of the abyss between the human and the supra-human or the extra-human, . . . she . . . defines the tragic experience of confronting the abyss and communicates her moral adjustment to the experience" (*In Defense of Reason*, p. 244). It is her simultaneous awareness of and withdrawal from "the abyss" represented by the nonhuman that especially moves him. It is precisely the attitude he claimed to have found in Baudelaire, and, as we shall see, in Tuckerman and Sturge Moore. The abyss is confronted, and as far as possible appraised, but it is not surrendered to. For Winters, great modern poetry existed chiefly on this precarious ledge of appraisal, the "shore" of his poem "The Slow Pacific Swell." Finally Winters, and the writers he admired, step back from the abyss in order to gain the perspective necessary for judgment: "It is possible to solve any

problem of insoluble experience by retreating a step and defining the
boundary at which comprehension ceases, and by then making the necessary moral adjustments to that boundary" (p. 290). But such a disjunction between the mind and the world inevitably involves the modern
poet in that "haunting sense of human isolation in a foreign universe"
(p. 288) which Winters considered the distinguishing mark of Emily
Dickinson's best poems.

Before passing on to examine Winters's view of Tuckerman and Sturge
Moore, which will take us into his writings on twentieth-century poetry,
it is worth drawing attention to his essay on Henry Adams as this is in
many ways a summation of his attitude towards the Puritan legacy to
nineteenth-century American thought, and it also provides a convenient
point at which to consider his views on historiography, a branch of literature he felt to be neglected by most critics.

Henry Adams and Historiography

Winters's treatment of Henry Adams, in *The Anatomy of Nonsense* (1943),
is the culmination of the thesis set out in *Maule's Curse*, published five
years earlier, that the preoccupations and difficulties of nineteenth-
century American writers had their origins in the religious history of
New England, and that these problems remained pressing well into the
twentieth century. He begins by noting that Adams "saw himself as the
product of an earlier New England . . . [and] he was correct" (*In Defense
of Reason*, p. 374), and this enables him to repeat the analysis of New England's cultural history, based largely on the writings of H. B. Parkes,
with which we are already familiar. The analysis is, however, more extensive than in the previous essays, and the influences at work are traced
(with the help of Gilson, for whose work Winters had a high regard)
back to Ockham (nominalism) and Augustine (voluntarism—the eleva-
tion of faith above reason). The principal results of this historical development were, according to Winters, (a) a propensity for allegory that
approached the obsessive, (b) Emersonian mysticism and the doctrine of
"equivalence," (c) an inclination to determinism, and (d) a "homeless"
(because cut off from its proper theological context) moral sense such as
he had discerned in Henry James's novels. All these traits Winters dis-
covers in Adams's work, and, as with his other analyses of nineteenth-
century writers, he is careful to point out the contemporary relevance of

his diagnosis (it is this relevance that is the chief cause of his concern). He writes, "My acquaintance with the minds of my literary contemporaries is extensive and I am sure that many of them derive an important part of their thought from Adams" (p. 401). And Adams's thought Winters considered to be largely an amalgam of the factors listed above as deriving from "an earlier New England":

> He possessed the acute moral sense of New England to which I have already referred and the New Englander's need to read the significance of every event which he saw. But he was of the Ockhamist tradition and as for the Mathers, so for him, the significance could not reside within the event but must reside back of it. . . . [His tradition] had lost the particular kind of intelligence and perception necessary to read the universe for what it is; and had developed instead a passion to read the universe for what it means as a system of divine shorthand or hieroglyphic, as a statement of ultimate intentions.
>
> He had no faith, however, and hence he could not believe that there was anything back of the event: the event was merely isolated and impenetrable. Yet he possessed the kind of mind which drove him to read every event with a kind of allegorical precision; and since every event was isolated and impenetrable he read in each new event the meaning that the universe was meaningless. [P. 391]

Adams's most characteristic response to events or people was to find them incomprehensible; the result was that "his frustrated passion for precise understanding drove him toward the dogmatic certainty . . . that no understanding of any kind was possible" (p. 396). This inclination to believe that understanding is impossible was combined with an admiration for James's later style, in which objective judgment of a character is unattainable because all the necessary information is suspect; the result was that "all judgements are relative, as Adams repeatedly states" (p. 395). Naturally Winters could find little to admire in such a passion for *not* arriving at objective truth.

If Adams's conclusion that judgment is relative and that reality is meaningless was the result of an allegorical nominalism derived from his New England background but cut off from the context of theological faith, similarly his determinism can be traced back to the fideistic traditions of Calvinism. It is this determinism, in particular, that Winters appears to have had in mind when he writes of those literary contemporaries who "derive an important part of their thought from Adams."

Adams's determinism was chiefly expressed in his belief that there had been an inevitable decay in the quality of civilization from the time of Aquinas to the present. Winters yields to few in his regard for Aquinas, but he sees him primarily as an individual rather than as a mere representative of his time: "I have the greatest respect for the mind of Aquinas . . . but I respectfully submit that had Aquinas felt himself determined by the stupidity and confusion of his time, he would probably have accomplished very little" (p. 411).

Winters's view of history was that an unregenerate barbarism is always present beyond the pale of civilization, but that in recent centuries there had been some success in pushing it back. This is a strenuous and difficult business and there is no cause for immense satisfaction; nevertheless,

> That we have done a good deal . . . anyone may discover by a
> moderately attentive reading of such writers as Chaucer, Defoe and
> Dickens. . . . the life of most of the lower classes on the land and
> in the cities equally, and perhaps well into the nineteenth century,
> beyond all argument in the middle ages and the Renaissance, was
> far more terrible than that of any considerable number of persons
> in North America or in Western Europe during the twentieth cen-
> tury, even at the lowest ebb of our social and economic life.
> [P. 410]

Winters could be termed a cautious meliorist; Adams considered decadence inevitable, and his determinism involved a direct link between social conditions and artistic activity, so that during his own time "Art had to be confused in order to express confusion; but perhaps it was truest so" (p. 414). For Winters this view was itself a confusion, of subject matter and method, and he elsewhere labeled it "the fallacy of imitative form." It is this supine abdication of will and reason that Winters saw as having had such a baleful influence on the writers of his own generation, in particular T. S. Eliot: "Art also is deteriorating, but it must deteriorate to express honestly the general deterioration of man; and thus we arrive at one of the central ideas of T. S. Eliot" (p. 414).

Adams's nominalism, which led him to take such a gloomy relish in the incomprehensibility of experience, and his determinism, which led him to preach inevitable decadence and the necessary confusion of contemporary art, were the two most important aspects of his thought for Winters. Both traits Winters saw as having been derived from Adams's New England background, and both he saw as influential and pernicious in his own time. However, at the close of his essay Winters praises

Adams's early historical writings very highly indeed; he calls the *History of the United States during the Administrations of Thomas Jefferson and James Madison* possibly "the greatest historical work in English with the probable exception of *The Decline and Fall of the Roman Empire.*" This leads him to a discussion of historiography as literature.

His enthusiasm for the art can be traced to three main causes. The first is its relatively objective nature when compared with, say, novel writing. Winters was frequently irritated by the excessively subjective nature of a great deal of literature (see, for example, his strictures on James's later novels), and the public and relatively verifiable nature of historical data must have appealed to him. If the historian's task was the recovery of truth from the oblivion of the past he could be regarded as an ally by one who saw literature as ideally a "quest for reality." Second, the historian needed to reduce a large number of facts to a coherent and manageable whole which would nevertheless not betray what he took to be the objective truth of the situation he was discussing. This reduction of minutiae to general principles is again consistent with Winters's view of art—the abstraction of universals from a mass of apparently inchoate particulars. Third, the art had a very serious subject, far more serious than "the personal adventures of the relatively young, in the private relationships arising from what is relatively the leisure time of the characters"—the subject matter of most novels—and Winters always maintained that great art cannot be written on a trivial matter. His instinct for the heroic, clearly apparent in his later poetry (and in scattered remarks in his criticism) was satisfied by history in a way that it could be only rarely by the novel. His interest in history, as is evident from the examples he gives, was chiefly a concern with ethical heroism.

His remarks on particular historians are also indicative of his wider preferences and beliefs. He admires Gibbon but, one suspects, does not feel quite comfortable with him. His analysis of the tone of Gibbon's description of the Empress Theodora's personal life strikes me as wholly mistaken: he sees it as "embarrassed" whereas I suspect that most readers would find Gibbon's mixture of condemnation and implied innuendo indicative of a kind of lascivious glee—a glee common in Gibbon, particularly in his footnotes. The English historian he appears to feel most sympathy for is Macaulay; the two passages he selects from the *History of England* for special commendation are the third chapter and the description of the Monmouth rebellion. Macaulay's general meliorism must have appealed to Winters (the third chapter, by invoking the depths of misery that *had* prevailed in English life, both supports the meliorist the-

THE LATER PROSE 189

sis and makes vivid the semibarbarism that appears in the absence of consciously maintained civilization) and so too must his liking for strenuous
heroism. Macaulay is a far less equivocal and ironic writer than Gibbon,
and is far more hopeful of the beneficial results of heroic individual
effort. Winters's liking for the American historians, such as Prescott and
Parkman, can partly be traced to a straightforward patriotism, a fascination with the past of his own continent. But is is significant that those
historians he particularly admired dealt with the early period of American history, that is, the encounter between man and the wilderness. This
encounter was of particular interest to Winters—indeed in his own
poems it can become a paradigm of all men's encounters with reality; further, it was solitary and heroic in a way that more recent history could
not be, and one of its chief characters was the American Indian, who had
fascinated Winters since his youth. The pathos and heroism contained in
the story of the destruction of the Indian civilization were obviously important factors in his high regard for William Carlos Williams's essay *The
Destruction of Tenochtitlan*. It is this combination of ingredients—the wilderness, the Indian, the solitary and heroic cast of the action, and the peculiarly American quality of the whole experience—that also accounts
for his advocacy of James Fenimore Cooper's novels.

Tuckerman and Sturge Moore

Winters wrote two essays on Tuckerman: the first appeared in 1950 in the
Hudson Review and is reprinted in *The Uncollected Essays and Reviews;* it is
concerned almost entirely with Tuckerman's long poem "The Cricket,"
to which Winters gives very high praise. The second was a foreword to
N. Scott Momaday's edition of Tuckerman's *Complete Poems*, issued in
1965. This too concentrates on "The Cricket," which has risen even further in Winters's estimation; he now calls it "the greatest poem in English
of the century." (The section on Tuckerman in *Forms of Discovery* is an
almost-verbatim reprint of the foreword to Momaday's edition of the
poems, with a few additions).

The judgment that Tuckerman's "The Cricket," a poem still probably
unknown to most casual readers of nineteenth-century poetry and but
slightly known to many specialists in the subject, is "the greatest poem in
English of the century" is certainly eccentric. The reasons for this judgment are, however, not difficult to discern. Though Winters praises
Tuckerman's skill in his gradual presentation of the cricket as a symbol

with very wide implications, and though he has a high regard for Tuck-erman's eye for natural detail (which he compares with Wordsworth's, considerably to Tuckerman's advantage), the main reason is clearly his estimation of the true subject of Tuckerman's poem. This is in essence the subject matter that he had already designated central to the work of Melville and Emily Dickinson (both are invoked as parallels), and Tuckerman's attitude towards this subject matter is even closer to Win-ters's preferred attitudes than are the views of Melville and Dickinson. Winters always insisted that great poetry could only be written on a great theme. For him, as we have seen, the chief subject of postromantic po-etry was the "cleavage" between the human and the nonhuman, between the mind and the world, meaning and experience; all these are facets of the same apprehension of man as isolated in a "foreign universe." Winters had little time for poets who did not see the cleavage, he was horrified by those who saw it and attempted to overcome it by a kind of deliberate delirium; his preferred attitude to the problem was an acceptance of the existence of the "cleavage," a recognition of the nostalgia we feel (our desire to overcome this separation), and a drawing back from the nostalgia, an understanding of it as an invitation to abandon our humanity.

These are precisely the concerns of Tuckerman's "The Cricket" (or at least they appear as such in Winters's analysis of the poem, which is no-where contradicted by the poem's meaning or tone). It is small wonder therefore that, given Tuckerman's skill, Winters should declare the poem "the greatest . . . in English of the century"; it could almost be taken as his own credo.

Here is Winters's analysis of the poem's symbolism:

> We meet the cricket in multiplicity spread throughout a summer
> landscape, in which heat, scent and sound are hypnotic and stun
> the sense to slumber; we approach a pantheistic trance; and at the
> end of the passage the sound of the crickets is compared to the
> sound of the sea. The sea is a traditional symbol of the changing
> physical universe from which we arise and to which we return,
> and it is often in addition a symbol of those elements in human
> nature which elude understanding and control, and which may be
> destructive. . . . the cricket has become a symbol for non-human
> nature and for the primitive and sub-human in human nature and
> has been used to create a deep longing for these qualities and for
> death. . . .

The poet longs to resemble the old enchanter who employed *evil* drugs to learn the language of the lower creatures. He would thus be unwise, would descend through denser stillness, would convert the world to the cricket's wisdom . . . would possess a great deal but would yield more. He then recognizes the impossibility of this choice, and accepts the necessity of living at the human level until the end of his life. The conclusion is similar to that of "Le Cimètiere Marin." [*The Complete Poems of Frederick Goddard Tuckerman*, pp. xiv–xv]

The drowsy haze, the invitation to pantheistic trance, is reminiscent of the atmosphere of Winters's own early poems; the mention of the sea enables him to set out his customary analysis of its symbolism as representing the nonhuman and destructive; the recognition of both the immense charm of the invitation to join the nonhuman and the impossibility of sanely doing so are the themes of many of his later poems. The approach to and rejection of pantheistic trance are an encapsulation of Winters's own early development. The poem fits his thesis of what is crucial in both life and poetry with hardly a wrinkle. It fits in too with his analysis of the important developments of nineteenth-century American literature: in the earlier essay the cricket is compared in its symbolic significance with the meaning of Melville's whale; and Tuckerman (like Emily Dickinson) is implicitly recruited to the ranks of the postsymbolists at the conclusion to the foreword of Momaday's edition of the poems.

Winters saw Sturge Moore as in many ways a more conscious Tuckerman. He defined Tuckerman against a background of romanticism and remarked on the similarity in tone of one aspect of his work (acuteness of sensory perception taken as an end and meaning in itself) with that of the French poets of the later nineteenth century, and Tuckerman had been attracted by a "progression into pure obscurity" but had withdrawn to the limits of consciousness at the last moment. His verdict on Moore is essentially similar—he sees him as a man influenced by but ultimately reacting against the romantic influences that surrounded him: "He was influenced by the French Parnassians and Symbolists, to some extent by Swinburne and the English poets of the nineties and (unfortunately) by the English nineteenth century: but his work is in a large measure and rather importantly a reaction against these influences" (*Forms of Discovery*, p. 235). Further in the same essay Winters calls Moore "a counter-Romantic, but not naively so," and elsewhere (*Uncollected Essays and Re-*

views, p. 151) "a regenerate Romantic" (as against Yeats, whom he calls
"an unregenerate Romantic"). In connection with this counterromanti-
cism Winters remarks that "Moore had a great deal of common sense in
an age that exhibits little"; it is a curious fact that Moore's brother, the
philosopher George Edward Moore, was also known for the meticulous
and painstaking common sense that he brought to another discipline then
lost in romantic solipsism.

In a review, written in 1933, of Moore's *Collected Poems*, Winters
quotes J. V. Cunningham's statement of Moore's chief theme, "spiritual
pride which would over-reach natural limits . . . the effort to violate human relationships by imposing one's identity on others." (*Uncollected Essays and Reviews*, p. 144). Winters's comment on this formulation is
revealing—he transfers the diagnosis from the human to the metaphysical, and Moore is assimilated to his own conceptions of classical restraint,
that sense of the separateness of the human mind from experience and
external reality which is so much a feature of his own poetry: "The
theme, however, is not limited to the ethical sphere in Mr. Moore, but
has its religious counterpart . . . which leads to the attempt to violate our
relationship with God, or with whatever myth we put in his place, even
with Nothingness" (p. 144).

The discussion of Moore in *In Defense of Reason* is largely an expansion
of the earlier review: the most interesting part of the new material is the
examination of Moore's poem "To Silence"—the poem is discussed in
terms almost identical to those Winters used of Tuckerman's "The
Cricket." The poem describes silence as being like a sea in which one
bathes to be refreshed; the "bather swims / To refresh and not dissolve
his limbs." Winters remarks on the "remarkable freshness and sensitivity" of the feeling and links it to what he calls "the hypersensitivity of
convalescence." He then explicates the poem's allegorical meaning: "Silence is equal to pure quality, unclassified sensation . . . and the immersion in sensation (or confusion) amounts to the dissolution of one's
previous standards in order to obtain a fresh sensibility. This is what the
Romantic movement amounted to, the degree of dissolution varying
with each poet. . . . Mr. Moore states explicitly, however, in this poem
and in others, not only the value of immersion but its peril and the need
of the return" (*In Defense of Reason*, p. 99).

As in his discussion of "The Cricket," Winters emphasizes the attractions of the proposed dissolution of consciousness (and in Moore's poem,
as in many of Winters's own, the element of dissolution is water) and the
necessity for "the return." Both poets—according to Winters—acknowl-

edge the attractions of romanticism, almost succumb to them (indeed gain in sensitivity of response as a result), but finally draw back from them. There is at times a suggestion—in Winters's emphasis on Moore's hypersensitivity, which he traces to the influence of late romanticism, *and* on his withdrawal from what this hypersensitivity implies—that one can both have one's cake and eat it.

On Twentieth-Century Poetry

Because many of the twentieth-century poets whom Winters most profoundly admired had begun their writing careers in the nineteenth century, and because he considered that the concerns and techniques of twentieth-century poetry had clear and immediate roots in nineteenth-century theory and practice (even when the modern poets saw themselves as in revolt against nineteenth-century beliefs), Winters did not draw any clear line between the poetry of the two centuries. He treats Emily Dickinson, for example, virtually as a contemporary, and he considers Sturge Moore, a largely twentieth-century poet, in much the same light as he considers the nineteenth-century Tuckerman. Interestingly the first third of Winters's first extended essay on Moore—the review of his *Collected Poems* in *Hound and Horn*—is as much an attack on modern "American experimentalists" as it is advocacy of Moore's own work. He took the same attitude toward a whole group of poets born in the nineteenth century but writing much of their poetry (most of it in traditional forms) in the twentieth, and his praise for their work is frequently joined with explicit condemnation of writers who had abandoned their principles. He holds up the work of this group—Moore, Bridges, Hardy, Robinson, Valéry—as a model and admonition to the "experimentalists."

Twentieth-Century Traditionalists: Bridges, Hardy, Robinson, Valéry

In 1932, in a review of *The Shorter Poems of Robert Bridges*, Winters praised Bridges for "restraint, economy, richness of feeling . . . and extreme generality or universality of import accomplished with no loss in the specification of the perception" (*Uncollected Essays and Reviews,*

p. 130) and found his language "free from any trace of personal idiosyncrasy" (p. 128), and this is clearly meant as praise. It was obviously
Bridges's impersonal classicism that particularly impressed Winters at
this time—Bridges provided an example of objective dignity in verse, a
way out of the solipsistic haze into which so many of his, and Winters's,
contemporaries had wandered. Winters calls him "the most valuable
model of poetic style to appear since Dryden" (p. 128). (That he utilized
this model is evident from his own "The Slow Pacific Swell," as I indicated in Chapter 4.) But it is not only the style that moves him: the emotional tone embodied in the style was clearly close to Winters's own
preferred mode of writing, "a more or less classical resignation . . . an
undercurrent of calm and carefully restrained bitterness" (p. 133).

It is significant that although at this time Bridges was usually discussed, if he was discussed at all, as an experimenter in original verse
forms, Winters is little interested in his experiments and judges his syl-
labics, by which Bridges himself set great store, to be something of a
failure (though he does admire the poems in classical meters). Winters
considered Bridges a traditionalist, not an experimenter. In *Primitivism
and Decadence*, Winters's characterization of and attack on "American experimentalism," Bridges is offered as an admonitory example to the ex-
perimenters, in particular to the imagists. Winters rejects both the idea
that imagism *could* produce poems as fine as Bridges's best and that
the revolution of Eliot and Pound was somehow inevitable or, once
achieved, mandatory in its effects: "There is current at present a very
general opinion that it is impossible to write good poetry in the mode, let
us say, of Bridges, either because of the kind of poetry that has been written since ('the stylistic advances of Eliot and Pound') or because of social
conditions ('the chaos of modern thought') or because of both, or because of something else. I believe this to be a form of group hypochondria" (*In Defense of Reason*, p. 101). In the critical writings of the thirties,
then, Bridges is praised largely for his diction and tone, and as a traditional model whom the experimentalists would do well to imitate. By
the time Winters came to write his last book, *Forms of Discovery*, the emphasis has shifted somewhat.

As is so often the case in this book, Winters's enthusiasm has become
more than a little qualified, particularly in regard to Bridges's diction. In
the 1932 review he had specifically praised "the purity of his diction," but
in the later work he remarks that "the bulk of his work is corrupted
by the facile diction of the nineteenth century," and commenting on
Bridges's regard for Shelley he writes that "much of his own diction is

just as bad [as Shelley's]" (*Forms of Discovery*, p. 194). However, Bridges
survives fairly well in Winters's estimation. He remarks that "the best
poems display a kind of passionate intellectuality comparable to nothing
else in English so much as the great poems of Fulke Greville, Ben Jonson
and George Herbert" (p. 194).

Readers familiar with Winters's criticism, and with his estimation of
these poets' work, will recognize this as high praise indeed. Three poems
are analyzed: "Low Barometer," "Eros," and "The Affliction of Richard."
The last deals with a theme that appears to have particularly attracted
Winters towards the end of his life—a questioning of God's purposes in
placing man in a situation he cannot understand, a species of loss of faith
that is nevertheless directed toward God. It is the theme of his own "To
the Holy Spirit" and is very close to the theme, as Winters describes it, of
his favorite poem, Valéry's "Ebauche d'un serpent." "Eros" is concerned
with the attractiveness and danger of physical passion and has something
of that tranced wonder (tinged with fear) before the compelling strangeness and beauty of the natural world that is apparent in certain of Winters's own poems (like "Midas"). Both the attractiveness and the danger
(the one almost seems an aspect of the other) of this state are brought out.
Here is Winters himself on "Low Barometer": "The poem deals with an
attack on Reason by the 'unconscious' mind, which is seen as an inheritance from a remote and savage past. . . . Bridges sees the humanity of
man as something recently acquired and precariously kept" (*Forms of Discovery*, p. 196). (There is a similar discussion of this poem in Winters's
essay on Hopkins in *The Function of Criticism*.)

Loss of faith, the attractiveness and danger of physical passion and
beauty, and the attack on reason were all themes of particular importance
to Winters, and it is clear that his later liking for Bridges's work was
largely a liking for Bridges's themes and his attitude towards those
themes. At the end of the section on Bridges in *Forms of Discovery* he
praises the plays on Nero; again it is difficult to resist the conclusion that
this is largely because of the central theme he discerns in them—the cor-
ruption of reason (represented by Seneca). If Winters was first drawn to
Bridges because of the "purity of his diction" and his "traditional mastery," his later respect for him was based on those few works explicitly
concerned with concepts that Winters considered important and that he
had largely made his own. This shift in emphasis is entirely typical of
Winters's development as a critic, though for him there was little dichotomy; the traditional forms and lucidity of language were themselves seen
as a paradigm of the author's commitment to reason.

It seems at first sight extraordinary that, given Winters's estimate of Hardy as, with Bridges, one of the "two most impressive writers of poetry in something like two centuries" (*Uncollected Essays and Reviews*, p. 271), he should have devoted no essay to his work; the only extended discussion of Hardy is the four pages in *Forms of Discovery*. However, this is partly explicable by the fact that Hardy did not, in general, deal with those specifically Wintersian themes which we have noticed in writers like Bridges, Tuckerman, and Sturge Moore, and partly by the fact that a great deal of Winters's criticism is given over to an explication of the concepts presupposed by a poem, what one might call the metaphysical groundwork of the piece, and that he believed Hardy's ideas to be more or less transparent, "a summation of folk-wisdom" (*Uncollected Essays and Reviews*, p. 271), in little need of explication. When he does discuss Hardy's philosophy he is impressed by what he takes to be its grasp on the realities of the human condition. Though he is mildly irritated by the "melodramatic" nature of Hardy's determinism, he claims that this "should not weaken for us those poems which do not deal too pugnaciously with the doctrines" (*In Defense of Reason*, p. 26).

Winters was obviously fascinated by Hardy's language and rhythmic virtuosity—he links Hardy's practice to Emily Dickinson's, remarking that they were both "naifs" and that their models were not the usual literary ones of most poets, but in Dickinson's case hymns and in Hardy's folk songs and ballads. What most fascinates him about Hardy's language is the range of its suggestion: "Hardy is able to utilize . . . great ranges of literary, historical, and other connotations in words and cadences. . . . Hardy gets somehow at the wealth of the race" (*In Defense of Reason*, p. 28), and again, "The gesture, cadence, the pauses, indicate a richness of wisdom and experience not defined in the meaning of the words: (*Uncollected Essays and Reviews*, p. 58). It is Hardy's ability to be plain yet to imply far more than is immediately apparent, colloquial yet deeply serious, that impresses Winters. He does not draw the parallel, but his discussion of Hardy frequently reminds us of his similar remarks on the poetry of Wyatt: there is an emphasis on similar techniques (plainness, colloquial language, rhythmic variation) and on a similar honesty of mind and fidelity to experience. Significantly, he remarks of Wyatt and Hardy that their best poems often contain very little imagery—and the implication is the same in both cases, of a mind too faithful to experience to be concerned with such relative dishonesty. As with Wyatt, Winters implies that Hardy's effects are achieved mainly by rhythm, by a uniquely subtle manipulation of metrical form.

But Hardy, even more than Bridges, exists mainly, in Winters's opinion, as an example of the continuing validity of traditional form in the modern period. He suggests that those spiritual crises suffered by Eliot and other modernists had also been suffered by Hardy and Baudelaire "even if they had not read Whitehead" and that this had not led to a collapse of either form or will: "Baudelaire, Thomas Hardy, Emily Dickinson found themselves in precisely the same predicament [as Eliot] and maintained their spiritual dignity and vigor" (*Uncollected Essays and Reviews*, p. 52).

I wrote above that Bridges's formal allegiances were themselves for Winters a paradigm of his commitment to reason, and Winters similarly remarks on Hardy's "sense of form, which we have seen to be, so far as writing is concerned, identical with the will or the ability to control and shape one's experience" (*In Defense of Reason*, p. 26). The notion of will was intimately bound up in Winters's mind with notions of reason (as is apparent from his remarks on Henry Adams); the exercise of the two were for him the sine qua non of sane existence. Hardy and Bridges he saw as exemplars of the continuing validity of both to poetry—they were the alternative to the "hypochondria" of those who preached inevitable formal dissolution and the submission of the self to a nebulous "spirit of the age." It is worth remarking that, although Hardy is now highly regarded as a poet, this was far less true when Winters was offering his example as an alternative to that of Pound and Eliot, in *Primitivism and Decadence*. Hardy's stock as a poet was then fairly low, and he was considered chiefly as a novelist, an aspect of his work Winters barely mentions.

Winters's first published review was of Edwin Arlington Robinson's *Collected Poems* (1922), and Robinson was the subject of his only book-length study of a single author. Though his enthusiasm is tempered in *Forms of Discovery*, Winters's favorable view of Robinson's work remained more or less constant, unaffected by the change of direction apparent in his own poetry.

Winters discerns in Robinson two philosophical attitudes: one he calls common sense or folk wisdom (reminding us of his descriptions of the work of Sturge Moore and Hardy), the other Emersonian. The former he sees as dominant in those poems he finds most successful and distinctively typical of their author; the latter as pervading the poorer poems, less the product of the author's own thought than a result of the "folk-atmosphere of the upper levels of New England society" (*Edwin Arlington Robinson*, p. 4). He finds the true direction of Robinson's thought to be "counter-Romantic," but sometimes vitiated by "a certain admixture of Emersonian doctrine" (p. 17). That is, poems that support his own preconceptions and preferences (such as "Hillcrest") he finds successful and typical of their author, while those that do not (such as "The Man against the Sky") he finds unsuccessful and less typical of their author than of the milieu in which his mind had been formed.

Winters traces Robinson's "moral curiosity," as well as the Emersonian tone of certain of his poorer poems, to his New England background, and chapter 2 of his book on Robinson is devoted to an exposition of New England cultural and religious history such as we have already encountered in his writings on Hawthorne, Melville, Adams, and Henry James. Winters frequently compares Robinson's allusive technique in his longer poems to James's procedures in his later novels, and he suggests that the moral ambiguity of both writers is a direct result of their common New England heritage.

As we have seen, two themes particularly attracted Winters in the work of Robinson's immediate predecessors and contemporaries: the theme of immersion in and withdrawal from experience, and the related theme of the threat which experience and the unconscious pose to the rational will. These are not Robinson's themes, but there are certain other preoccupations in Robinson's work which Winters singles out and which are typical of Winters's own concerns. These are, chiefly, the recognition of the twin realities of man's metaphysical ignorance and his suffering, and the poet's consequent turning to stoicism as an ideal of behavior. Linked to this latter theme is Robinson's (and Winters's) abiding interest in failure, in "characters who are weak or insignificant in the eyes of the world, but who sustain themselves in loneliness on some kind of inner integrity" (*Edwin Arlington Robinson*, p. 17). Winters frequently writes sympathetically of authors whom he sees in this position—it is an important factor in his estimate of, for example, Greville and Gascoigne among sixteenth-century poets, and Johnson and Churchill among eighteenth-century writers. The reader cannot resist the suspicion that Winters saw himself as, in some degree, their fellow. Most of the poems by Robinson which Winters singles out as being particularly fine are concerned either with stoicism, or with the apparent failure of an artist, or both.

A further and connected motif which moves Winters in Robinson's work is that of renunciation coupled with understanding: as with his comments on Robinson's stoicism, his remarks on "Lancelot," for example, carry a note of conviction that seems to come from personal experience: "Lancelot is not free, because of the Light; that is, because he has acquired understanding which before he lacked, and of understanding one cannot divest oneself. Having acquired understanding which conflicts with previous habits or desires, one can sacrifice the habits and desires and achieve growth through tragedy, or one can try to sacrifice the understanding by refusing to live in accordance with it and corrupt one's existence" (*Edwin Arlington Robinson*, p. 94). This has a tone of auto-biographical certainty: the comments on understanding and the subsequent choices it entails are made with such authority that the reader surmises Winters had found what he took to be the theme of "Lancelot" confirmed by his own experience. The particular experience behind this conviction was perhaps the crisis of Winters's late twenties, when he believed he had gained understanding and renounced an intellectually lazier and more confused position. This escape from a more or less sentimental and self-regarding solipsism, grounded in a refusal to recognize the limits of one's own ego and the independent existence of external reality, is also an important factor in Winters's regard for Robinson's "The Wandering Jew" ("one of the great poems not only of our time but of our language," [p. 38]), the theme of which he describes as "the vice of pride in one's own identity, a pride which will not allow one to accept a greater wisdom from without even when one recognizes that the wisdom is there and is greater than one's own: the result is spiritual sickness" (p. 42).

With Sturge Moore, Bridges, and Hardy, Robinson was invoked by Winters as an ally against the experimentalists. The chief rhetorical device of the experimentalists was the use of the suspended image, and their criticism frequently implies that poetry is imagery or it is nothing: Winters, as a counterclaim, draws attention to the relative lack of imagery in poets as various as Wyatt, Churchill, and Hardy, and he does the same with Robinson: "Most of Robinson's great poetry contains very little sensory imagery, this poem ('The Wandering Jew') contains less than most, it is almost purely a poem of ideas" (p. 37). This is praise, and should be read against the background of Pound's "Damn ideas, anyhow" and his "Go in fear of abstractions" (*Literary Essays of Ezra Pound*, pp. 267, 5).

However, though given a choice between a plain style written in relatively abstract and discursive language, and an imagist, pointilliste style devoid of abstraction, he would undoubtedly choose the former. Winters's true preference, especially at the end of his life, was for that style which he believed combined the virtues of both abstraction and "sensory imagery," which he calls postsymbolist. Though the work of Emily Dickinson, Tuckerman, Sturge Moore and Bridges can (with more or less success) be characterized as postsymbolist, Robinson's cannot, and in *Forms of Discovery* Winters does not accord him quite the high place he gives these other poets.

A small incident in Robinson's life, referred to by Winters with the remark, "Of these facts the reader is free to make what he can," may also give us a clue to Winters's special interest in this writer: "Of his father's last two weeks, Hagerdorn writes, 'His interest in spiritualism deepened, and, in the slow disintegration of his organism, detached and eerie energies seemed to be released. There were table rappings and once the table came off the floor, "cutting my universe" as Robinson told a friend later, "clean in half"'" (*Edwin Arlington Robinson*, p. 5). His mother's spiritualism similarly disturbed Winters, and it is probable that he saw in Robinson's dogged abstractions and exact rhythms just that armed reaction to the undefined and possibly supernatural that he himself adopted. For both writers the alternative to order and a trust in reason would seem to have been too appalling to contemplate.

Towards the end of Winters's life, Valéry appears to have been the twentieth-century poet he most admired; he calls the two poems "Cimetière Marin" and "Ebauche d'un serpent" "as far as my knowledge and judgement will guide me . . . the two greatest short poems ever written" (*Function of Criticism*, p. 63). Valéry's subjects in these two poems were precisely those which Winters found most fascinating: in "Cimetière Marin" the nature of time and death, experience as endless flux, radically divided from the mind which attempts to order and comprehend it; in "Ebauche d'un serpent" what one may call the tragedy of reason—that desire to understand which is the uniquely human aspect of man's nature, the frustration of this desire by the inscrutability of our data (here, God's purposes), and the stoicism that such an acceptance of our metaphysical ignorance entails. A large number of the poems written in Winters's thirties are concerned with the themes of "Cimetière Marin"; his subsequent poems hint at the theme of "Ebauche d'un serpent" continually, and it is the explicit subject of one of his finest late poems, "To the Holy Spirit." Winters's explication of "Ebauche d'un serpent" evokes with extraordinary fidelity the atmosphere of questing but frustrated reason, of barely resigned intellectual passion, that is a distinguishing tone of most of his own later poems.

But, in Valéry's work, it is not only the stoical adventures of reason confronted by the inscrutable, whether physical or divine, which wins Winters's admiration. Valéry's subject matter, so sympathetic to Winters's own concerns, was, he believed, presented, indeed manifested, in a style that he found wholly admirable. Like Sturge Moore, Valéry had learned from the romantics a hypersensitivity to the phenomena of the natural world, and he often used this hypersensitivity to suggest that haze of sunlight in which the observer approaches a kind of hallucinated trance. We are reminded of the "haze" of Winters's own poems and the tranced descriptions of his early work, as well as of Tuckerman's "The Cricket," which Winters compares to Valéry's poems. Valéry could invoke exactly that sense of dissolution that had been sought by the romantics, and he could invoke it by the same tranced descriptions of the natural world. But the independence of the observer is never quite abandoned; the mind is always aware of its separation from the reality it contemplates. The evidence is the firm metrical control of the language, itself a paradigm of the poet's will to order and comprehend this experience rather than submit to it. As in Winters's poetry, the primary impulse is to understand rather than to dissolve the mind in beatitude.

Valéry's subject matter, his commitment to reason and the strategies of reason (syntax, logic, ordered form) and his simultaneous ability to evoke the sensuous reality of the world are all factors in Winters's admiration for him. The commitment to reason *and* the simultaneous evocation of sensuous reality make Valéry, for Winters, the exemplar par excellence of the postsymbolist style. In *Forms of Discovery* Winters analyzes an image from "Cimetière Marin" and concludes, "As a visual image, the line is brilliant; as an intellectual perception it is profound; the visual and the intellectual are simultaneous—they cannot be separated in fact" (*Forms of Discovery*, p. 252). It is this simultaneity of visual and intellectual process that Winters sees as the distinguishing mark of the postsymbolist style.

Like Bridges and Hardy, Valéry appears in *In Defense of Reason* largely as a stick with which to beat the experimentalists, and in comparing Valéry with Pound Winters points out that Valéry's imagery—every bit as fine as Pound's *as* imagery—is also a part of an intellectual structure that he finds lacking in Pound's "blur of revery": "Its [the opening of Pound's 'Fourth Canto'] tenuity becomes apparent if we compare it . . . to the poetry of Paul Valéry, which achieves effects of imagery quite as extraordinary, along with precision, depth of meaning, and the power that comes of close and inalterable organization" (*In Defense of Reason*, p. 59).

Twentieth-Century Experimentalists: Pound, Eliot, Stevens, Williams

Winters's notoriety as a critic rests largely on his rejection of the claims of the "Poundian Revolution." The animosity aroused by his polemical critical style has sometimes led to the assumption that he was simply deaf to the talents of those of his immediate elders and contemporaries who participated in this revolution. This is not so; as we have seen, he considered himself as a member of its vanguard during his early twenties, and it cannot be emphasized too firmly that he was as aware as anyone else—even after his own change of poetic direction—that its leaders were among the best poets then writing. He was far ahead of contemporary taste in his recognition of such diverse poets as William Carlos Williams and Wallace Stevens (his favorable review of Williams's *Sour Grapes* was published when Winters was only 22, at a time when Williams had very few supporters—even the admirers of Eliot and Pound tended to dismiss him). In the same year (1922) Winters called Stevens "this greatest of living and of American poets." This was the year before Stevens's first book, *Harmonium*, was published and some ten years before he began to receive general critical recognition. Again in 1922 he wrote of "a tradition of culture and clean workmanship" associated with "Stevens, Eliot, Pound, H.D. and Marianne Moore" (*Uncollected Essays and Reviews*, p. 10). In 1930 he wrote, "The best poets of Mr. Aiken's generation are Robert Frost . . . William Carlos Williams, Ezra Pound, T. S. Eliot, Marianne Moore, Mina Loy, Archibald Macleish, John Crowe Ransom, Wallace Stevens and possibly H.D." (p. 87), and in 1937 (well after his own change of taste) he wrote, "The masters of free verse of the Experimental generation are William Carlos Williams, Ezra Pound, Marianne Moore, Wallace Stevens, H.D. and perhaps Mina Loy in a few poems" (*In Defense of Reason*, p. 124). The only unfamiliar name in the lists is Mina Loy, and she has become problematic on her second appearance. The notion that Winters did not recognize the talent of these poets is therefore quite false; further, he recognized it before most other critics and was able to separate sheep and goats with a remarkably sure hand. His lists are not cluttered with names that were merely in vogue during the 1920s and 1930s and have since suffered eclipse.

As we have seen, Winters owed a certain amount to Pound's criticism—his own early critical essays bear the clear imprint of Pound's influence, and he retained characteristically Poundian qualities in his later writings, in particular Pound's emphasis on poems rather than poets and his habit of treating all poetry as at least potentially contemporary. In many ways Winters remained faithful to Poundian criteria, specifically those of clarity and the importance of objective truth in poetry; Pound's famous dictum that poetry should be at least as well written as prose could be very slightly adapted to "poetry should have at least as much denotative meaning as prose" in order to indicate a distinguishing obsession of Winters's criticism. It is on the question of meaning that Winters and Pound part company; for Winters meaning involved universals, for Pound it resided in particulars and a concern with universals could only result in a loss of immediacy.

Pound had been the acknowledged leader of the American experimentalists to whose ideals Winters himself had owed brief allegiance, and his example must have been, in Winters's youth, something in the nature of a call to arms. Even when Winters had quite rejected the aims of the experimentalists he still found it difficult to wholly reject Pound's poetry (his rejection of Pound's work is far less thoroughgoing than his rejection of Eliot's, for example). One can sense throughout his strictures a nagging awareness of the sheer magnitude of the Poundian revolution; there is a hint, too, wryly recorded in "The Critiad," of the temerity involved in taking on Pound as an antagonist:

> Each fool was breathless not to make a sound,
> Sweating with terror lest he waken Pound.

Primitivism and Decadence, published in 1937, is Winters's chief formulation of what he thought was wrong with the experimentalists of American poetry. Through the typically taxonomic structure of the book the main thesis is clear: the carefully enumerated faults of the school are all traceable to its romantic origins. Pound was, for Winters, a classic example of the decadent poet, defined as "those who display a fine sensitivity to language and who may have a very wide scope, but whose work is incomplete formally" (*In Defense of Reason*, p. 90). Elsewhere he remarks that "this kind of poetry is not a 'new kind of poetry. . . .' It is the old kind with half the meaning removed" (p. 56).

Winters sees Pound's verse as an example of the excessive development of certain aspects of poetry encouraged by romantic concerns—in particular a hypersensitivity to feeling and visual effects, and a consequent diminution of other aspects, for example, logical structure and paraphrasable meaning. In Valéry's work Winters discerned the gain in sensitivity with no loss of logical rigor; in Pound's the sensitivity has smothered logic in a haze of association. This appears in the language of the poetry as an attempt to depend as far as possible on the connotative nuances of words rather than on their actual denotative meanings: as connotations are dependent on contexts in which meaning is plain, the procedure becomes, in one of Winters's favorite formulations for procedures of which he disapproves, "parasitic." In all this Pound is, Winters insists, in the direct romantic tradition against which he considered himself to be in revolt: "Sensory impression replaces idea. Pound early in his career adopted the inversion derived from Locke by the associationists: since all ideas arise from sensory impressions, all ideas can be expressed in terms of sensory impressions. But of course they cannot be: when we attempt this method, what we get is sensory impression alone, and we have no way of knowing whether we have any ideas or not" (*Function of Criticism*, p. 47).

Pound's replacing of idea by sensory impression is for Winters merely the natural result of following romantic teachings. He does not even allow Pound his rejection of late romantic vocabulary, calling his early verse "superior Swinburne." Pound's trouble, for Winters, was at root philosophical—he had not emancipated himself from romantic theories of the mind and poetry. His remarkable sensitivity, itself the product of his romantic inheritance, operates, Winters believes, in an intellectual vacuum; he is "a trained and refined sensibility unsupported by a unifying intellect" (*In Defense of Reason*, p. 494). A few pages later, employing the same formula, he calls Pound "a sensibility without a mind" (p. 496); more graphically, "Mr. Pound resembles a village loafer who sees much and understands little" (p. 58), and (perhaps the best-known expression of the idea) he is "a barbarian on the loose in a museum" (p. 480). Winters's opinion of Pound's verse is very like that of the Scottish lord quoted by John Aubrey who, when he was asked what he thought of a sermon preached by Lancelot Andrewes, answered, "He was learned, but he did play with his text, as a Jack-an-apes does, who takes up a thing and tosses and plays with it, and then he takes up another and plays a little with it. Here's a pretty thing, and there's a pretty thing!"

An interesting footnote to Winters's view of Pound is his view of Milton, whose skills he significantly compares to Pound's; his characterization of Milton's position in the seventeenth century as a brilliant and eccentric experimenter who led lesser minds astray is in essence his characterization of Pound's position in the twentieth century—and I am sure Winters meant the parallel to occur to his readers.

Damning though all this is we should remember that Winters emphasized Pound's remarkable abilities ("The loveliness of such poetry appears to me indubitable" [*In Defense of Reason*, p. 59]) and merely deplored the abandonment of reason and coherent meaning—and therefore of any form other than associational revery—evident in his poetry: "Since there is neither structure nor very much in the way of meaning what we have is the ghost of poetry, though I am willing to admit that it is often the ghost of great poetry" (*Function of Criticism*, p. 47). Winters is perturbed by what he understands as the implicit antiintellectualism of Pound's work, its rejection of abstraction, its insistence that "the natural object is always the adequate symbol." Winters considers Pound a person who has made himself as responsive as possible, but who refuses to think. This would seem to be borne out by Pound's political career, and Winters hints obliquely at this: "Within relatively recent years, we have had two tragic examples, in Hart Crane and Ezra Pound, of what a man of genius can do to himself by energetically living the life of impulse" (*Function of Criticism*, p. 166).

Winters calls Pound "a man of genius," but sensitivity unsupported by reason was for Winters a disastrously unstable guide. Pound's career, like Crane's, he could trace to the catastrophic results of taking romantic doctrine seriously. In the lives of both, ideas that Winters believed to be typically romantic are evident: the desire for the "unrelated thrill" of Babbitt, the denial of reason, the emotional need to lose oneself—and especially the discriminating self—in a greater "whole." Winters's warnings of the ethical results of romantic doctrine must have seemed to him to be amply confirmed by Pound's career.

In *Primitivism and Decadence* T. S. Eliot is, as often as not, the chief exemplar of the vices of the experimentalists. The passage on "qualitative progression" begins with a discussion of a passage from Pound's *Cantos* but then moves on to *The Waste Land*, and reserves its chief scorn for Eliot's theoretical defense of the method. The method is described as proceeding "from image to image wholly through the coherence of feeling: [the] sole principle of unity is mood. . . . It is the progression either of random conversation or of revery" (*In Defense of Reason*, p. 57). Winters then quotes Eliot to the effect that "there is a logic of the imagination as well as a logic of concepts" in defense of the practice. He accuses Eliot of fudging the issue by blurring the meaning of the word *logic*: "The word *logic* is used figuratively, to indicate qualitative progression, and the figure is one which it is hard to pardon a professed classicist for using at the present time" (pp. 62–63).

Eliot is also a prize exhibit in the section on pseudoreference—that is, the laying claim to more meaning than is actually discernible given the poem as it stands. Winters quotes the passage of proper names (Mr. Silvero, and so forth) from "Gerontion" and comments: "Each one of these persons is denoted in the performance of an act, and each act . . . implies an anterior situation. . . . Yet we have no hint of the nature of the history implied. A feeling is claimed by the poet, the motivation, or meaning, of which is withheld" (*In Defense of Reason*, p. 46). Winters elsewhere suggests that the practice may have arisen from Eliot's use of dramatic verse as a model for his poetry. In such verse the references would be to other personages or events in the play—they would point to an actual context; in a discrete poem they imply a context that simply does not exist.

Later in *Primitivism and Decadence* Winters comments that the most impressive passages of "Gerontion" (which he considers Eliot's best poem) are made up of moments "which, on first glance appear to have more meaning than they really have. The success . . . depends very largely on the reader's being more or less deluded" (p. 87). Here Winters accuses Eliot of deluding the reader; at other points he accuses him of "evasive dallying" and "taking refuge in mystery." His most common response to Eliot is that of the little boy who shouted that the emperor had no clothes; he refuses to be party to what he perceives as deception. Now although Winters frequently refers to the generally accepted belief that Eliot's practice was almost wholly derived from Pound, he does not accuse Pound of actual bad faith as he does Eliot. He retained a lingering regard for Pound, but his attitude to Eliot stops little short of contempt. Why is this? A phrase in Winters's rebuttal of Eliot's defense of "qualitative progression" gives us a clue: the phrase is "a professed classicist."

Eliot, like Winters, concerned himself with ethical and metaphysical problems, and the two came to superficially very similar conclusions. But however alike their positions may have seemed to be at first glance, they were in reality radically divergent; Winters is at pains to maintain the divergence, to distance himself from one who, he believed, was claiming a position to which he had no right. As in a religious war the maintenance of the purity of the faith can seem more important than crusades against total outsiders; the Roman and Byzantine Christians were usually more ready to fight each other than do battle against the armies of Islam. The heretic is a greater threat than the unbeliever because he claims to have the true interpretation of a belief one holds oneself. Eliot called himself a classicist and an Anglo-Catholic; Winters called himself a classicist and a Thomist. It is the apparent proximity of positions Winters believed in reality to be opposed to each other which leads him to attack Eliot's position so emphatically. Eliot, Winters believed, had usurped classicism, Christian intellectual traditions, and logic, and was prepared to use them for ends unclassical, un-Christian, and illogical.

The complexity of the situation is compounded in that both authors declared themselves to have been converted to this classicist stance from a thoroughgoing modernist or experimentalist position. And by a remarkable coincidence the change of heart occurred at virtually the same moment. Winters first gave clear expression to his new allegiances in 1929 (though they had been hinted at in a review of *Fugitives* published in 1928 [*Uncollected Essays and Reviews*, pp. 51–55]). In 1943 Winters wrote of Eliot, "The year 1928 should be held in mind as a crucial one . . . for it was in this year . . . that he announced his conversion to Catholicism and classicism" (*In Defense of Reason*, p. 460). Though he could easily have distinguished his own Thomism from Eliot's Anglo-Catholicism (Eliot's conversion was to a dogma, Winters's to a method of inquiry), he was more interested in Eliot's claim to classicism.

As we have seen, the classical temper was for Winters, following Babbitt, bound up with notions of decorum and human dignity. These notions depended on a recognition of the efficacy of the human will, at least in its ability to control the self, and the desirability of the will's being guided by reason rather than emotion or instinct. Winters detects as the basis of a great deal of Eliot's theoretical writing, and of the whole of his poetry, the notion that the will and reason play no part in the creation of poetry. He quotes with incredulity Eliot's contention that Dante and Shakespeare did not think, and Eliot's representation of the process of writing: "At the moment when one writes, one is what one is, and the damage of a lifetime, and of having been born into an unsettled society, cannot be repaired at the moment of composition" (*In Defense of Reason*, p. 486). Winters is naturally appalled at such supine determinism:

> At the moment when one writes one is what one is: one has, in other words no power over that moment; one must surrender to one's feelings and one's habits at that moment if one is to achieve sincerity. . . . Obviously one will not change one's literary habits between moments of composition; one will change them if at all in writing. And if one's conversion to Catholicism and to classicism is worth a flourish of the pen, it is worth risking a few years of unsatisfactory composition in order to form new habits. . . . Eliot's position is one of unmitigated determinism. [P. 487]

The phrase "having been born into an unsettled society" is seen as a sign of a distinctively modern brand of poetic determinism—the notion of a gradual disintegration of the splendors of a once-coherent Christian society—traced by Winters to its source in Henry Adams. Winters will have none of this, and suggests that if Dante and Aquinas achieved any eminence it was by their own efforts, not as a result of submitting to "the vast underworld of sluggishly brutal paganism which surrounded them" (p. 487). He also traces to Adams one of Eliot's most typical (and influential) beliefs, that poetry should be "chaotic in order to express chaos." He sarcastically remarks that such a notion would mean Dryden's writing like Shadwell in order to expose his deficiencies; he sees such a blurring of subject and method as a surrender to experience rather than an evaluation of it. He frequently compares Eliot to Baudelaire; after a comparison of *The Waste Land* and *Les fleurs du mal* he concludes, "Eliot, in brief, has surrendered to the accedia which Baudelaire was able to judge; Eliot suffers from the delusion that he is judging it when he is merely exhibiting it" (p. 500). The notion of surrender, of a lack of moral control, is central to Winters's view of Eliot, and he sees it as the source of Eliot's lax, quasi-iambic meters: "The rather limp versification of Mr. Eliot . . . is inseparable from the spiritual limpness that one feels behind the poem" (p. 22).

Occasionally Eliot will, as a Christian, rebuke another author for his lack of spiritual fiber; in the same way he claims that art is autotelic but will sometimes rebuke an author for some ethical solecism. Such self-contradictions particularly annoy Winters: "Andrews . . . is praised because he adheres to my principles, whereas Donne is blamed because he adheres to those of Eliot. Eliot does not explain his self-contradiction, nor does he give any evidence that he is aware of it" (p. 469).

Winters therefore sees Eliot's claim to classicism as spurious. On the contrary, he considered Eliot's ideas as a collection of romantic notions: the idea that art must be chaotic in order to express chaos he traces to Adams; that it is autotelic to Poe and Mallarmé; that the artist searches for an objective correlative to his emotion to the archetypally romantic belief that the purpose of art is the expression of emotion rather than the understanding and evaluation of reality. Classicism for Winters involved clarity and control, the exercise of the will in the service of reason, a suspicion of the vague and inexplicable—particularly if it threatened to assume any kind of sway over an author's identity. The submission to the *Zeitgeist* which he believed was the gist of Eliot's criticism and the attempted practice of his poetry could only be seen by Winters as the reverse of classicism.

Winters's attitude towards Wallace Stevens was ambivalent: on the one hand he saw Stevens as one of those traditional poets whom he had admired throughout his own experimental stage, almost, as it were, against his own conscious practice (the others were Baudelaire, Valéry, Hardy, Bridges, and Robinson) and whose example led him to question experimentalism; on the other hand he saw much of Stevens's poetry—especially his later poetry—as being vitiated by the neoromantic ideas he discerned in the work of the experimentalists.

I remarked above that Winters was one of the first critics to draw attention to the excellence of Stevens's work. He was also one of the first to draw attention to the central importance of "Sunday Morning" in Stevens's oeuvre: he saw it as the principal statement of Stevens's chief, perhaps only, theme.

This theme he defines as "the situation of the isolated man in a meaningless universe." The definition comes from *Forms of Discovery* (p. 277), by which time Winters's own concerns had come to include the ethical situation of man in just such a universe; he shows some irritation with Stevens for not progressing beyond a repeated statement of his premise. But if we consider the theme we can see that it is, in essence, a statement of the presuppositions that lie behind Winters's own poetry. The isolation of man, his separation from the rest of the universe by reason of his consciousness, is crucial to Winters's poetry: in his early poems it is a flaw to be smoothed away in hallucinatory trance; in the later work it is an indication of man's essential difference from the rest of the world, a distinction that should be maintained and the destruction of which involves a loss of the essentially human. Winters begins from the fact of this isolation which, with Stevens, he sees as tragic and unavoidable. The "meaningless universe" is an apt equivalent for that chaos of experience existing over against man's consciousness which Winters continually posits. Thus Stevens's initial appraisal of man's situation is similar to Winters's, and not only the appraisal but also the attitude of wondering concern which he adopts towards it. And there are further parallels, for example, in their refusal of the consolation of religion, combined with a deeply nostalgic feeling for the religious myths they reject.

Despite Winters's early advocacy of Stevens's verse, he found much to criticize in it. It is the differing responses of the two poets to an initially similar apprehension of the human condition which led Winters to find so much of Stevens's work unsatisfactory. Significantly, Winters considered Stevens's early work, with one or two exceptions, to be his best: the early work states the theme, as Winters understood it, and Winters agrees with this statement. There then arises the problem of what to do next. According to Winters, Stevens's reaction is one of hedonism; his own reaction was stoical and classical. He traces Stevens's hedonism to romantic models, in particular to Poe, and finds it inimical and intellectually flimsy. Discussing "The Man Whose Pharynx Was Bad," he writes: "The situation in which Stevens may here be observed is similar to a difficulty in which Poe found himself. Poe, like Stevens, sought only emotional stimulation in the arts, and hence he considered novelty, and novelty of a fairly crude kind, to be essential to good art. . . . Both men are in search of intense feeling: neither is in search of just feeling, of feeling properly motivated" (*In Defense of Reason*, pp. 438–39).

Stevens thus becomes another of those romantic poets whom Winters had characterized in his book on Edwin Arlington Robinson as being "on a tour in search of emotion." The search for emotional stimulation, if it did not result in insanity, could only end, Winters believed, in the besetting sin of romanticism—ennui—and it is this ennui which he sees as the source of Stevens's whimsicality and dandyism: "The hedonism . . . led to boredom, romantic ennui, and to alleviate the boredom the poet was moved to greater and greater indulgence in stylistic excess" (*Forms of Discovery*, p. 273).

But though Winters could only deplore what he took to be Stevens's romantic reaction to his initial apprehension of the human condition, he was profoundly moved by Stevens's expression of this condition, by the rhetoric Stevens brought to bear on his diagnosis. He discusses the closing stanza of "Sunday Morning," for example, with a sympathy that—as in some of his discussions of Robinson's work—seems autobiographical in its intensity. The terms of the discussion, the meaning apprehended by Winters in the poem, and the sense we have of his convinced acquiescence in the truth of that meaning recall to us how close the poem's concerns are to the preoccupations of Winters's own poetry, both his earlier poetry with its intimations of "beatitude" and his later work's concern with "invading impersonality":

> The "water without sound," the "wide water inescapable," is not only an image representing infinite space; it is an image, established in the first stanza, representing a state of mind, a kind of bright and empty beatitude, over which the thought of death may darken suddenly and without warning. . . . The mind perceives, as by a kind of metaphysical sense, the approach of invading impersonality; yet knowing the invasion to be inevitable and its own identity . . . the only source of good whatever, maintains that identity in its full calm and clarity. . . . This combination of calm and terror, in dealing with this particular theme, will be found in only one other poet in English, in Shakespeare. [*In Defense of Reason*, p. 447]

The "combination of calm and terror" might be found only in Shakespeare, but it is, I would suggest, precisely the effect Winters himself tries for in his own poems that deal with "invading impersonality," and I have indicated already that Stevens was probably an important influence in

Winters's choice of symbols, for example, his use of the sea and moon-light as symbols of experience and the imagination, respectively.

Further he saw in Stevens, as in Valéry, a perfect example of the post-symbolist method—the fusing of the sensuous and the intellectual in an identity beyond the arbitrary mechanics of allegory—to which he devoted so much of his last book, *Forms of Discovery*. Of the pigeons at the end of "Sunday Morning" he wrote: "The pigeons embody an idea as well as a feeling, and the idea motivates the feeling. The pigeons cannot be separated from the idea: they are a part of the universe which the poet is trying to understand, and at this point they are an efficiently representative part. The rational soul and the sensible soul are united: we do not have the purely rational soul of Jonson nor the purely sensible soul of Pound; and there is no decoration" (*Forms of Discovery*, p. 276).

Despite Stevens's lack of interest in Winters's own brand of ethical stoicism, the basic premises of Stevens's position were close enough in origin, and the suavity of his rhetoric was close enough in intention, to Winters's own perceptions and aims for Winters to feel a strong and abiding sympathy with his work. As so often in Winters's perception of the work of his contemporaries or near contemporaries, it is this very proximity that seems to provoke from him his most contemptuous comments when he feels that a position he discerned and shared has been betrayed. It is this that accounts for remarks like, "The heir of Milton and Jonson is endeavouring, in his old age, to *épater les bourgeois*" (*In Defense of Reason*, p. 446).

Winters's initial enthusiasm for Stevens's work grew more qualified as he discerned in it an emerging trait of romantic hedonism; his early advocacy of William Carlos Williams's poetry was equally forthright, and his later disappointment with this work was even more profound. In the case of Stevens the cooling of Winters's youthful ardor was, he believed, because of developments within Stevens's poetry; in Williams's case it was the change in Winters himself, rather than any change in the nature of Williams's work, that led Winters to revise his opinion. Williams is one of the three poets about whom Winters most radically (in print at least) changed his mind. The other two were Hart Crane and Gerard Manley Hopkins, for analogous reasons.

It is clear that the sharply defined perception of the natural world evident in Williams's early work was an influence on Winters's own experimentalist verse. In an essay published in 1948, long after he had repudiated his own experimentalism, together with much of Williams's work, he wrote, "Had it not been for my academic career, it is quite possible that I should still be a minor disciple of W. C. Williams, doing little impressionistic notes on landscapes" (*Uncollected Essays and Reviews*, p. 308). For a while, during the 1920s, the two poets corresponded.

But despite Winters's advocacy of Williams's best work (in 1931 he wrote of him as "a writer who has seemed to me for ten years or so one of the principal geniuses of our time, and whose work has been stupidly neglected and ridiculed" [*Uncollected Essays and Reviews*, p. 111]), Williams's rallying cry of "no ideas but in things" could not be expected to endear him to Winters, and by the beginning of the 1930s Winters was obviously beginning to be alarmed by Williams's unrepentant nominalism. At first he merely remarks that "the range is limited" (1931) and that "half or more of an intelligent man's experience is unintelligible to [Williams] and is ruled out of his poetry" (1932), but by the time he published *Primitivism and Decadence* (1937) he had become decidedly suspicious of the antiintellectual implications of Williams's practice and theories, which, he claimed, led to "a sentimental debauchery of self-indulgence" (*In Defense of Reason*, p. 55).

If Pound is the typical decadent in Winters's characterization, Williams is an archetypal primitive:

> Dr. Williams is a good example of the type of poet whom I should call the contemporary primitive. . . . Such poems as "The Widow's Lament" or "To Waken an Old Lady" are fully realized; the form is complete and perfect; the feeling is sound. Dr. Williams has a surer feeling for language than any other poet of his generation, save, perhaps, Stevens at his best. But he is wholly incapable of coherent thought and he had not the good fortune to receive a coherent system as his birthright. [*In Defense of Reason*, p. 93]

In Winters's later comments this lack of any intellectual framework in Williams's work, his insistence on the sufficiency of the natural world as it is immediately visible as the adequate and proper subject for poetry, becomes, as one would expect, more and more of an irritant to Winters. The evasion of abstraction he naturally sees as a product of romanticism, and the fragmentary and imagistic structure of Williams's verse he traces to the associationism of Shaftesbury and Locke. His 1939 review of Williams's *Collected Poems* begins, "W. C. Williams, in his view of life and poetry, is an uncompromising Romantic," and the rest of the review follows the line one would expect from Winters given such an opening. However, he retained an admiration for certain of Williams's poems (as with his view of Pound's verse he could not quite shake off his first enthusiastic youthful response to the new voice) within what he took to be their very narrow and primitive limits, and he praised Williams's use of rhythm as being more accomplished than that of any other free-verse writer. (He included six poems by Williams in *Quest for Reality*, the anthology of poems he edited shortly before his death; the book contains no poems by either Crane or Hopkins, the two other poets whose work he radically revalued after his own change of poetic direction). He also had a high regard for Williams's prose piece *The Destruction of Tenochtitlan*, combining as it does heroic history, pathos, and a fine threnody for a lost Indian civilization.

His early advocacy and later rejection of Williams's verse (typically, both were maintained against the current of received opinion) is a particularly clear example of how Winters's own development as a poet, and his own perception of the problems and needs of the modern poet, radically influenced his perception of another man's work. He began as a disciple, or at the least a sympathetic imitator, of Williams; his later position was opposed to almost everything in which Williams believed.

Winters did not deny the talent of the experimentalists. As I indicated above he was in many cases one of the first to draw attention to this talent, but a talent for language, even as remarkable as that he discerned in Pound, Williams, and Crane, did not of itself for Winters guarantee the production of great poetry. For him great poetry could only be written within an intellectually sound theoretical framework. Poetry, he believed, was involved with notions of truth and wisdom, and the to him romantic preconceptions of the various primitives and decadents who participated in the experimentalist revolution led, he was sure, to neither truth nor wisdom. He greatly admired their talent for language—of Yeats for example he wrote, "The sonority is real, and I can appreciate it as well as the next man"—but he could not rest as a mere sensibility, a finely tuned register of linguistic subtlety. The acknowledgment of Yeats's "sonority" continues, "but it takes more than sonority to make a great poem. Pure sonority comes to seem pompous and empty" (*Forms of Discovery*, p. 212). His sensitivity to nuances of rhythm and meaning was complemented by a highly idiosyncratic complex of needs which grew on him as he became older, until he found it almost impossible to tolerate poetry that did not satisfy them. These needs were rooted in his deep distrust of the cultivation of emotion for its own sake and of the exploration of areas of experience that were ipso facto indefinable. He demanded of the poet clarity of thought, a consciously maintained control over subject matter and significance, and from the poem a clear indication of the poet's ethical bearings. (As his own poetry, from the David Lamson poems on, became more and more concerned with ethical problems, so his later criticism too is careful to indicate the ethical implications of a poet's beliefs; his essays on Frost and Yeats, for example, are relatively late, and both take issue with their subjects mainly because of what Winters sees as the sentimental (in Frost's case) or vicious (in Yeats's case) ethical and social implications of their work). He was suspicious of anything that could be construed as a surrender to the "chaos of experience," as a sign that the poet had stopped thinking, either because he considered thought irrelevant (Pound, Williams) or because he considered it predestined—his mind an Eliotic sponge reproducing the Spirit of the Age unconsciously, as Eliot believed Dante and Shakespeare to have done. Allied to his notion of authorial control is his distrust of unmotivated feeling, the vague floating moods that engulf the romantic poets in subjective confusion. Ideally he desired from poetry an appraisal, explicit or implicit, of the human condition, and his own inability to accept revealed religion, coupled with a strong desire for absolute standards, gave him a clear predeliction for poets in whose work he discerned that same classical stoicism that he himself considered the appropriate response to man's isolation in a universe at once beautiful and incomprehensible. He believed his own stance to be not dissimilar to that of a clerisy he traced from Aristotle through Aquinas to the more logical poets of the Renaissance, and he considered that the attack on this logical and dignified stoicism by the ideas of romanticism was an invitation to social and cultural barbarism—the mind resigning itself to a welter of meaningless sensation. In his own poetry this fear is generally represented by a terror of personal disintegration, either through "the invasion of the impersonal" or in the more beguiling form of pantheistic trance; in his criticism, especially his later criticism, it is more usually expressed in a concern for the ethical ideas embodied in the poetry under discussion. It is the concepts of what human life is and means which underlie the poems of Pound, Eliot, Williams, Stevens, Yeats, and Frost that lead him to so often reject their work, and in every case he traces these concepts to romanticism of one kind or another. His strictures on particular modernist poetic techniques, pseudoreference and the rest, are the anatomizing of symptoms. The disease is what he takes to be a metaphysical misapprehension, or willful ignoring, of the nature of human life, which he believed to be demonstrably obscured or perverted by romantic notions of the evil of reason and the sacredness of unreflective impulse. These notions had become the unchallenged presuppositions of literature, and to that extent literature was, he believed, vitiated. His particular scorn was reserved for Eliot, whom Winters saw to be as much a child of Emerson and Poe as the rest of them, yet who considered himself a classicist. His case against these poets was not that they lacked talent, but that they had used their talent, through muddled thinking, in the service of an untenable view of human life. If asked for evidence he could point to the (to him paradigmatic) careers of Hart Crane and Ezra Pound.

The lists of fine poets that Winters made in the 1920s and 1930s are now everyone's lists, and he is frequently taken to task for not recognizing the subtleties of work he championed before his latter-day detractors were born. But the lists he made later, mainly after the Second World War, of his contemporaries and juniors, are another matter. Many of these poets are still writing, and there is little critical agreement about their stature, but in general it is true to say that Winters's preferences have not been shared by other critics. His criteria of what constituted good poetry certainly hardened over the years; in his early twenties he had been able to acclaim poets as various as Robinson *and* Stevens *and* Williams *and* Pound—poets who, with the exception of Williams and Pound, probably found little to admire in each other's work. The younger poets he championed later in his life have much more of a family likeness about them, and many of them were directly associated with him either as students or friends or both. His interest in the possibilities of experimentalism clearly waned as he grew older, and he looked for a counterrevolution. Even before the Second World War he thought he had discerned its vanguard in the work of J. V. Cunningham and Louise Bogan (Louise Bogan was in fact slightly older then Winters; nevertheless, he clearly considered her work as indicative of a new and hopeful development rather than as a representative of an older, waning tradition). Of the new poets whose work he championed after the war, certainly the most important were Edgar Bowers and Thom Gunn. It is an unfortunate reflection on modern literary journalism that the work of these major poets (Cunningham, Bogan, Bowers, Gunn) has too often—with the exception of Gunn—been considered largely in terms of the proof it offers of the validity or absurdity of Winters's critical theories, rather than on its own merits.

Winters's criticism on the literatures of the nineteenth and twentieth centuries was, as I hope I have sufficiently demonstrated, intimately involved with those problems which he considered to be of particular importance to a modern poet. That is, it was criticism written by a poet, and by a poet deeply perturbed by what he considered the deleterious effects of the preconceptions that underlay most contemporary literature. His prose writings on the literature of earlier ages may at first sight appear to be more purely objective exercises in literary history; however, we should remember that Winters, like his early mentor Pound, had a habit of considering all poetry as in some sense contemporary, lifted from its peculiar context. In particular, the stylistic problems faced by poets varied, Winters believed, very little from age to age (the chief variation being that though the principles by which good poetry is written are constant these principles are sometimes part of the folk wisdom of an age and sometimes disastrously obscured by that folk wisdom). His writings on earlier poetry are therefore remarkably of a piece with his writings on more recent literature, and this is easily verifiable by a glance at his criticism on, for example, the poets of the eighteenth century. In a work of this scope it would be redundant to demonstrate how Winters's writings on each poet he mentions are in fact imbued with his own often very personal preconceptions and standards. I shall confine myself to a discussion of his work on the late sixteenth and early seventeenth centuries, and on the drama; the reader may take it as axiomatic that the same principles at work in these writings are equally at work in his writings on the later seventeenth and eighteenth centuries. I should perhaps point out that I do not consider the fact that Winters wrote criticism as a poet, and one with very idiosyncratic needs and preoccupations, in any way invalidates his judgments; on the contrary, he brings to his task, particularly in the criticism written during his thirties, such vitality and fresh intelligence—and (which very few critics can bring) such a profound knowledge of the sheer mechanics of writing poetry and of the reasons why men write poetry—that his criticism has in general a continuously cogent authority. His analyses of, for example, the nature of poetry in England in the late sixteenth century seem, to me at least, to be quite simply true.

Criticism on Sixteenth- and Early Seventeenth-Century Literature and on the Drama

Winters's three major essays on the sixteenth century are "The Sixteenth Century Lyric in England: A Critical and Historical Reinterpretation" (published in *Poetry*, 1939), "English Literature in the Sixteenth Century" (the last chapter of *The Function of Criticism* (1957, previously published in the *Hudson Review*, 1955), and "Aspects of the Short Poem in the English Renaissance" (the opening chapter of his last book, *Forms of Discovery* (1967). This last essay is partly a revision of the 1939 essay and partly a conflation of that essay with passages from his contribution to *Four Poets on Poetry* (1959). The first essay seems to me to be by far the best of the three, although it is nowhere reprinted in a collection of Winters's essays. The second is largely a review of books on the sixteenth century and is only incidentally concerned with the literature itself. The chapter in *Forms of Discovery*, though it does have very fine passages, is an altogether more rigidly exclusive and wearily dogmatic affair than the enthusiastic rediscovery of the plain stylists which forms the central argument of the 1939 essay. In 1939 he was mainly interested in persuading his readers to consider forgotten poets; the emphasis in the later book is as much on defining faults as introducing virtues, and the effect is more crabbed than generous. The general argument of the essays is the same in each case—Winters was, with some (usually more negative) modifications, content to let his insights of the 1930s stand—and this pattern is repeated throughout his criticism. When we remember that a large number of his major poems also belong to this decade it is apparent that this was not only the most productive period of his life, in terms of the sheer quantity of work produced, but also the most intellectually vital. Thereafter the insights of his criticism were more and more fitted to already-elaborated theories of literary history and the nature of literary genres. In so far as Winters modified his critical opinions after 1940 it was almost always in the direction of a more rigid definition, a further exclusion of what seemed to him less than first rate (this is clearly discernible in his developing attitude to Shakespeare, for example). But in general it is remarkable how consistent his views of, for example, which are the great poems of the sixteenth century remained—the lists of recommended works given in the 1939 essay differ very slightly from those given in *Forms of Discovery*, though the essays were separated by more than twenty-five years. And if we can say that the creativity of his criticism was succeeded by decades of clarification and exposition, there is too a similar diminution of poetic creativity—the lessons of the 1930s are repeated and consolidated in the poems of the 1940s, and thereafter he wrote very few poems.

Winters called his 1939 essay "a critical and historical reinterpretation," which indeed it was, and to many readers may still be. His epigraph, from Ben Jonson, alerts us to his concerns:

> And it is not always the face,
> Clothes or Fortune gives the grace;

Or the feature, or the youth;
But the Language and the Truth.

Like Jonson, Winters is less interested in the superficially elegant and charming than in "the Truth": the sixteenth-century poetry that attracted him, and which he felt he was rescuing from centuries of comparative neglect, was a poetry of direct integrity. Its subject was the truth (whether external or psychological) and often a truism, and its language exhibited the qualities apparent in the last line of the quotation from Jonson—a straightforwardness that eschews decoration and puts its trust in the unvarnished statement of its meaning.

Winters's basic thesis is that there were two traditions at work in English poetry in the sixteenth century: the Petrarchan style, imported from Italy, and the plain style (though he does not refer to it by this name until the essay included in *The Function of Criticism*), which was native to England. Certain poets wrote almost entirely in the plain style and others almost entirely in the Petrarchan; in the work of some (Drayton, for example) we can perceive an uneasy, unassimilated mixture of the two. The greatest poets, toward the end of the century, were able to combine the preoccupation with truth, a fidelity to the facts of human experience (characteristic of the plain stylists) with the linguistic subtlety of the Petrarchans. Though Winters attempts to be evenhanded in his descriptions of the characteristics of these two styles, and though he reserves his highest praise for those who were able to combine the virtues of both methods, it is nevertheless obvious that given a choice between the average Petrarchan—say, Sidney—and the average plain stylist—say, Gascoigne —he felt a strong temperamental affinity for the latter.

As the passage illuminates not only its subject matter but also, I believe, Winters's own predelictions, I quote his description of the plain style at length:

> The characteristics of the typical poem of the school are these: a theme usually broad, simple and obvious, even tending toward the proverbial, but usually a theme of some importance, humanly speaking; a feeling restrained to the minimum required by its subject; a rhetoric restrained to a similar minimum, the poet being interested in his rhetoric as a means of stating his matter as economically as possible, and not, as are the Petrarchans, in the pleasures of rhetoric for its own sake. . . .
> . . . Only a master of style can deal successfully in a plain manner with obvious matter: we are concerned with the type of poetry

which is perhaps the hardest to compose and the last to be recognized, a poetry not striking nor original as to subject, but merely true and universal, that is, in a sense, commonplace; not striking nor original in rhetorical procedure, but direct and economical, a poetry which permits itself originality, that is the breath of life, only in the most restrained and refined subtleties in diction and in cadence, but which by virtue of those subtleties inspires its universals with their full value as experience. The best poems in the early school are among the most perfect examples of the classical virtues to be found in English poetry. ["Sixteenth Century Lyric," pp. 95–96]

We recognize, particularly in the second paragraph of the extract, not merely exposition but advocacy and sympathy. When Winters writes of "a theme of some importance, humanly speaking," we are sure that he prefers such a theme to the often slight subject matter of the Petrarchans: subject matter he usually refers to as "trivial" or "charming." In the remarks on the restraint of feeling and rhetoric to the "minimum required" we recognize his own distrust of excessive emotion and his strong instinct for decorum and sane balance in the arts—a bias which I believe to have been fundamentally temperamental, so deeply is it embedded in the matrix of his own poetry, but which received theoretical confirmation from his reading of Babbitt.

Further, his description of the plain stylist as one who is "interested in rhetoric as a means of stating his matter as economically as possible, and not . . . in the pleasures of rhetoric for its own sake" can be matched by commendatory remarks scattered throughout his criticism: it was always axiomatic for Winters that the good poet keeps his eye firmly on his subject matter. If for the Elizabethans the temptation to be avoided was the proliferation of "charming" (but essentially "trivial") decoration, the parallel temptation for the more modern poet (made suspicious of decoration by the romantic notion that it is inorganic) was often an excessive interest in his own subjectivity, which would lead to similarly colorful and willful language which obscured rather than clarified the poet's ostensible theme. Winters's linguistic preferences remained constant, whether writing of sixteenth- or twentieth-century poetry: he looked for clarity, definition, and language that was wholly apposite to the subject. He wanted language to reveal subject matter, not to blur it—neither with the *fioritura* of the Elizabethans, nor with the veils of moody personality affected by the romantics and their successors.

If we accept Buffon's "*Le style est l'homme même*," we can more fully understand Winters's advocacy of such predominantly plain stylists as Wyatt, Gascoigne, Googe, and Raleigh. He clearly felt an admiration for the moral plain speaking and integrity of these men, an integrity (of which their poetic style is merely the "ocular proof") which extends beyond their accomplishment as poets. Two extracts from his criticism demonstrate this. The first (on Wyatt) occurs only in the later (from *Forms of Discovery*) version of his essay on sixteenth-century poetry; the second (itself a quotation, from Fulke Greville) appears in both this version and in the earlier (1939) version.

On Wyatt he wrote:

> "Blame not my lute," "It was my choice" and "Is it possible" and many lesser poems deal with Wyatt's dislike of the poetic style variously known as ornate, aureate, sugared or Petrarchan, and with the corresponding form of making love—the courtly or affected way. Wyatt was a believer in the plain style in both activities. The relationship between these activities is close and is not trivial. If poetry is, as I believe it to be, a form of moral judgement, then the poetic form, in regard to this matter, is merely a more refined and precise embodiment of the social form: poetry and morality are one. Wyatt, if we may accept his explicit comments, believed in an honest and permanent love and in a style which would deal with such love in an honest and plain way. [*Forms of Discovery*, pp. 8–9]

And on Greville:

> Of himself Greville wrote in his life of Sidney, "For my own part I found my creeping genius more fixed upon the images of life, than the images of wit, and therefore chose not to write to them on whose foot the black ox had not already trod, as the proverb is, but to those only that are weather beaten in the sea of this world, such as having lost sight of their gardens and groves, study to sail on a right course among rocks and quicksands." [*Forms of Discovery*, p. 52]

The contempt for the merely decorative (and by implication morally oblique) of the passage on Wyatt, together with the "images of life" and the disillusion and quiet stoicism of the passage by Greville, imply a type of character (in life as in poetry) which Winters, from the evidence of his writings, found profoundly sympathetic and indeed appears to have adopted as a conscious model.

One of the most impressive passages celebrating the poetry of disillusion and retreat from the world is Winters's discussion of Gascoigne's work; the sympathy here evinced for the plain man's failure, and sense of being haunted by failure, is—as I have indicated—repeated elsewhere in his criticism, for example, throughout his study of Robinson. Winters's predeliction for such poetry goes deeper than his own skirmishes with the world of his day. The moral and metaphysical darkness that we find in, for example, the later poems of Fulke Greville, a darkness only mitigated at the last moment by Greville's "saving God of mine," that sense of moral frustration apparent in Greville's lines

> Oh wearisome condition of humanity!
> Born under one law, to another bound:
> Vainly begot, and yet forbidden vanity,
> Created sick, commanded to be sound:

is echoed, albeit mutedly, throughout Winters's writings. This disillusion, which so often elicited a commendatory response when he found it in other poets, was not merely a disillusion with the ways of the world (with the "dead living") but also with man's capacity to understand his condition. His admiration for stoicism, derived from his dislike of undefined emotion and his classical instinct for decorum, precluded any great emotional fuss about this ignorance, but the fact of it pervades his writings, and he was clearly drawn to writers who had experienced this same darkness and who had assumed the stance of stoicism as a result.

His temperamental affinity for the plain stylists did not blind him to the achievements of a predominantly Petrarchan poet like Sidney. But his praise of Sidney's work is everywhere tempered by moral impatience, a sense that he is drawing attention to brilliant talent wasted, frittered away on trivialities. Of "Highway, since you my chief Parnassus be," he wrote, "Sidney is concerned here with obtaining what he regards as a graceful manner, a polished surface" ("Sixteenth Century Lyric," p. 108), and though he allows that the "polished surface" is frequently achieved, his objection is that a poet who devotes his energies to the production of superficial effects cannot fail to produce superficial poetry. Nevertheless he conceded that Sidney's technical facility surpassed that of most of the early plain stylists and was the model for later poets like Jonson and Greville. These two (and in the 1939 essay Shakespeare and Donne, though both have rather slipped from grace by the time Forms of Discovery came to be written) combined, in Winters's view, the virtues of both schools—the technical subtlety of the better Petrarchans and the integrity and concern for truth of the better plain stylists.

The fusion of qualities from the two schools produced the finest poetry of the late Elizabethan and Jacobean periods. In the 1939 essay he wrote extensively on three poets whose work exemplified this fusion—Jonson, Donne, and Shakespeare. Greville is seen in the earlier essay as primarily a plain stylist, though in *Forms of Discovery* he too is considered as combining the virtues of both styles, and he has to some extent replaced Donne and Shakespeare as the peer of Jonson.

Jonson is praised as "plain and direct . . . likewise polished and urbane" (that is, combining the virtues of both styles) and is characterized as "a classicist in the best sense" ("Sixteenth Century Lyric," p. 116). It is apparent from the context that by "classicist" Winters means one who takes the mean between eccentric extremes—that is, he saw the classicist in Babbitt's terms, as a man who looks for the centrally and perennially human while eschewing the willful and affected. Jonson's subject matter is described as "chiefly ethical in the narrowest sense of the term . . . his devotional poetry concerns itself explicitly with man's moral relationship to God." The discussion continues: "His view of life is both dramatic and heroic; it is seldom devout; it excludes the mysterious. . . . His language is accurate . . . there is an exact correlation between motive and feeling that may easily be mistaken for coldness . . . by the reader accustomed to more florid enticements" (p. 117). Again, the context defines "dramatic." It indicates Jonson's concern with ethical relations between individuals; it does not refer to the obsessive and colloquial tone often described by the epithet, for which Winters reserves the word *melodramatic*.

It is easy to see from this description why Jonson remained one of Winters's two or three favorite English poets. There is the ethical subject matter, the suggestion of integrity and individualism preserved against odds in the word *heroic*, the eschewing of the mysterious with its attendant stylistic and metaphysical dangers—and above all there is the instinct for propriety manifested in both subject matter and language, and in their relation to each other. This view of Jonson is borne out by the more extensive discussion of his work in *Forms of Discovery* (the additions are largely analyses of particular poems). In this later essay he is compared favorably to Shakespeare and Donne: "Shakespeare, in comparison, succumbed to excessive and uncontrolled sensitivity; Donne shows the vices of both Gascoigne and Sidney, the affectation of harshness on the one hand and of sophisticated ingenuity on the other" (*Forms of Discovery*, p. 63).

His view of Donne remained fairly constant, though the faults noted in the 1939 essay ("his meters are sometimes grossly incorrect. . . . an affectation of directness . . . though genuinely profound [he] often affects profundity, sometimes with grotesque results" ["Sixteenth Century Lyric," p. 119]) are more fully discussed in *Forms of Discovery*. It is clear from the list of faults that it is to those very qualities for which Donne has been most highly praised in this century that Winters took strongest exception—especially his metrical eccentricity (Winters quotes Jonson with approval on Donne's "misplacing of accents"), his use of colloquial diction, and the elaboration of his conceits (if this is what is meant by Donne's "affecting profundity"). The conclusion to the later version of the essay is a definite demotion: "Great as he is, one can find greater poems than any of Donne's in Greville, Jonson and the two Herberts, and one can find more great poems in the first two of these" (*Forms of Discovery*, p. 80).

Winters's view of Shakespeare is especially interesting; it is highly idiosyncratic, and its very idiosyncrasy is an indication of Winters's fundamental views on the nature of poetry, which were violated by much of Shakespeare's work. In general his opinion of Shakespeare's oeuvre became less favorable as he grew older. In *Primitivism and Decadence* (1937) Shakespeare's sonnets are "our standard of the greatest possible poetry" (*In Defense of Reason*, p. 131); but in the 1939 essay we perceive an uneasy truce between Shakespeare's vast reputation and the principles Winters obviously felt he could not abandon even when faced with Shakespeare's apparent dereliction. In *Forms of Discovery* the principles have, as we might expect, won outright. The treatment in the 1939 essay seems to me the most illuminating, and I shall concentrate on that.

Near the opening of the essay Winters remarks, "We tend to find in poetry what we are looking for," and it is notorious that Shakespeare is the writer par excellence into whose works readers peer only to make out their own rather murky reflection. Winters does not seem to be an exception; he writes that Shakespeare "displays in certain poems an obsession with certain metaphysical notions of time and destruction, particularly in their subtle impingement upon the human consciousness. [He] is minutely aware—almost sensuously aware—of the invading chaos, the unmanageable and absorptive continuum, amid which the ethical man, the man of free choice and of usable distinctions, exists" ("Sixteenth Century Lyric," p. 120).

Three points emerge: the emphasis on man as an ethical being threatened by an unmanageable universe, the sense of external reality as "an invading chaos," and, as a particular example of the latter, an obsession with the attrition of time. These are all preoccupations which—as the reader must be aware—permeate Winters's own poetry. The essay then goes on to compare Shakespeare and Donne in a passage which again parallels Winters's own poetic concerns:

> Shakespeare's difficulties are pre-Christian; his sensibility is metaphysical at times but not theological; his mood is perplexed, awed, and at times astounded, but it is practically never devout. . . .
>
> Donne tends to deal with the recognition of definitions. His best poetry is composed mainly of explicit definitions, or of explicit and definite figurative excursions from definitions. . . . I should say that Shakespeare tends to approach the metaphysical in a more direct and immediate fashion, as regards the experience, an approach which paradoxically leads to a more evasive, or at least elusive, expression. That is, he constantly sees the matter that haunts him, as a quality, and frequently as an almost sensuous quality, of something else, and so treats it indirectly. . . . Shakespeare's method makes for a richer sensuous texture, for greater and more elusive suggestion. Donne's makes for a greater certainty and for greater concentration and completeness. Of the two methods Donne's appears to me, abstractly considered, the sounder, or at least the safer. ["Sixteenth Century Lyric," p. 121]

Winters here draws a distinction between the "metaphysical" sensibility haunted by its problems but lacking a structure with which to apprehend or define them, and the "theological" sensibility that has to hand a syntax or system by which the numinous or mysterious is at least categorized if not tamed. This distinction is remarkably like that we perceive between Winters's earlier poetry, where both subject matter and style convey just such a haunted sensibility, and the later verse, where logic and syntax are the outer expression of a rational and categorizing approach to reality. Winters claims that the haunted, metaphysical sensibility is reduced to hints and comparisons to convey its meaning, whereas the theological sensibility can present meaning more directly through the built-in grid of its system. Direct contact with the numinous produces verse which is sensuously rich but "evasive or at least elusive" when it comes to paraphrasable meaning. Winters is here arguing against that absorption in the numinous which had been the goal of his own early work; he is demanding a perspective rather than absorption. This is in line with his own change of direction, which was in essence from the method he here ascribes to Shakespeare to the method he ascribes to Donne. Interestingly, he says that Donne's method seems to him "the sounder, or at least the safer." Though he goes on to describe this safety in terms of the subsequent development of English verse, we can see in his choice of the word a hint of his own sense of danger associated with the haunted sensibility.

The indirectness of Shakespeare's approach led him, Winters believed, to invest the connotative power of language with a disproportionate emphasis; unable or unwilling to state meaning directly, he obliquely suggests it. Winters analyzes the sonnet "Thy glass will show thee how thy beauties wear," concentrating particularly on the word *waste* to demonstrate this. The demonstration is one carried out very much in terms of Winters's own version of man's relations with reality:

> In the ninth line the enemy invades the mind, the centre of being; it was the conceit of the blank book that enabled the poet to extend the familiar figure to this brilliant and terrifying conclusion. This terrifying subject, the loss of identity before the uncontrollable invasion of the impersonal, is no sooner suggested than it is dropped. . . .
>
> . . . We may consider especially the adjective "waste," in the phrase "Commit to these waste blanks." The word is obviously a pun, with the emphasis on the secondary meaning. It means not only "unused" or "blank," but it means "desert" or "uninhabited" or "uninhabitable," a sense reinforced by the word "waste" in the second line. It carries over the feeling of the invading chaos from the preceding line; but rationally considered the pages are not waste in this sense, but are the instruments offered for actually checking the invasion of the waste. A feeling, in other words, is carried over from its proper motive to a motive irrelevant to it.
>
> . . . we have a discreet example of the most perilous of all procedures, the use of expressive or imitative form; in order to express the invasion of confusion the poet for a moment actually enters the realm of confusion instead of describing it. ["Sixteenth Century Lyric," p. 122]

Winters's obsession with "the invading chaos" is clear enough; clear too is his preference that the poet step back from the flux of experience in order to describe it, that to "enter the realm of confusion" is "the most perilous of all procedures." And he is suspicious of meanings that conflict with the logical meaning of the words; he distrusts connotation if it begins to lead an independent existence of its own, implying a meaning that subverts or contradicts the denotative meaning. In this sonnet the blur of meaning surrounding the word *waste* worries him—it smacks too much

of the unexplained metaphysical frisson and not enough of ordered theological comprehension. An examination of Winters's later writing on
Shakespeare will quickly show the reader that he came more and more to
distrust the aura of suggestion which is so typical of Shakespeare's language and to which Shakespeare certainly owes much of his immense
reputation. He also distrusted the form to which Shakespeare gave most
of his attention, the drama.

Winters's main discussion of the drama as a form is in the opening essay
of *The Function of Criticism*. This essay, "Problems for the Modern Critic
of Literature," was first published in 1956—quite late in Winters's career
and well after the period during which he produced most of his best critical work. It is, inter alia, a discussion of the virtues and defects, seen by
Winters as inherent, of particular literary genres. The discussion of the
drama, which is brief, concentrates on three plays, *Macbeth*, *Volpone*, and
Phèdre. As the authors of two of these fall within the Elizabethan-Jaco-
bean period I mention the discussion here.

   Winters is certainly unhappy with the drama as a form, and indeed
everything to do with it seems to have prompted a kind of revulsion
in him—some fairly vituperative remarks about actors are scattered
throughout his writings. I would guess that the element of dishonesty
inherent in the very idea of acting revolted both his love of plainness and
his sense of decorum and tact. His minimal concern seems prompted
only by the attention given to it by authors whom he admired, often for
quite other reasons (Shakespeare, though his admiration was waning by
the time this essay was written; Racine, whose Jansenism—a doctrine
close to Winters's own views—appears to have attracted him; and Jonson, who was simply his favorite English poet with the possible exception of Greville).

   He begins his discussion with a general exposition of what he believed
a work of literature to be: "In each work there is a content which is rationally apprehensible, and each work endeavors to communicate the
emotion which is appropriate to the rational apprehension of the subject.
The work is thus a judgement, rational and emotional, of the experience"
(*Function of Criticism*, p. 26). It is in the word *judgment* that Winters's objection to the drama lies. Phèdre, for example, lives out the particularity
of her experience before us. When she speaks we are not given Racine's
judgment of her situation, or even her own judgment. We are merely
presented with the situation, unjudged; "the speeches are expressions of

suffering only, and almost of self-pity" (p. 27). It is this lack of distance between text and experience that troubles Winters. Turning to Macbeth, he makes the same point more elaborately:

> Let us suppose that the dramatist is imitating the speech of a character of moderate intelligence in a situation of which the character does not in any serious sense understand the meaning. This presents an almost insoluble problem. If a poet is endeavoring to communicate his own best understanding of a human situation, that is one thing. If he is endeavoring to communicate approximately a plausible misunderstanding of a situation on the part of an imaginary character much less intelligent than himself, that is quite another. . . .
>
> In Act II Scene 1 of *Macbeth*, for example, Macbeth leaves the stage to kill Duncan. Just before he goes out there occurs the dagger speech. Macbeth is, at this point in the action, uneducated by his sin.. . . . His character here is that of a competent but rough opportunist, somewhat more intelligent than most men of his kind but far less intelligent than he is shortly to become. . . . The situation calls for powerful statement; but the statement must be made by an imperfect intelligence. [P. 53]

By speaking through his characters who are caught in the flux of life and limited by their partial apprehension of their circumstances and actions, the dramatist cannot speak to us directly with his full intelligence; he must involve his meaning in particulars whose immediacy can only blur any possible judgment. It is the objection that we have already noted Winters held to dramatic verse—truth is given to us through a distorted medium, through the obsessive emotion of a "character." Of the end of Macbeth's dagger speech he wrote, "The poet surrenders the form of his statement to the formlessness of his subject-matter" (p. 54). This involvement of form with subject matter, the confusion of distinction between experience and the mind that apprehends the experience, was anathema to Winters. He appears to be demanding that the speeches of a play function according to the criteria he has demonstrated as desirable for the short poem. In fact he is not demanding this because he knows it to be impossible, but precisely because it is impossible he considers the drama as an inherently flawed form. This had not always been his view: almost twenty years previously, in *Maule's Curse*, he had stated that the great passages of epic or the drama "must be read in their context if they are not to seem inferior in quality to the shorter poems. This does not mean that they are an inferior kind of poetry; it means that they are a different kind of poetry" (*In Defense of Reason*, p. 219).

To most of us the particular attraction and power of the drama lie precisely in the inextricable involvement of the mind with the particulars of experience. But to Winters this is seen as a lack of perspective, an emotional pressure that precludes the clear presentation of reality. Comparing *Macbeth* to *Phèdre* he wrote: "The play is not merely an account of the tragic consequences of a particular irrational passion, as is *Phèdre*; it is an account of the tragic consequences of irrational passion. It is thus the greater play" (*Function of Criticism*, p. 28). For Winters art approaches greatness as it approaches the universal. And he prefers that this universal be directly stated rather than merely suggested. The speeches of disillusionment uttered by Macbeth toward the end of the play are very generalized indeed, and for Winters the worth of the play lies in this transcending of the particular circumstances which to most readers *are* the play, and a necessary matrix for the generalized speeches.

Another aspect of the drama, apart from the necessarily embroiled nature of its language, seems worth considering if we are to account for Winters's distaste for the form. The multiplicity of characters in a play (especially a Shakespearean play), each with its own implied values and version of reality, points to a relativism that seems fundamental to the very idea of drama. It is a cliché that drama depends on conflict: if there is to be conflict it is usually between two or more sets of values, and if we are to be engaged in the play's action we must be able, at least theoretically, to sympathize with both aspects of the struggle. Though Winters does not discuss this problem it is significant that he deals with plays (which he regards very highly, with the caveat that he disapproves of the genre as such) in which this relativism is fairly subdued, and where the conclusion of the play points to a clear moral position. It is significant too that he takes it as axiomatic that tragedy is superior to comedy: the focus in tragedy is usually more sharply defined than in comedy, if only because it concentrates on the sensibility of the protagonist, whose apprehension of reality and downfall are the play's raison d'être. The ironies and conflicting implications of Shakespearean comedy are more fundamentally irresolvable and frequently suggest that the audience and players must necessarily live in the relative and that a hunger for absolutes is a disease to be cured. This relativism, implicit in tragedy, clearly visible in comedy (and occupying the center of the stage in Shakespeare's problem plays) acounts in large part, I believe, for Winters's antagonism toward the drama. And it seems no accident that the moral Winters sees in the three plays he chooses to discuss as the best of a bad category—*Phèdre*, *Macbeth*, and *Volpone*—is identical in each case: the deleterious effects of an obsessive and irrational passion. Though he could agree with such a conclusion, the vivid portrayal of extreme emotions which we frequently encounter in drama (emotions which are presented unjudged and as being of compelling interest for their own sake), cannot have recommended the form to him.

But though, given his own criteria, Winters's distaste for the drama is explicable, it is a judgment that is particularly difficult to endorse. His declared preference for reading plays rather than seeing them should give us pause, particularly in the case of Shakespeare, whose plays were undoubtedly written to be seen rather than read. Further, Winters only fleetingly considers the notion that judgment—if that is what we are looking for—may reside elsewhere than in a line-by-line perusal of the text. The sense of an epiphany of meaning, arising from the flux of relative values embodied in character and plot, and which is the product only of a particularly fine live presentation of a play (as against private reading of the play) appears to have held little interest for Winters. His concern was with the text, and he was suspicious of such indefinable manifestations of meaning.

Winters's view of seventeenth-century poetry was similar to that of many of his contemporaries, in that he saw it as a gradual decadence after the achievements of the generation of Donne and Jonson—a decadence accelerated rather than retarded by Milton. Or, to use the metaphor he himself used of later and similar developments, the latter part of the century was parasitic on the work of its first decades.

For Winters, the sound logical structure of the plain style and a rhetorical sophistication derived from the ornate or Petrarchan style united to form a medium of unequaled suavity and power. No sooner had this marriage been effected, however, than it began to break down. Or rather the unity began to break down in another direction, in the cleavage between pietism and worldliness. Winters saw this as symbolized by the careers of the two Herberts: George Herbert displaying (except in his best poems) "a cloying and almost infantile pietism" and his brother Edward representing a "worldliness which is beginning to leave religion behind" (*Forms of Discovery*, pp. 81, 88). He then goes on to demonstrate how the style too began to break down under this pressure, the religious verse inheriting the conceits and suavity of the ornate style, the secular verse continuing the plain style's traditions.

It is possible to see a parallel here with T. S. Eliot's doctrine of a "dissociation of sensibility"; both see the generation after Donne as establishing a compartmentalizing of experience, an inability, or refusal, to "see life whole." Winters nowhere adduces social reasons for this compartmentalization. The religious and social state of an England preparing itself for religious and political civil war is not mentioned. He rarely indulged in considerations of why poetry followed a particular course at a particular time, preferring, like Babbitt, to concentrate on the influence of specifically intellectual events such as Locke's associationism or the influence of New England transcendentalism. Influences for Winters were almost invariably intellectual, and even then his opposition to any suggestion of determinism led him to emphasize that they are, given sufficient awareness and will, resistable.

Despite the irritation shown with the majority of George Herbert's poems, Winters singled out one, "Church Monuments"; this and Jonson's "To Heaven" are "the most impressive short poems of the English renaissance" (*Forms of Discovery*, p. 84). Winters analyzes the poem at length, and it is difficult to resist the impression that the poem has been chosen very largely for its subject matter—for the stoicism evinced, the acceptances of the limits of human knowledge, above all for the apprehension of the fact of death (Winters was always particularly sensitive to poetry that claimed such an apprehension, death being the clearest manifestation of that hallucinated sense of time passing which pervades his earlier poems, and also of the natural destruction of consciousness, an important theme in his later poetry). All these are subjects which we recognize as being of particular concern to Winters. Our sense of Winters's personal involvement with the poem's themes is confirmed when he claims that "there is nothing explicitly Christian in the poem, no reference to any exclusively Christian doctrine or attitude. The poem deals with the vanity of life and the necessity of preparing for death" (p. 86). He attempts to rescue the poem from its intellectual milieu, which he does not share, so that it becomes more accessible, more a paradigm of anyone's experience rather than specifically the Christian's.

According to Winters, the substructure of the seventeenth-century lyric survived with sufficient strength for there to be a considerable number of poets able to write fine poems within the tradition established by Jonson and Donne. In *Forms of Discovery* Winters praises, and frequently analyzes, poems by King, Crashaw, Herrick, Vaughan, Traherne, and Marvell. The poems chosen sometimes seem idiosyncratic and hardly representative of their authors: Vaughan, for example, is praised for "To His Books" and "The Lamp." Neither poem is typical of Vaughan's concerns, but both are typical of Winters's. "To His Books" describes "the struggle toward the intellectual life and, at the end, the desperate awareness of one's own limitations" (p. 101). As with Herbert's "Church Monuments" Winters remarks that "we do not have the explicitly Christian context." "The Lamp" concerns "a speaker who is confronting death, alone, in a remote countryside, and laboring with the tools of his religion to adjust himself" (p. 100). It is noticeable that in those cases where Winters had recorded his opinion of a poet's work before *Forms of Discovery* the later discussion is almost invariably less enthusiastic, less open, more concerned with the exact definition of an impersonal excellence rather than with the acceptance of whatever individual contribution a particular writer may have to make (see, for example, the discussions of Crashaw in *Primitivism and Decadence* and *Forms of Discovery*).

I believe that the best of Winters's later criticism is to be found in the three books *Primitivism and Decadence*, *Maule's Curse*, and *The Anatomy of Nonsense*, collected together under the title *In Defense of Reason*. The criticism contained in this volume was written within the period subsequent to his own change of poetic direction; it has a cogency of insight which is inextricably involved with the importance—and not merely the literary importance but the psychological and metaphysical importance as well—which Winters at this time attached to the issues it addresses. As I hope I have demonstrated, it is criticism written by a poet reading the literature of the immediate and more distant past as well as that of his contemporaries with his own distinctive poetic, psychological, and metaphysical concerns vitally informing the process. This is not to imply that the criticism written after 1947 is greatly inferior to *In Defense of Reason*, but a diminution of intellectual urgency and vitality is detectable, particularly in parts of *Forms of Discovery*. This last volume contains excellent analyses of particular poems, as fine as any to be found elsewhere in Winters's criticism, but it can also be more querulous than incisive, more concerned to exclude than to define. It is, of course, impossible to define without excluding and the shift is one of emphasis and tone rather than of substance, but it is nevertheless real. The reader should perhaps bear in mind that Winters was dying, and knew he was dying, while he wrote *Forms of Discovery*; it was to be his last literary testament (together with its companion volume, the anthology *Quest for Reality*), and he perhaps deliberately sacrificed the vivacity and generosity of spirit evident in, for example, the 1939 essay on Elizabethan verse, for what he saw as a more lapidary, albeit exclusive and minatory, final statement of his position.

Throughout this study I have emphasized that Winters was first and foremost a poet, but it would be foolish and churlish to regret the criticism, which has greatly enriched our understanding of areas as diverse as nineteenth-century American literature, the sixteenth-century lyric and modern American verse. The criticism gains, rather than loses, by having been written by a poet with such a precise and subtly intimate knowledge of style, technique, and the nature of literary creation. In matters of intellectual history he was often content to follow mentors whom he trusted (Babbitt, Parkes); in matters of style he had his own thorough knowledge of technique to draw on. Quite simply, he knew—and knew more profoundly than any save a few other great poet-critics like Johnson and Arnold have done—what he was talking about.

Conclusion

It is ironic that a man committed to a vision of the classical, to what is central and constant in the human experience of the world, should have found himself so much at odds with the poetic practice and critical theory of his own day. In *Maule's Curse*, published in 1938, he ridiculed Poe's "process of systematic exclusion, in the course of which he eliminates from the field of English poetry nearly all of the greatest acknowledged masters, reserving the field very largely to Coleridge, Tennyson, Thomas Moore, himself and R. H. Horne." At the time this was written his own judgments had a breadth of sympathy and understanding that made Poe's ad hoc tradition seem absurdly exclusive and eccentric: and yet there are moments in Winters's last book, *Forms of Discovery*, where he appears to have painted himself into a similarly lonely corner. The concern with the classical vision gradually gave place to a related concern with those few who, Winters believed, could discern this vision: in the work of poets as various as Gascoigne, Churchill, Very, and Robinson, it was as much their stoic sense of being disregarded by fortune and men's eyes as the actual vision they recorded that moved Winters's interest. In a similar way, though Winters's version of the poet (after 1929) was always of a man embattled with reality, the metaphysical battles of the criticism of his thirties—with time, death and the "invasion of the impersonal"—were often replaced, as he became more concerned with ethical and social issues, by battles with the "dead living." Yet his achievement remains, when all is said and done, major. The best of his early verse has a freshness and limpidity, and a sensitivity to rhythm, unequaled save in the best work of William Carlos Williams. What he considered to be his major important poetry—that written after 1929—has been unjustly neglected, largely I suspect because of his reputation as a pugnaciously antimodernist critic, rather than for reasons intrinsic to the verse itself. To live with these poems is to be aware of a mind intensely sensitive to the reality of both the life of the intellect, and the nature of the physical world in which that intellect must live. The consciousness that informs the poetry is perpetually attuned to the claims of both spirit and world; it works toward balance, toward a just vision, toward a true

233

and clear understanding of the nature of our life. The "massive calm" of these poems is intensely moving to one who has experienced the reality of their premises and who can sympathize with Winters's temperamental need to define the limits of our understanding with lapidary certainty. His best poems, "Apollo and Daphne," "The Slow Pacific Swell," "The Marriage," "On a View of Pasadena from the Hills," "John Sutter," "The California Oaks," "Sir Gawaine and the Green Knight," present us with sensory experience—a sense of the mind drenched in the physical reality of the world—and, simultaneously, an intellectual passion for understanding rarely equaled in the poetry of this century.

The significance of his criticism was, for Winters, as I have attempted to demonstrate, intimately bound up with his notions of what was wrong with modern literature, in particular modern poetry. He read literature as a poet, looking for warnings, models, pitfalls. Again his ideal was one of balance, and his dislike of so much modern literature was largely a regret for what it had sacrificed rather than disdain for what it had achieved. He welcomed the increase in sensitivity that he discerned in the work of the late romantics, he merely regretted that this increase had been gained at the expense of logical form, of denotative meaning. His ideal was a combination of such sensitivity with rigorous and verifiable logical structure; he claimed to have found such a combination in the best work of Valéry and Wallace Stevens. Yet to a reader more interested in Winters's ostensible subjects than in his own poetic preoccupations, his writings—especially on sixteenth-century poetry and nineteenth-century American literature—are among the clearest and most useful available. It is time he was accorded his true place, as one of the major figures of twentieth-century American literature.

As we have seen (from his remarks, for example, on the poetry of Frost and Yeats) Winters became more and more concerned, as he grew older, with the social and ethical implications of poetry. He characterized himself as a "reactionary," and it has even been suggested that his concern with order and form was somehow indicative of an incipient fascism. The charge was somewhat nebulously made by Robert Gorham Davis in the Winter 1949–50 issue of the *American Scholar*. In the April issue Winters wrote an angry and pained reply, setting out his theoretical opposition to fascist beliefs and listing his (impeccably liberal) practical political activities and affiliations. His answer, in part, is as follows:

> I believe in the reality of absolute truth; and since I am not a Platonist, I accept the theistic explanation of this reality offered by

Averroes, Avicenna and Aquinas—namely that true judgement and true knowledge reside in God, that it is the duty of every man to approximate them as closely as his particular talents permit. Now if this is actually or potentially a fascistic notion, then every believing Christian and Jew is a fascist, to say nothing of many others. Actually this belief is immovably anti-fascist, for it places the responsibility for his own development (and perhaps salvation) solidly on the individual, and it indicates that any arbitrary interference with his assuming the responsibility is evil. The fascist, (or any totalitarian) state, however, indicates that true knowledge and judgement reside in the Leader, and that it is the duty of the citizen to accept his verdicts without question. There is no conceivable reconciliation of these points of view. [P. 299]

In fact, Winters's concern with individual ethical responsibility, with his view of poetry as a process of moral evaluation whose chief end is the modification of the reader's sensibility so that he understands more clearly and fully the nature of human existence in the world, both point to a moral sensitivity hardly compatible with either the glorification of violence or the demand that the individual merge his being in that of a greater whole, be it state or race, endemic in fascism. Further, as we have seen from his own poetry, his ideals of human existence in the world were deeply imbued with notions of self-restraint, dignity and moral decorum. He viewed all suggestions of violation, spoliation, and trespass beyond natural and abiding limits with horror. The whole tenor of his writings indicates that the individual is responsible for his own spiritual state—his ideal is the rational man who understands and chooses, and he frequently seems impatient with determinist psychological models of human behavior which concentrate on the neurotic and the child, both categories in which the role of reason is diminished.

My chief concern in mentioning this aspect of Winters's work is not to refute the absurd charge of his potential fascism—a charge which his own actions and writings amply refute without outside help—but to draw attention to the fact that Winters's classicism and concern for reason and ethical probity were of a piece and prevented his being deluded, either in part or wholly (as so many of the major literary figures of this century have been deluded) by any of the versions of totalitarianism and moral and political nihilism peddled in his lifetime. This in itself should give significant pause to those readers who would dismiss his message and preoccupations as outmoded or trivial. His concern was with the centrally and perennially human, with the individual's apprehension of the nature of his life, here, in time and in the flesh. The focus of his vision was unwaveringly clear, undisturbed by notions, whether political or literary or both, of what Borges has called "energetic barbarism."

Selected Bibliography

Primary Sources

Russell, Frances Theresa, and Winters, Yvor. *The Case of David Lamson: A Summary*. San Francisco: Lamson Defense Committee, 1934.

Winters, Yvor. "Alan Swallow, 1915–66." *Southern Review* 3 (Summer 1967): 796–98.

———. "By Way of Clarification." *Twentieth Century Literature* 10 (October 1964): 130–35.

———. *Collected Poems*. London: Routledge and Kegan Paul, 1960. This is the edition prepared by Winters himself.

———. *The Collected Poems of Yvor Winters*. Introduction by Donald Davie. Manchester, England: Carcanet, 1978. This includes Winters's introduction to his *Early Poems 1920–28*, and his short story "The Brink of Darkness." Page references in the text are to this edition.

———. "The Critical Method of T. Weiss." *Quarterly Review of Literature* 2 (Winter 1945): 133–41.

———. *Edwin Arlington Robinson*. Norfolk, Conn.: New Directions, 1946.

———. *Forms of Discovery*. Chicago: Alan Swallow, 1967.

———. *The Function of Criticism*. Denver: Alan Swallow, 1957.

———. *In Defense of Reason*. Chicago: Swallow Press, 1947. This includes the texts of *Primitivism and Decadence*, 1937; *Maule's Curse*, 1938; *The Anatomy of Nonsense*, 1943; *The Significance of The Bridge*, 1947.

———. *The Journey*. Ithaca, N.Y.: Dragon Press, 1931.

———. "The New Criticism and the Democratic Tradition, A Protest." *American Scholar* 19 (Spring 1950): 227–30.

———. "Poetry, Morality, and Criticism." In *The Critique of Humanism, A Symposium*, edited by Clinton Hartley. New York: Brewer and Warren, 1930.

———. "The Poetry of T. Sturge Moore." *Southern Review* 2 (Winter 1966): 1–16.

———. "The Sixteenth Century Lyric in England: A Critical and Historical Reinterpretation." 1939. Reprinted in *Elizabethan Poetry: Modern Essays in Criticism*, edited by Paul J. Alpers. New York: Oxford University Press, 1967.

———. *Quest for Reality*. Edited by Yvor Winters and Kenneth Fields. Chicago: Swallow Press, 1969.

———. *The Uncollected Essays and Reviews of Yvor Winters*. Edited and introduced by Francis Murphy. Chicago: Swallow Press, 1973.

Secondary Sources

Aquinas, Thomas. *On the Truth of the Catholic Faith* [*Summa contra gentiles*]. Translated by Anton C. Pegis et al. New York: Doubleday, 1956.

———. *An Aquinas Reader*. Edited by Mary T. Clark. London: Hodder and Stoughton, 1972.

Babbitt, Irving. *Rousseau and Romanticism*. New York: Houghton Mifflin, 1919.

Blackmur, R. P. "A Note on Yvor Winters." *Poetry* 57 (November 1940): 144–52.

———. *Language as Gesture*. New York: Harcourt, Brace, 1952.

Bogan, Louise. "Review of *The Giant Weapon*." *New Yorker*, July 22, 1944, pp. 57–58.

Davie, Donald. "Winters and Leavis: Memories and Reflections." *Sewanee Review* 87 (Fall 1979): 608–18.

Davis, Robert Gorham. "The New Criticism and the Democratic Tradition." *American Scholar* 19 (Winter 1949–50): 9–19.

Fields, Kenneth. "The Free Verse of Yvor Winters and William Carlos Williams." *Southern Review* 3 (Summer 1967): 764–75.

Fraser, John. "Winters' *Summa*." *Southern Review* 5 (Winter 1969): 184–202.

———. "Leavis, Winters and 'Tradition,'" *Southern Review* 7 (Autumn 1971): 963–85.

Freer, Agnes Lee. "A Poet-Philosopher." *Poetry* 32 (April 1928): 41–47.

Graff, Gerald. "Yvor Winters of Stanford." *American Scholar* 44 (Spring 1975): 291–98.

Isaacs, Elizabeth. *An Introduction to the Poetry of Yvor Winters*. Athens, Ohio: Swallow Press/University of Ohio Press, 1981.

Kaye, Howard. "The Post-Symbolist Poetry of Yvor Winters." *Southern Review* 7 (Winter 1971): 176–97.

———. "Yvor Winters' Criticism." *Southern Review* 11 (Summer 1975): 652–57.

Lohf, Kenneth A., and Sheehy, Eugene P. *Yvor Winters, A Bibliography*. Denver: Alan Swallow, 1959.

Malcolm, Norman. *Ludwig Wittgenstein: A Memoir*. Oxford: Oxford University Press, 1967.

Maxeiner, Tom. "The Poetry of Yvor Winters." *Sequoia* (Spring 1967): 37–47.

McKean, Keith. "Yvor Winters and the New Humanists." *University of Kansas City Review* 22 (Winter 1955): 131–33.

Parkes, Henry B. *The Pragmatic Test*. San Francisco: Colt Press, 1941.

———. "Ralph Waldo Emerson." *Hound and Horn* 5 (July–September 1932): 581–601.

———. "The Puritan Heresy." *Hound and Horn* 5 (January–March 1932): 165–90.

Parkinson, Thomas. *Hart Crane and Yvor Winters: Their Literary Correspondence*. Berkeley: University of California Press, 1978.

Pound, Ezra. *Literary Essays of Ezra Pound*. London: Faber and Faber, 1974.

Powell, Grosvenor. *Language as Being in the Poetry of Yvor Winters*. Baton Rouge: Louisiana State University Press, 1980.

Ransom, John Crowe. "Yvor Winters, the Logical Critic." In *New Criticism*. Norfolk, Conn.: New Directions, 1941.

Sexton, Richard J. *The Complex of Yvor Winters' Criticism*. The Hague: Mouton, 1973.

Stanford, Donald E. "Yvor Winters, 1900–1968." *Southern Review* 4 (Summer 1968): 861–63.

Tuckerman, Frederic Goddard. *The Complete Poems of Frederick Goddard Tuckerman*. Edited and with an introduction by N. Scott Momaday, and with a critical foreword by Yvor Winters. New York: Oxford University Press, 1965.

Weiss, Theodore. "The Nonsense of Winters' *Anatomy*," *Quarterly Review of Literature* 1 (Spring 1944): 212–34, (Summer 1944): 300–318.

Wellek, René. "Yvor Winters Rehearsed and Reconsidered," *Denver Quarterly* 10 (Autumn 1975): 1–28.

Wittgenstein, Ludwig. *Philosophical Investigations*. Translated by G. E. M. Anscombe. Oxford: Blackwell, 1974.

Index

241

Experimentalism (*continued*)
  ters's attitude to, in other poets' work,
  193, 194, 201–5, 211, 215

Fascism, 234–35
Fletcher, John, 63–64
Freer, Agnes Lee, 22, 135–36
Frost, Robert, 30, 42, 214, 234

Gascoigne, George, 56, 198, 218, 220, 221,
  233
Genet, Jean, 62
Gibbon, Edward, 188, 189
Gilson, Étienne, 185
God, Winters's conception of, 21, 62, 68,
  113, 115, 195, 200
Googe, Barnabe, 56, 146, 220
Gourmont, Rémy de, 161
Gray, Thomas, 152
Greville, Fulke, 53, 168, 195, 198, 220,
  221, 223, 226
Gunn, Thom, 103, 215

Hardy, Thomas, 30, 40, 50, 60, 61, 62,
  133, 168, 193, 196–97, 199
Hawthorne, Nathaniel, 150, 169, 173,
  176–78, 198
H. D. *See* Doolittle, Hilda
Hegel, Georg Wilhelm Friedrich, 49
Herbert, Edward, 223, 229
Herbert, George, 195, 223, 229
Herrick, Robert, 56, 231
Historiography, 188–89
Hoffmannsthal, Hugo von, 72
Hopkins, Gerard Manley, 51, 195, 211

Imagism, 154, 159, 165, 199; in Winters's
  early verse, 3, 6, 37, 40, 41, 43, 46, 51,
  58, 74, 79, 174, 175, 178

James, Henry, 2, 64, 150, 163, 169, 173,
  176, 178–80, 185, 198
Jansenism, 167, 226
Jeffers, Robinson, 68, 69, 71
Johnson, Samuel, 198, 232
Jolas, Eugene, 65, 68, 69, 71
Jones, Richard Foster, 8
Jonson, Ben, 56, 57, 168, 195, 217–18,

221, 222, 223, 226, 229, 230
Joyce, James, 65, 75

Kaye, Howard, 97–98, 101, 103
Keats, John, 13, 168, 169
Kennedy, A. G., 7, 8
King, Henry, 231

Laforgue, Jules, 47
Lamson, David, 7, 133, 136, 137–43; Winters's poems on, 3, 74, 93, 213
Landor, Walter Savage, 168
Lawrence, David Herbert, 42
Lewis, Janet, 6, 8, 9, 38, 56, 114
Locke, John, 203, 212, 230
Logical method, of structuring a poem,
  62–63, 66
Loy, Mina, 202
Luther, Martin, 172

Macaulay, Thomas Babington, 188–89
McKenzie, Edwin V., 139–40, 142
Macleish, Archibald, 59, 202
Mallarmé, Stéphane, 65, 88, 208
Manicheism, 76, 167
Marvell, Andrew, 63, 231
Matthews, Washington, 16
Melville, Herman, 3, 94, 151, 168, 170,
  173, 180–83, 198
Milton, John, 204, 229
Momaday, N. Scott, 189
Monroe, Harriet, 5, 70
Moon, and moonlight as symbols in Winters's verse, 25, 35, 36, 116–20, 121,
  136, 211
Moore, George Edward, 192
Moore, Marianne, 6, 42, 45, 202
Moore, Thomas Sturge, 13, 116, 176, 184,
  189, 191–93, 196, 199

Narrative method, of structuring a poem,
  62, 64
Nashe, Thomas, 62
Natural world, Winters's ambivalent attitude toward, 75, 98, 101, 102, 106, 109,
  110, 130, 167, 175
Nature mysticism, in Winters's early verse,
  15–16, 46, 48, 59, 76

New England, intellectual history of, 150–51, 169, 170, 178, 185, 186, 198, 230
New Mexico, 5, 11, 44, 45, 51, 57
Nominalism, 75, 176, 185, 186

Ockham, William, 185
Overbury, Thomas, 83, 85

Pantheism, 13, 22, 29, 61, 68, 69, 71, 72, 89, 92, 98, 104, 169, 173, 174, 184, 191, 214
Parkes, H. B., 164, 170–73, 174, 185, 232
Parkinson, Thomas, 6, 20, 32, 55, 57
Parkman, Francis, 189
Petrarchan style, 162, 218, 221, 229, 230
Plain style, 146, 162, 164, 199, 217, 218–21, 229, 230
Plato, and Platonism, 26, 27, 39, 45, 112
Poe, Edgar Allan, 42, 101, 151, 208, 209, 214, 233
Pope, Alexander, 152
Porter, Katherine Anne, 8
Postsymbolism, 13, 97–98, 102, 147, 148, 177, 191, 199, 201, 211
Pound, Ezra, 12, 42, 45, 46, 47, 70, 152, 160–64, 194, 199, 201, 202–5, 215
Powell, Grosvenor, 47, 121, 125, 131
Prescott, William H., 189
Primitivism, 154–55, 158, 159, 165, 212
Psychological method, of structuring a poem, 62, 64–65
Puritanism, 171–72, 178, 185

Racine, Jean, 60, 61, 62, 70, 76, 226
Raleigh, Sir Walter, 146, 220
Ransom, John Crowe, 202
Rape, as a theme in Winters's verse, 91, 123–26, 130, 182–83
Resurrection, as a theme in Winters's early verse, 18, 20, 33, 54, 96
Richards, I. A., 164
Rimbaud, Arthur, 5, 16, 58, 63, 65, 69, 72
Robinson, Edwin Arlington, 42, 43, 44, 45, 48, 51, 147, 163, 169, 193, 197–200, 210, 215, 221, 233
Roman Catholicism, 21, 66–67, 171
Romanticism, 46, 68, 101, 106, 123, 150,

151–60, 163, 169, 170, 173, 174, 191, 192–93, 203, 205, 212, 214
Ronsard, Pierre de, 11, 12, 76
Rousseau, Jean Jacques, 154
Ruskin, John, 49
Russell, Frances Theresa, 137

Santayana, George, 158
Scattered method, of constructing a poem, 62
Schopenhauer, Arthur, 49
Sea, as a symbol in Winters's writings, 94, 96–99, 101, 181–83, 184, 191, 211
Shaftesbury, Anthony Ashley Cooper, third earl of, 152, 174, 212
Shakespeare, William, 60, 61, 150, 210, 214, 217, 221, 223–26, 227–29
Shelley, Percy Bysshe, 152, 163, 168, 194
Sidney, Sir Philip, 218, 221
Socrates, 67, 145, 159; Winters's poem on, 143
Solipsism, 13, 14, 15, 30, 32, 37, 49, 79, 104, 125, 150, 173, 194, 199
Stanford University, 6, 7, 8, 56
Stendhal (Henri Beyle) 161
Stevens, Wallace, 22, 27, 35, 40, 42, 50, 64, 70, 94, 133, 150, 168, 182, 202, 208–11, 215, 234
Swinburne, Algernon Charles, 191

Tact, as a value in Winters's later verse, 82, 85, 90, 92, 104, 106–7, 123, 127, 130, 144, 182
Tate, Allen, 6, 29, 64, 69, 132, 133
Technique, poetic: as an indication of poet's moral and philosophical presuppositions, 51, 64, 66, 72, 149
Tennyson, Alfred, Lord, 49
Time, in Winters's verse, 11, 17, 21–22, 26, 39, 90, 111–15, 145, 167; in Winters's criticism, 169, 223
Traherne, Thomas, 231
Transcendentalism, 173, 176, 230
Tuberculosis, 5, 6, 11, 13, 17, 18, 55, 169
Tuckerman, Frederick Goddard, 46, 150, 180, 184, 189–91, 193, 196, 199, 201

University of Chicago, 5
University of Colorado, 6, 51
University of Idaho, 6